the culture of design
guy julier

SAGE Publications

London • Thousand Oaks • New Delhi

© Guy Julier 2000

First published 2000

SAGE Publications Ltd
6 Bonhill Street London EC2A 4PU

SAGE Publications Inc.
2455 Teller Road Thousand Oaks, California 91320

SAGE Publications India Pvt Ltd
32, M-Block Market Greater Kailash - I
New Delhi 110 048

British Library Cataloguing in Publication data
A catalogue record for this book is available from the British
Library

ISBN 0 7619 6866 0
ISBN 0 7619 6867 (pbk)

Library of Congress catalog card number available

Text and cover design: barkerhilsdon
Typeset by Photoprint Typesetters, Torquay
Printed in Great Britain by The Cromwell Press Ltd, Trowbridge,
Wiltshire

contents

list of figures

list of illustrations

acknowledgements The Arts and Humanities Research Board supported the preparation of this book with a Research Leave award which was match-funded by Leeds Metropolitan University.

I warmly thank the many talented colleagues and students I have worked alongside in the School of Art, Architecture and Design at Leeds Metropolitan University in recent years. They have been a constant source of inspiration. Former colleagues Ken Dixon, Marq Smith and Viviana Narotzky also continued to share valuable insights from their respective positions in the creative industries. As ever, my wife Sue and children Joe and Becca have been supportive of this project.

Many design professionals have contributed to this book by giving interviews and informal discussions. They have generously shared their personal viewpoints on the precarious and demanding industry in which they are engaged. I thank all who have helped me with the development of this book. As its author, any ticks, glitches or gaffes are, ultimately, my responsibility.

introduction   Design is a highly entrepreneurial profession. It is also a maturing academic discipline. As a focus of leisure and consumption, it has become a source of public entertainment. It is and has been a vehicle of political coercion and symbolism, appropriated and employed by the darkest or most benign of power structures. It serves as an informal indicator of economic performance, cultural regeneration and social well-being. Spectacular displays of youth subcultures, the accumulation of wealth, mid-life crises and retirement plans all produce design. Few practices of intellectual and commercial human activity reach into so many areas of everyday private and public life. Few industries in the West have grown in terms of economic presence and cultural import as design has in the past two decades.

Design has become a global phenomenon. Thus to take Central and Eastern Europe alone, following the collapse of state socialism there, some 350 million citizens have been drawn into liberal democracy and market capitalism. A new global generation of consumers of design within a capitalist context is emerging. The remit of design practice itself has extended during the same period. It is no longer a 'value-added' extra applied to a restricted range of domestic objects; rather it extends, for example, to the planning and shaping of digital interfaces in computer games and websites, to large-scale leisure and retail spaces and even the creation of a city's public image.

Design is represented and talked about at a range of levels. A more conservative notion of it as a commodity signifying modernity and desirability resides in the pages of lifestyle magazines. On the television, the plethora of home-improvement shows which emerged in the late 1990s, while drawing something from this notion, also began to represent design as a process of expert decision-making and implementation. Since the early 1980s a range of professional journals have become firmly established with the growth of the industry. They have presented design variously as business news (e.g. *Design Week*) or an avant-garde cultural activity (e.g. *Blueprint*) and all points between. Design history and design studies have taken their place as discrete academic disciplines in universities with their own scholastic journals, conference circuits and key figures. At the same time, academics from other disciplines in the humanities and social sciences have, though often tentatively, stepped into design territory. This has stemmed from discussions of consumption in cultural studies, anthropology and geography (e.g. Miller 1987; Jackson and Thrift 1995; du Gay et al. 1997). Some sociologists and economists have recognized the importance of design in a wider global economic growth in the first world of 'cultural goods' and creative industries within this (e.g. Lash and Urry 1994; Molotch 1996). In either case, they have provided a wealth of theoretical frameworks for the investigation of design. Generally speaking, however, many of them do not approach specific design examples against which these formal perspectives may be contextualized and deconstructed. It is hoped, then, that this book will have a two-way use. For those with a specialist knowledge of design it should broaden the field of their enquiry by relating it to a wide net of theoretical discourses. For those with an interest in cultural studies, sociology, anthropology, ethnography and geography, it should introduce them to the more focused activities and issues of design and the way that it brokers the material and visual relationships of production and consumption.

The interdisciplinarity of this project is in parallel with a similar trend in design practice itself. This precarious, creative activity has in recent years undergone perhaps its most fundamental revolution yet. It has shifted from being a problem-solving activity to a problem-processing one and thus from a multidisciplinary to interdisciplinary activity. A typical larger design consultancy may bring 'together materials, manufacturing, software and "futures" specialists, with the big ideas flowing from that chemistry' (Hollington 1998: 63). Designers also work closely with product managers and researchers, marketing specialists, advertising agents, public relations consultants and many others involved in the generation, mediation and control of the flows of images, objects and information around a product or service. Technological change, the globalization of economies and the growth of the importance of the brand (all three of which are in themselves related) have played vital roles in this process. Many design consultancies have also moved from the consideration of objects, images and spaces to the investigation and provision of relationships and structures. The traditional demarcations between disciplines such as graphic, product and interior design have receded. Designers increasingly market themselves not by the visual style they create, but by their business approach or, more loosely speaking, the way they structure and manage the design process. Meanwhile, studies in design history and criticism have struggled, mostly unsuccesfully, to keep up with these changes. Thus the richness of contemporary design must be met in its discussion by a strident and robust spectrum of academic disciplines.

Equally, much work in media and cultural studies takes an overly reductionist approach to the discussion of the strategies of producing and selling things. Often the study is narrowed down to skilful, but limiting, image analysis. In particular, the dominance of advertising analysis, stemming from literary criticism, has served to divert attention from the fact that these days it only represents just one of many strategies employed by corporations and institutions to colonize the consumer's world. So, for example, despite their insightful and worthy exploration of the production and meanings of Nike's advertising campaigns, Goldman and Papson are forced to admit that this approach, 'none the less risks leaving other aspects of the story in the background. Matters central to the operation of *Nike*, such as sports marketing and shoe design [both of which are highly interrelated], remain out of sight' (1998: v). As I argue in the final chapter of this book, the centring of production, the designer's labour and, indeed, consumption around brand values in the 1990s drastically reconfigure the role and status of advertising.

In view of these shortfalls, my interest is in the instigation of a concept of design culture. In the first instance this is animated by the evermore pervasive role of design in contemporary Western society. It takes design as a culturally specific practice which is driven almost entirely by strategies of differentiation. This process appropriates and employs a wide range of discursive features: not just ones of modernity, but also risk, heritage, subculture, public space, Europeanity, consumer empowerment and many others. Design culture is not fixed, homogeneous or homogenizing; rather it embraces a complex matrix of human activities, perceptions and articulations. Careful analysis of its visual, material, spatial and textual manifestations provides routes into this complexity.

The following chapters are structured into two parts. The first (see Figure I.1) maps out an extended introduction to thinking about contemporary design culture by considering each of its three key domains: production, the designer and consumption into which the design artefact, be it an object, space or image, may be inserted.

Production not only includes manufacture but all forms of *conscious* intervention in the origination, execution, distribution and circulation of goods and services. Thus it would incorporate the influence of materials, technologies and manfacturing systems but also the effects of marketing, advertising and distribution channels. The design industry is structured within this both to reproduce it and to modify it: Chapter 1 concentrates mostly on the interaction of design practice with wider changes in commerce.

Figure I.1

Domains of design

culture

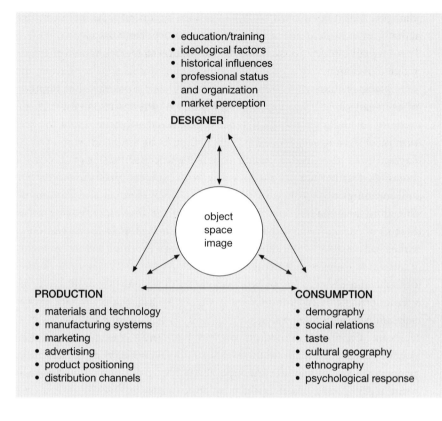

The designer is clearly bound up in this process, however it is given a separate nexus in this triangle. This honours the designer's role in shaping the form and content of the visual and material artefacts which are produced and consumed. But it also allows us to pay special attention to the less conscious features which inform and structure this process. Thus heed to the peculiarities of the professional status of design and the discourses which influence and mediate among designers and between them and their public must be paid: Chapter 2 largely focuses on these aspects through a discussion of the professional, historiographical and discursive questions which are articulated by design historians and critics and that provide a set of reference points for designers.

Consumption completes this triumvirate. This would not only include quantitative data regarding, say, the degree of acquisition or use of particular designs in relation to demographic trends. It involves the discussion of qualitative questions concerning the reasons and meanings of consumption. Why are certain goods which do not perform a utilitarian function accorded special status over others? Does consuming involve an active or even subversive practice? How are places consumed? These are some of the many questions which have interested academics in the humanities and social sciences in the past two decades. Chapter Three outlines some of the key thinkers in this area and considers them alongside the practice of design.

None of these three nexi of production, designers and consumption exists in isolation. They constantly inform each other in an endless cycle of exchange. Equally, they all individually have some influence to play on the form of objects, spaces and images. But these in turn are not neutral: they play an active part in influencing or making sense of the systems of their provision. Furthermore, contemporary conditions of production, design and consumption bring the three domains ever closer so that at times aspects of them may even overlap. It is the interaction and intersection of these domains within the culture of design that is of prime interest to the author.

The remaining six chapters provide more detailed analysis of specific visual and material theatres of design culture. Onto each of these the interactions and intersections of production, designer and consumption are mapped, although one or other of these is perhaps given more emphasis in each case. Chapter 4 discusses the more conservative conception of design in what has been termed 'high design' and the manoeuvres of the avant-garde in design to mediate that meaning. Chapter 5 considers developments in the design of consumer goods. It reveals the design processes by which material artefacts are shaped within the framework of achieving coherence between the use of contemporary materials, manufacturing systems and marketing practices. In particular it shows how quantitative and qualitative consumer information is reconciled with brand identities of clients by designers. In a final section, the discussion sets this against the more experiential world of using products.

Chapter 6 continues to investigate the role of designers and design managers in orchestrating coherence between different manifestations, but this time in the context of the shaping and selling of geographical locations. Initially it considers the city as design product, arguing against architecture as the primary expression of urban identity; instead, a web of features, including the material and visual design hardware of cities and their emotional and experiential software interlock and vie with each other. This is further problematized in the context of shifting regional, national and global power structures. Chapter 7 investigates branded leisure spaces and the challenges of designing and consuming place and placelessness in locations which are largely disembedded from traditional spatial geography. It considers the problems of differentiating leisure experiences when they are dislocated from place identities and consumed by a progressively critical and knowing audience.

Chapter 8 looks into the design of interactive digital environments including computer games, educational packages and websites. It begins by discussing the effect that this area is having on the structural organization of design practice itself. It then contrasts some of the exaggerated expectations of these media with the pragmatic realities of its limitations. Much of this chapter hinges on the relationships this digital world has with the material world. Chapter 9 discusses case studies where design is used to communicate and consolidate the internal identity of corporations. This is something that the public does not see, but it indirectly influences the external corporate image. Furthermore, this strategy reconfigures employees of organizations as both its workers and consumers. As such it adds further credence to the notion of design conspiring to blur the distinction between producer and consumer. The chapter concludes with remarks to recapitulate on the recurrent themes of the book.

Each chapter of the second part of this book features a key case study. At times the authorial voice of the text shifts towards a more literary style, acknowledging the subjectivity of experiencing these design artefacts. Subsidiary case studies are also discussed, acknowledging that the key examples cannot provide an exhaustive platform to explore all the issues which adhere to the chapter's theme. It is hoped that the debates which relate to the specific examples discussed may subsequently be carried to others outside the scope of this book. They have been chosen for the richness of data they bring to their respective theme and are also all relatively well-known ones. It is hoped that the reader may have some personal experience of them to compare with. Furthermore, nearly all of them have been experienced by myself as a consumer before being considered for this book. This is not to declare any experiential neutrality. Clearly as a specialist in the design field my response to goods and services may be coloured by my own academic baggage: I am a 'knowing consumer' whether I like the feelings this brings up or not.

None the less, the examples are not presented as paradigms of either good or bad design. Much publishing has been devoted to establishing expert canons of good design taste and criticism (e.g. Bayley 1979; Sudjic 1985). Conversely, some critics have drawn up vehement attacks on this canon and offered alternative approaches to the practice and appreciation of design framed by environmental concerns (e.g. Papanek 1972; Whitely 1993). Some important discussions of the role of gender in both design production and its consumption have emerged recently (e.g. Attfield 1989; Sparke 1995; Buckley 1998). While questions around gender emerge lightly within the text of this book, I am concerned not to separate it out as an issue and thereby restrict it. In choosing case studies, then, my primary interest is that objects, spaces and images exist in the mainstream of design production and consumption, and because they exist we are required to build a measure of objective understanding of their purpose. After all, only by understanding the current state of design culture can we then begin to look at routes towards its ethical and practical amelioration.

design production   If the design profession is concerned with innovation, change and invention, then during its relatively short lifespan it has consistently reinvented itself. This has happened in both haphazard and systematic ways: its ability to dodge-and-weave, wheel-and-deal in the face of economic ups and downs is matched, in some quarters, by an ambition to systemize its practice. In this context, it is difficult to generalize about its various phases: tendencies in its organization and aims are often multi-layered. The exponential growth of the design profession from 1980, alongside that of other creative industries, has produced a point of 'critical mass' whereby it now takes a prominent public and commercial role.

At the same time, this expansion is matched by ever-increasing diversification of its practices. The breadth and heterogeneity of design markets coupled with the need for design consultancies and designers to differentiate themselves from each other mean that it is difficult to ascertain singular models of design consultancy.

However, there have been broad structural trends in the practice of design brought about, not least, by global economic changes. In short, these have involved a convergence between design and other commercial practices such as advertising, management consultancy and public relations. Secondly, we have witnessed a growing trend within the profession to 'move up a gear' by specializing in the development of approaches, structures and relationships within which the object, image and space consequently play a role (Mitchell 1993). Rather than centre the design process on the solving of specific individualized visual and material problems then, there has been a move towards the integration of various levels of practice along with the 'systems of provision' (Fine and Leopold 1993) of goods and services. Thus many designers enter into a more sophisticated dialogue with clients in which product development is assessed in a broader context of corporate and brand ambitions.

This chapter traces recent developments in design consultancy. Through a discussion of the shifting commercial, economic and technological contexts in which it is produced, it is primarily concerned with moving popular concepts away from design as an artesanal, problem-solving activity towards a more complex model which integrates hardware and software thinking 'beyond the object'.

design consultancy reaches 'critical mass': setting the scene with some statistics   Since the mid-1980s there has been an increasing interest in measuring the size, structure and impact of the design profession on the wider economy of developed nations and regions. This has been taken both by state government bodies and institutions (e.g. McAlhone 1987; Netherlands Design Institute (NDI) 1994; Design Exchange 1995; Creative Industries Task Force (CITF) 1998) and independent business analysts (e.g. *Design Week* annually from 1987; Business Ratio Plus from 1987; KeyNote from 1995). Two pointers emerge from this. First, it is significant that the design profession has recently been deemed large enough to be measured and a structure within itself determined. Attempts to quantify the design industry had historically been dogged by its fragmentation and small-scale practice. It is estimated that fewer than 200 design firms in Europe employ more than 25 designers (NDI 1994: 8). By the close of the twentieth century, however, it seems that the design industry had reached a point of 'critical mass'. Secondly, these reports were produced by institutions dedicated to the promotion of the public and commercial profile of design, and yet, their findings stressed the current, actual importance of design in the wider economy, rather than their potential impact. The British journal *Design Week* in its 1998 design consultancy survey went as far as to state that, 'Design is finally coming of age' (*Design Week* 1998: 62).

It is widely acknowledged that accurate figures for the total value of design activity are difficult to calculate (NDI 1994; CITF 1998). This is because many design consultancies are engaged in non-design activities; much of their value is hidden within the activities of other industries; the design function cannot be consistently bounded – different sectors use different definitions of design; and therefore definitive statistics are often not collected. As Mike Jones, put it, 'Despite the hugely sophisticated network of rumour and gossip, nobody is entirely sure just how many small consultancies there are, or how many people are employed, let alone unemployed' (Jones 1991: 13).

However, the 1980s and 1990s certainly registered exponential growth in design incomes. Annual fees earned by UK consultancies doubled from £175 million to £350 million between 1985 and 1995 (CITF 1998). Put more prosaically, when the Yellow Pages were launched in 1966, there were just three design consultants listed in Central London; in 1999 there were 536 listed in Central London. Likewise, the European design market grew at an estimated 25 per cent between 1982 and 1989 (NDI 1994: 10).

Within the European market, the United Kingdom has maintained the highest expenditure on design services with $2.4 billion spent in 1994, followed by Germany with $2.2 billion and then both France and Spain with $0.9 billion (see Figure 1.1).

Much of the British growth has been in graphic communication and environmental design whereas the German market relies more on product development and civic or institutional design projects. The economic importance of 'DesignUK' is matched by an infrastructural dominance. For instance, of the 30,000 annual graduates of design in Europe during the 1990s, 30 per cent were trained in the UK. Similarly, the growth of 'DesignUK' was matched by educational growth. The years 1993–8 saw a 12 per cent rise in design degree applications and in 1998 a 63 per cent rise in students sitting the GCSE examination in Design and Technology (Design Council 1998: 24). By the end of the 1990s, there were 62,000 students specializing in design in higher education where over 900 courses were available (CITF 1998).

Despite the concentration in Britain and Germany, the design industry is highly internationalized. Some 75 per cent of British consultancies were active in overseas markets, their main market being the United States and Northern Europe. Exports by British design consultancies rose from £175 million in 1987 to £385 million in 1997; in one survey, 45 per cent of consultancies reported that exporting their services was more profitable than UK projects (Design Council 1998: 14).

In 1994, there were about 8,000 design firms within the then 12 member-states of the European Union (NDI 1994). In 1998, Britain had some 4,000 design consultancies employing over 20,000. A further 3,000 worked as sole-traders or in non-design specific organizations or, in other words, as in-house designers to companies and institutions (CITF 1998). Thus it appears that the bulk of design activity was carried out in consul-

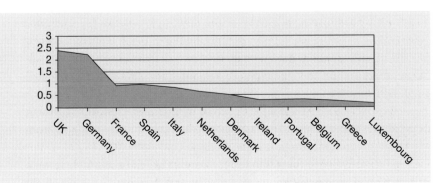

Figure 1.1

European design services expenditure, 1994 ($b.)

Statistical source: Netherlands Design Institute 1994

Figure 1.2

European design

market by sector

and discipline

Statistical source:

Netherlands Design

Institute 1994

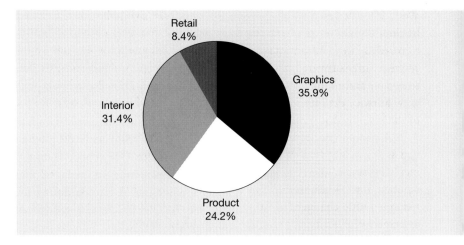

tancies rather than on a freelance basis, although, again, statistics on the number of freelance designers are rarely accurate (see Figure 1.2).

The majority of design practice is in graphics and interior related fields, embracing corporate identity, corporate literature, packaging and/or branding, consumer literature, exhibitions, multimedia, advertising, retail and information design, while only 19 per cent of UK consultancies offer product design and only 6 per cent offer furniture design (CITF 1998). (We shall see in Chapter 2 how a hierarchy of design in its public presentation, through exhibitions, books and journals is skewed in exactly the opposite direction in favour of product and furniture.) This in part reflects a general trend in the UK economy away from manufacturing towards the service sector in the late twentieth century. But it also confirms the fact that design is bound up not just in the origination of products, but also their marketing, promotion, packaging, distribution or dissemination. Generally speaking, a similar pattern is felt in Europe as a whole, though product design occupies a larger proportion than in the UK specifically: in 1993 graphic communication occupied 35.9 per cent of design business, product 24.2 per cent and interior and retail 39.9 per cent (NDI 1994: 17).

The high concentration of design practices in Britain is explained by a number of historical factors. These would include: the earlier industrial revolution and subsequently, the establishment of a design schools system in the nineteenth century; the fact that Britain resisted invasion in the two World Wars ensuring greater cultural continuity, or, indeed, a consolidation of design practice; the geographical and commercial position of Britain between America and Europe, thus acting as a strategic, mediating bridge between the two markets. The last of these becomes of vital importance as we begin to consider the emergence of design consultancy.

The growth of the design industry may also be read alongside a general economic and political shift in favour of the 'cultural goods' sector in the

West. Thus design is mapped alongside other 'creative industries' identified by the UK government's Creative Industries Task Force as advertising, architecture, the art and antiques market, crafts, designer fashion, film, interactive leisure software, music, the performing arts, publishing, software and television and radio. Collectively in the UK the creative industries' revenue grew at twice the rate of the economy as a whole and represented 5 per cent of the employed workforce by the late 1990s (CITF 1998).

Clearly some sectors, such as leisure software, were newer than others and were still in the process of establishing their own structures and commercial systems. Conversely, the Creative Industries Task Force reported that a potential weakness of the advertising industry was that its agency structure remained little changed for 50 years. Design consultancy fell between these extremes: it could not be described as 'nascent', but it was still in a state of flux. A review of the historical development of design consultancy is thus useful in order to understand its contemporary nature.

the establishment of design consultancy Throughout its history, design consultancy has echoed – with some years' time lapse – the business approach and organization found in advertising. Advertising agencies first appeared in the second half of the nineteenth century when their mandate was to provide everything from posters to the frames in which to hang them. Thus from the outset their activities brought together an array of specialist activities. By the 1920s, their ranks included copywriters, art directors, account executives and media space buyers. The modern advertising agency, which was expected to coordinate aspects of a campaign across a range of advertising media came into being with the medium of television. In the case of America, this was consolidated in the 1930s while this model did not take shape in Europe until the early 1960s.

A clear model for the structure and actions of advertising was therefore forged in the USA and transplanted, primarily by the establishment of subsidiary offices of American agencies, to Western Europe. In 1937 only four American advertising agencies had branches outside the United States. By 1960, 36 had foreign branches with a total of 281 offices (Nevett 1987: 195).

In design consultancy, similar models of interdisciplinarity were developed in America. Most well-known among these was Raymond Loewy Associates, founded in 1929. By 1938 it employed 18 designers; in 1941 there were 56 and between 1947 and the mid-1960s, it expanded from 150 to 180 employees (Julier 1993: 120). Loewy himself combined a background in engineering with illustration and he sought to coordinate all aspects of design provision, from product origination to its styling and brand identity.

His no-nonsense book *Never Leave Well Enough Alone* (1951) positioned the role of design at the service of the corporation and consumerism. A client's market position could thus be matched with consumer trends to competitively position products through both their visual appearance and promotional strategy.

Compatriots Walter Dorwin Teague and Norman Bel Geddes also ran sizeable, complex studios which during the 1930s employed up to 30 individuals in design, drafting, modelling and technical activities respectively. They also drafted in specialists as required. Woodham (1997: 70) notes that undue emphasis on the individuals who headed the studios is thus misleading.

In bringing product, graphic and interior designers alongside advertising, marketing and management specialists, Raymond Loewy Associates was an important forerunner of much later European developments in design consultancy. Certainly his texts, and also Harold Van Doren's *Industrial Design: A Practical Guide* (1940) which also stressed the need for vertical and horizontal integration in design practice, were read in Europe. Nevertheless, design critics denigrated Loewy's activities as the mere styling and packaging of products for maximum sales with little social benefit (e.g. Mañà 1983). This may partially account for the relatively slow take-up of this American approach in Europe, though we must also take into consideration the economic disruption of the Second World War and the fact that markets in Europe continued to be more segmented than in the USA until the 1960s. After all, Loewy, Teague and Bel Geddes had been servicing a more stable, homogenized and affluent market with a wider distribution base than Europe since the 1930s.

By contrast, then, early design consultancy in Europe, and in particular in Britain, was a more 'gentlemanly' affair. The Design Research Unit, set up in 1943 by the Ministry of Information sought to bring designers and engineers together in order to provide practical advice for industry, equipping it for competition in postwar markets. The bulk of its activities, however, lay in exhibition design such as projects for the 1951 Festival of Britain.

It was not until the early 1960s that consultancies approaching the American model began to be established in Europe. In London notable among this first wave were Allied International Designers and Fletcher Forbes Gill, both founded in 1959, Cambridge Consultants begun in 1960, Minale-Tattersfield founded in 1964 and Wolff Olins which began work in 1965. In the same year, Unimark was founded in Milan.

Of these, James Pilditch's Allied International Designers set the pace for other consultancies. It began as a packaging consultancy but within 18 months was undertaking corporate identity projects; a year later was joined by Douglas Scott, designer of London's Routemaster bus. Pilditch is also important for the books he published on product development and corporate identity (1965; 1970). Mixing anecdote and analysis, these publications helped give a voice to the emergent multidisciplinary design industry in the UK which was, according to one of its key participants, Wally Olins, 'learning as it went along' (Olins 1982: 221).

While the general buoyancy of European economies during the 1960s provided a subsequent basis for the growth of the design sector, the structural changes in commerce which took place were of more direct importance. During this decade many of the corporate giants emerged, forcing either takeover, liquidation or repositioning of many smaller businesses. Thus Wolff Olins's first major corporate identity scheme in the early 1960s was for the paint manufacturer Hadfields. With the emergence of ICI's Dulux brand and Hoechsts's Berger, both with high quality product, blanket distribution and massive advertising, a corporate identity for Hadfields had to be developed which made the company equally visible but also emphasized its stealth and flexibility. Hence a fox motif was adopted for its corporate logo (Olins 1982).

Peter York viewed this trend during the 1960s more satirically:

This business of designing corporate identity was all rather abstract and high-flown. When knighted artists who knew the chairman's wife had done out the head-office hall in 1935 ... there'd been none of this. But these sixties designers were completely different. They'd ask you what your company really did, what its philosophy was and how people related to it, and ask to see the company archives and talk to the senior management. And they sent memos about it all. You'd think they were management consultants from the way they carried on, not sign-painters.

(York 1984: 34)

the 1980s design consultancy boom   Despite economic recession brought on by the 1973 international oil crisis, several other larger-scale consultancies became established during that decade. These would include Michael Peters & Partners (founded 1970), Enterprise IG (founded 1976), Fitch (founded 1972) and Addison (founded 1978).

It was in the 1980s that design practice got onto a solid coporate footing in terms of size, structure and distribution, though. The most significant and debatable feature of this decade was the flotation of some design consultancies on the stock market. The first of these was Allied International Designers: when Pilditch took the consultancy to the market in 1980 it had a turnover of £23 million, with 16 companies and a staff of 600. The move was strategic in that it encouraged clients to view the design consultancy, 'as a proper business' (Jones 1991: 17). When Addison took over Allied International Designers in 1984, it expanded it to a group of 1,600 employees offering market research, public relations and recruitment specialisms alongside design.

The tendency of some design consultancies' outward growth was matched by marketing services groups which also began to acquire design companies. These would include the WPP Group, Euro RSCG, Havas, Aegis, Gruner & Jahr and Saatchi & Saatchi. In 1983 when it began buying design businesses, the WPP Group encompassed 54 companies employing 22,500 staff (Jones 1991: 18). Its portfolio ranged across advertising agencies, public relations and public affairs consultancies to media planning and research groups. The publicly-quoted core group remained relatively small, with around 60 employees. It wholly or part owned companies, their payoff being increased capitalization and the sharing of clients across the group according to required specializations. These companies continue to be allowed managerial independence; their sole remit to WPP is profitability. Thus during the 1980s many larger design consultancies were driven by the imperative for high profits, either coming from the stock market or from their parent group.

This clearly matches a general ideological condition of that decade. In 1982 the British Prime Minister and leader of the Conservative Party, Margaret Thatcher, hosted a seminar at 10 Downing Street for designers and their advocates. She subsequently 'wrote' an article for *Design* in which she stated, 'The profit potential of product design and development is considerable. Designers themselves should be more aggressive in selling themselves to industry as wealth creators' (Thatcher quoted in Whitely 1991: 196). In 1983 the Design Council launched its 'Design for Profit' slogan. Its 1986 *Profit by Design* pamphlet echoed Thatcher's views, starkly pointing out that, 'the design process is a planning exercise to maximize sales and profits' (Design Council quoted in Whitely 1991: 196).

Thatcher's, and the Design Council's, emphasis on the development of innovatory products for manufacture was somewhat out of kilter with the prevailing growth in design opportunities of the 1980s, however. After all, Britain, and indeed most of the developed world, with the exception of Germany and Japan, had seen a steady decline in the *presence* of manufacturing since the mid-1960s. Employment in manufacturing dropped in the UK from 38.4 per cent in 1960 to 22.5 per cent in 1990 and in the USA from 26.4 per cent to 18.0 per cent over the same period; Britain's share of world manufacturing exports dropped from 14.2 per cent in 1964 to 7.6 per cent in 1986 (Barberis and May 1993: 31–2). This trend has been referred to as 'de-industrialization', although in effect we are talking about the decline of just one particular sector of industry, it being manufacturing. Furthermore, during the 1980s many activities formerly carried out by manufacturers were subcontracted out, so that what had traditionally been included as part of manufacturing was being seen as service sector commerce. None the less, during the 'Thatcher decade' of 1979–89, employment in the service sector grew by two million, roughly the same figure as the decline in manufacturing employment. Output in the services sector grew by 28.8 per cent as against nearly 10 per cent in manufacturing (Wells 1989: 25–6).

The chief growth area for design practice during the 1980s, then, was not in design for manufacture – though this discipline did not decline – but in design for the service sector in general and the mediation and distribution of goods and services in particular. Retail design, packaging and corporate identity, annual report design, events and exhibition design were the real boom areas.

Retail design expanded with the rapid growth of multiples in Britain during the early 1980s. This was an acceleration of a process which had been underway from the 1960s whereby the independently owned shops in the high street were gradually replaced by the larger retail chains. A study of the principal shopping street in Newcastle showed that in 1980 28 per cent of the shops were independents; by 1986 only 6 per cent were independent. Meanwhile the percentage of multiples in the same street rose from 26 per cent to 41 per cent (Howard and Davies 1988: 10). This was coupled with an exponential rise in retail expenditure, facilitated by a credit boom and a rise of consumer mobility through greater affluence and car ownership meant that shopping habits changed. Retail design was accordingly expansive and lucrative in the 1980s.

Packaging design was fuelled by the massification of shopping. To take a focused example of this trend: in 1972, the supermarket chain Tesco had 800 stores in the UK with an average floorspace of 4,500 square feet; in 1992 they had just 400 stores, but with an average floorspace of 27,000 square feet (Sparks 1994: 323). Fewer but larger shops in turn means that there is less brand loyalty among consumers and more competition between brands. A large shop is capable of stocking a wider range of competing products, thus the need for packaging redesign in order to help maintain market-share on the pure basis of visual attractiveness.

Corporate identity opportunities grew due to two basic phenomena. The first was the growth of mergers. During four years of the 1980s, the number of annual mergers and acquisitions in the UK exceeded the total for the whole of the 1970s (Napier 1994: 89). As the structure, size and nature of corporations changed, then so would their identity, often with the help of design consultancies. Secondly, the privatization programmes of state industries and services required the repositioning of these entities in a competitive market. This meant that they would be responsible to their shareholders rather than the state and that their public became their consumers. Those who remained as employees of newly privatized companies would have to relate to them as commercial, corporatized concerns rather than as state industries. Even if state services were not privatized, a clear shift in the relationship between them and their public took place. The wholesale change of public service, be it health, education, the Civil Service, the police force or social services, was based upon the application of market principles. Thus performance measurement and ratings, responsiveness to public demand and contracting out to competitive tendering gradually became features which brought the culture of public services closer to the private sector. Ultimately this led to the establishment of the Citizen's Charter in 1991, establishing levels of expectation of public services and thus repositioning their users as consumers. As such, the *presentation* of public services to either national or local government as their paymasters, and to tax-payers as their consumers has gained greater importance. This has been taken to the extent that London's Metropolitan Police commissioned an audit of its 'corporate identity' from Wolff Olins. Following the design consultancy's report entitled *A Force for Change* (Olins 1988), there was little modification of the Met.'s visual identity. However, subsequently, attention was paid to projecting greater cohesion, courtesy and sensitivity. Heward (1994) goes as far as to argue that through subsequent small-scale design changes – such as the use of calling cards by officers on the beat – repositioned the force within a retail-like 'service ethos'.

The design of annual reports perhaps did not require the complexity of project management that corporate identity demanded; none the less it became a significant and highly visible source of design employment during the 1980s. The removal of foreign exchange controls in 1979, the establishment of the Unlisted Securities Market in 1980 which allowed smaller and less well-established companies to issue shares and the progressive ending of demarcations between financial institutions, which freed up the movement of investment all contributed to the stock market boom of the 1980s. Employment associated with corporate finance grew by 45 per cent between 1979 and 1986 (Toporowski 1989: 243). There was thus a burgeoning design market for corporate finance literature. The freedom of capital during this decade also led to more mergers and takeovers, in turn requiring more communications design. To this we must add the deregulation of banks and building societies in the mid-1980s which allowed each to provide mortgage and banking facilities respectively, again all requiring newly designed literature.

Finally, an indirect cause of the changing cultural and economic landscape of Britain in the 1980s was the growth in events and exhibition design. As regional centres lost their manufacturing base, then they invented new forms of representing themselves. One result of this was the growth of the 'heritage industry' whereby localities were repackaged for tourist and leisure consumption. By the late 1980s a new museum was opened, on average, in the UK every two weeks (Woodham 1997: 217).

'neo-Fordist' design consultancy   The opportunities for the expansion of design businesses during the 1980s did not, on the whole, impact on the strategic approach they took, it just meant more, much more of the same. The sheer volume of commissions implied that a publicly quoted consultancy could acquire larger premises and add more drawing boards to their studios. At the larger consultancy end (studios of over 50 employees), design businesses exhibited some of the classic features of Fordist production to deal with the explosive market. Employees undertook specialized tasks, output was relatively standardized and they reached a mass clientele. Furthermore, clients were relatively inexperienced and thus uncritical employers of design consultancies. While there was high street competition, for many clients it was their first experience of commissioning design. As Mark Landini who worked for retail specialists Fitch during much of the 1980s remarked,

> One would say: well, we'll design a cash desk, but that was the end of the discussion. The cash desk would be presented to the people who had commissioned the design and then it would be built and then you'd find out that it didn't work. One just assumed that one could design a cash desk and the client assumed that you could because there was this great sense of euphoria.
>
> (Landini quoted in Jones 1991: 18)

Again, this tendency towards Fordist structural organization and economies of scale in design consultancy was prefigured on a grander scale in advertising. Dominant in this mode was Saatchi & Saatchi who developed a particular 'philosophy' of advertising, promoted an ethos of 'business principles' and underwent a series of acquisitions of other firms in order to operate a full range of marketing services – including design consultancy, public relations, market research, direct marketing – as part of what they called a 'commercial communications' package (Lash and Urry 1994: 140). None the less, unlike WPP, Saatchi stitched its various companies together under a tight 'brand' identity.

This identity was part of what has been described as the 'second wave' of advertising which developed from the late 1960s. In terms of product, this involved a more creative, humorous approach to advertising communications on the part of British agencies by comparison with the more 'hard-sell' approach of their American counterparts. In terms of process, this approach was systematized through the development of what is known as 'account planning'. The 'planner' originated in the efforts of Boase Massimmi Pollit and J. Walter Thompson and was predicated on the assumption that the client was too close to the brand being advertised to have an objective view of the consumer's experience. Thus the planner commissioned and analysed market research, undertook qualitative surveys by testing ads out on small samples of consumers and developed tracking studies to measure the impact of ad and promotion campaigns. From this the planner developed a 'creative brief' which gives specific guidelines for the creative team as to the target audience and the message of the ad (Davidson 1992; Lash and Urry 1994). However, this approach did not only focus on the creation of specific advertisements but was used to develop a longer-term strategic view of the creative direction of a product. It was also used to prove the effectiveness of campaigns. In this way the planner played a crucial role in reconciling the creative and market research approaches to advertising and, latterly, design. Ad-agency style planning was introduced in the Michael Peters Group in 1986 in the design of packaging (Southgate 1994: 87) and was used more frequently among design consultancies during the 1990s.

'post-Fordist' design consultancy: the 1990s This euphoria was broken by the 1990–3 economic recession. The European design market contracted from a total client expenditure of $10.5 billion in 1990 to $8.5 billion in 1992 (NDI 1994: 9). A handful of UK design consultancies such as Fitch, Addison and Wolff Olins sought a buffer zone from the effects of recession by seeking markets abroad. Thus, for instance, Spain became a favourite destination with its Barcelona Olympic Games and Seville World Expo year of 1992 suspending the effects of European-wide recession. However, this was only a delaying tactic.

The larger consultancies drastically reduced their staffing or the size of their operations. Both Crighton and the Michael Peters Group went into receivership while Conran axed 43 staff in 1990. Fitch drastically reduced from a 1987 peak of 300 staff to less than 50 by 1991. Stories of this period abound, for instance, of staff subsequently making themselves unavailable ('out at lunch') in order to avoid random sacking. If this sounds like a desperate situation, then it illustrates the design industry's high responsiveness to economic fluctuations and dips in commercial confidence. Design business is not highly capitalized: apart from premises, which are rarely of high value, there are few assets onto which risk can be spread. Its self-proclaimed flexibility and stealth could also be its weakness. Clearly for larger consultancies there was a conflict between their business position and the needs of running a creative studio. Share prices in design consultancies dropped dramatically in 1989: it is an industry which is too small to be of interest to the City (Jones 1991: 18).

As consultancies scaled down during the recession, many of their representatives spoke of a return to 'creative work'. However, at the same time, the recession actually provided an opportunity for smaller studios to move into the gap. Clients who had been round the first time with large-scale consultancies during the mid-1980s, and had both the experience of commissioning and had at least established a design identity for themselves, could now more confidently contract individuals and small studios to carry out design consultancy work at a much reduced cost.

So far, this chapter has focused on the development of large-scale design consultancy. However, it is important to note that this sector has historically been interdependent with a halo of smaller-scale activity undertaken by individuals and small groups. Little quantitative research has been carried out on their contribution to the creative industries. Many of them work on smaller-scale design projects for smaller clients. But they may also provide specialist subcontracted services to larger design consultancies and advertising agencies. These may include specialist strategic advice, technical skills and/or creative styles. Equally they may be employed simply to help out larger consultancies with the high volumes of work in times of buoyant business.

The structural relationship of the consultancy to freelancer might be viewed in a similar way to the core–periphery model of industry developed in the 1980s by economists (Berger and Piore 1980; Sabel 1982; Best 1990). Their interest was in the break-up of Fordist manufacture and product development. They identified the emergence of a dualistic economy, most spectacularly evident in Italy, whereby core mass manufacturing entities were dependent on a periphery of workshop-based industries. While the core corporation controlled product origination, assembly and distribution, the peripheral smaller workshops produced components under subcontracted conditions. This putting-out arrangement meant that specialist areas of manufacture could be drawn on according to fluctuations in demand, both in terms of volume and design: hence the term 'flexible specialization' was appended to this practice.

A step on from this, realized in the so-called Third Italy (being neither the poor agricultural south nor the heavily industrialized north) where the subcontractee workshops began to forge their own networks, undertaking their own product development and manufacture, independently of the core heavy industries. Thus a highly innovative, entrepreneurial, creative, profitable and commercially flexible cottage-industry was developed from the late 1970s in Italy. Indeed much of the avant-garde design in Italy, of the Memphis movement and Solid, drew from this manufacturing culture during the 1980s. A similar dualistic model may be discerned in the design industry. Larger design consultancies are invariably dependent on the flexible support of subcontracted freelance individuals. They provide a critical, creative edge.

Furthermore, the ever-diminishing price of computer equipment (Moore's law which has held for 40 years, suggests that the near-annual doubling of density of transitors on a microchip is accompanied by a halving of its cost (see Wollen 1998)) allowed individual designers increasing access to the production tools capable of dealing with complex visual problem-solving. The mid-1990s thus saw the growth of small-scale but well-known design groups such as Anti-Rom or Tomato working within flexible networks working for a multinationalized corporate infrastructure. Thus while they operated out of cramped studios, their clients may be Nike, Coca-Cola or Warner Brothers.

To briefly return to advertising, once again we find developments in this sector prefiguring the design industry, broadly speaking. Towards the end of the 1980s, the Fordist scale of agencies began to be supplanted by a proliferation of much smaller ad agencies. Additionally, there was a disintegration of the production side of advertising, so that there was an increased outsourcing of media buying, design and video production business (Key Note 1990). This has been called the 'third wave' in the advertising industry.

This disintegration, then, may be read as part and parcel of a wider shift in the culture industries to a post-Fordist mode. Lash and Urry (1994: 113–16) argue that in itself, Fordism arrived particularly late in the culture industries, with the exception of cinema. Thus while classic Fordism is ascribed in manufacture to the 1920s onwards in the USA and in Britain from around the Second World War, the record industry did not take on such characteristics until the 1960s, publishing and advertising until the 1970s, and, as we have seen, design until the 1980s. In each of these cases, a system of vertical integration was sought according to divisions of labour. Thus in this model a large design consultancy might incorporate account managers who liaise with the client, account planners who refine the brief for the design teams, and an artwork production team which is responsible for refining the design work for presentation to the client (Southgate 1994: 90). Within each of these teams, one would find subspecialisms, so that the design team might have to bring together product, interior or graphic design, and the artwork production department may include specialist model-makers or computer graphics experts.

In design, the early 1990s recession initiated a partial disintegration of this Fordist system in design. In order to maintain clients in lean times, design consultants would offer an increasing range of services: this meant, for instance, that graphics specialists would offer more three-dimensional orientated facilities such as exhibition stand design, while product designers would diversify to graphic design. Furthermore, some consultancies began to offer other strategic services, carrying out, for instance, design audits of companies, assessing their product and market. Indeed, many of the more prominent design consultancies dropped the word 'design' from their name altogether or added the word 'strategy' (Relph-Knight 1998: 33). None the less, for the smaller consultancies there was an emergent polarization between the growing sophistication of client demand in terms of the services required and the design industry's capabilities. One design industry analyst noted that, 'as clients demand more strategic input, greater use of technology, more multidisciplinary skills and increased international capability, design consultants will of necessity become larger. However a significant proportion of consultants will choose to remain small' (Key Note 1996: 37). Indeed, while a few of the larger consultancies, such as Fitch with 305 employees in 1997, grew back to their 1980s size, the majority remained as small concerns without significant expansion in the 1990s (Business Ratio Plus 1998: 287, 366). After all, clients may have demanded more sophisticated services from designers but they expected to pay fees at pre-recessionary rates, thus tightening profit margins and pressurizing them to work longer hours instead of expanding their businesses (Key Note 1996: 3). This diversification required individuals to work within a more complex system than the specialized demands of the (1980s) Fordist design era and to locate their practice within the frameworks of business and commercial culture more rigorously.

towards a brand ethos Implicit, here, is a convergence between advertising and design in the 1990s. In the first instance, this came about as the result of the growing dominance of the 'brand' as the driving value in the creation and mediation of goods and services. If the 1980s was dominated by an increased market in and sophistication of corporate identity design then the 1990s saw the growth of design for a brand identity. In its most general, and perhaps over-simplified sense, one might argue that once new corporate identities had been established in the 1980s, then companies could move on to the more focused characteristics of the product.

At its most basic, corporate identity is concerned with the development of a system which packages the visual style of a company and gives it a distinct and unified identity by means of design. Classically, corporate identity design has centred on the logo of a company, but its application, from its use in letterheads to advertising is important. Leading advocates of corporate identity, such as Wally Olins, are concerned that the system of corporate identity, in large companies, extends to all its visual features to the point that it becomes the embodiment of its personality (Olins 1978). Thus the 'softer' notions of values or corporate image – the more intangible impression given by a company – are paramount. Olins promoted the notion that corporate identity was not about window-dressing a company, but a tool to modify its own behaviour, bringing cohesion to its self-image.

Corporate identity, in essence, is manifestly productivist: in the first instance it is concerned with identifying the originators and distributors of goods and services.

Many similar strategies and concepts of corporate identity design are employed in branding. Its specialists equally talk of the need for in-depth research, identifying the longevity of the design, the importance of values and personality. However, the crucial difference is that in branding the designer is concerned with the actual products and services *to be consumed*, rather than the producing corporation that originates and distributes them. Sometimes these might be the same, most famously in the case of Richard Branson's Virgin Group whose corporate identity and brand identity coincide across a range of goods and services, from a cola drink, to air and rail travel to financial services and internet provision. Conversely, a corporation, might own and distribute a range of goods: thus the multinational Procter & Gamble produces a range of soap brands, some of which may even 'compete' with each other.

The burgeoning literature on branding in the 1990s uniformly proclaimed the primacy of the consumer. Nicholas Kochan of leading brand specialists Interbrand wrote, 'The brand will not attach to the group of products but to the buyers, to the consumers themselves' (Kochan 1996: xiv). Paul Southgate of Wickens Tutt Southgate puts this attachment into a process when, 'there comes a point in a brand's life when ownership is subtly transferred to the consumer. Beyond this point, perception is reality. The brand's values are no more and no less than what the consumer *believes* them to be' (Southgate 1994: 19). It seems, then, that the job of the branding expert is to manage the closing of the separation between the producer and the consumer. This narrowing of the producer/consumer gap requires a vigorous understanding of the brand's audience. Indeed, while design management in the 1980s centred on the systematizing of the design innovation process, in the 1990s it progressively veered towards the discussion of the problems of managing the interrelationship between the brand and the market.

Within this move there is a marked shift towards valuing the intangible aspects of design production. Brand identity incorporates many features: the names that products are given, the abstract sound that name invokes, the typeface employed to communicate it, the 'trade dress' in terms of colours, forms and textures employed, unique design details which identify a particular brand, the patina of copywriting ... a complex mesh of visual, material and/or textual factors. These may be the tangible expression of immaterial concepts which revolve around the brand's personality. Since the mid-1980s, intangible assets of corporations, which very much include the brand have been incorporated with increasing frequency into the company accounts (Napier 1994). How these assets are actually evidenced through design has sometimes led to complex legal battles where the extent to which these values are actually expressed in design terms has come under close scrutiny (see Schmitt and Simonson 1997: Ch. 8).

concurrent design   If the rise of branding in design draws attention further to the packaging or mediation then it is important to recognize that a fully-fledged brand-led design approach brings together a wide range of design and marketing skills. With regard to the actual products it is useful to take note of the growth of 'concurrent design' in facilitating this process. This approach to design and manufacture effectively does away with a linear system of development whereby in a corporation, departments worked in a chain of command. Instead, teams from different departments work simultaneously on the development of products, continuously interchanging information and the results of development. Of crucial importance in this process was the use of Computer Aided Design packages to speed the exchange of complex design information between individuals and groups within the development team (see Nevins and Whitney 1989).

In culture and manufacturing industries, a distinction between 'above' and 'below the line' elements of creative production is made. The 'above the line' parts are those that the product's audience directly experiences while the 'below the line' activities are those in the development of the product which are not encountered. In design terms, above the line would include packaging, branding, advertising and the product itself; the below the line work would be in the engineering of an object, the design of tooling for its manufacture, the market research and interpretation. Concurrent design effectively brought the above and below the line aspects together. It meant that data on market trends could be incorporated into the design process at various levels, not merely in the external styling of the object. Changes in functional needs, be they aesthetic or utilitarian, could be more cheaply, quickly and effectively responded to. In this way, the producer/consumer gap was drawn together by yet another route.

The development of 'just-in-time' methods – pioneered by Toyota in Japan from the 1950s onwards – further closed this producer/consumer gap. Under this system, goods are manufactured and distributed according to demand rather than being held in stock. Thus market fluctuations in volume and taste can be responded to more cheaply while capital is not tied up in holding components and finished products in stock. This requires a sophisticated production control system and a more flexible tooling able to change output rapidly.

The introduction of concurrent design, just-in-time methods and flexible specialization, either in large-scale manufacture, such as the car industry, or in the case of high-technology cottage industries of a Third Italy model form part of the productive chain of what Offe (1985) called 'disorganized capitalism'. Offe, and subsequently Lash and Urry (1987), reflected on a broad condition of late-twentieth-century society in the developed world wherein shifts from regulation, order and concentration to independence, disorder and fragmentation in economic, political and cultural life are experienced. While these writers differ in their approach, they share several conceptual shifts which are useful for understanding the growth and character of design production in recent years (see Figure 1.3).

Lash and Urry later note (1994: 123) the importance of the culture industries – which would include design – in activating this shift from organized to disorganized capitalism. Apart from the brief Fordist interlude of the 1980s already noted, the design business's propensity to constant flexibility and fragmentation, its increasing client and consumer responsiveness and its

Figure 1.3

Fordist and flexible production: transitions in economic, political and ideological realms

Source: adapted from Moulaert and Swyngedouw 1989

Fordist production	Just-in-time production
PRODUCTION PROCESS	
mass production of homogeneous goods	small batch production
uniformity and standardization	flexible and small batch production of a variety of product types
resource-driven	demand-driven
vertical and (in some cases) horizontal integration	(quasi-) vertical integration subcontracting
LABOUR	
single task performance by worker	multiple tasks
high degree of job specialization	elimination of job demarcation
vertical labour organization	more horizontal labour organization
SPACE	
functional spatial specialization	spatial clustering and agglomeration
spatial division of labour	spatial integration
homogenization of regional labour markets	labour market diversification
STATE	
regulation	deregulation
rigidity	flexibility
socialization of welfare	privatization of collective needs
centralization	decentralization and sharpened interregional /intercity competition
'subsidy' state/city	'entrepreneurial' state/city
national regional policies	'territorial' regional policies
IDEOLOGY	
mass consumption of consumer durables: the consumption of society	individualized consumption: 'yuppie' culture
modernism	postmodernism
socialization	individualization
	the 'spectacle society'

championing of visual, semantic, intuitive and creative values represent important steps in this development.

If attempts have been made to systematize the creative process in concurrent design and branding, then more intuitive, though equally consumer-orientated design work emerged in software-related fields. In this context, the design work is as close to the finished article as one might get, with the possible exception of traditional craft practice. In other words, there are few or no intermediary elements of production involved. What the designer sees on screen, is what the end-user will see. In this case, 'what the culture sector entails is not cognitive knowledge but a hermeneutic sensibility . . . or [an ability] to intuit the semantic needs of their public' (Lash and Urry 1994: 123). Thus the designer is involved in the interpretation of popular culture, fuelling it with further inflexions and innovations. The designer's understanding of the software-product's audience is filtered and synthesized with his or her creativity, itself a synthesis of influences.

conclusion   The 1980s and 1990s were fundamental decades for design practice. As a growth sector it enjoyed the freedom to test its own limits: initially consultancies developed to an unprecedented and subsequently unsurpassed size. Alongside this growth, graphics and interior related design emerged dominant as against product design, reflecting the structural changes in the economy and commerce at large. Simultaneously they began to develop systems for processing commissions, some of which were adopted from models employed by advertising agencies. Such systematizing placed many design practices into a neo-Fordist mode which ultimately would not allow them the flexibility required in a changing market. Maintaining a balance between creative and strategic practices has been, perhaps, the central concern of design in the late twentieth century.

The subsequent fragmentation of the design industry as the result of the economic recession of the early 1990s in turn led to a disembedding of its actors so that new alliances between design, advertising and other creative industries were formed. This fragmentation further encouraged the diversity of design practices: the parameters of what a design consultancy might actually do widened to overlap with other sectors such as public relations, management consultancy and advertising. Thus a combination of designers increasingly working alongside marketing-related sectors with the growing dominance of the brand – which in itself demands the amalgamation of marketing and design – and the globalization of markets meant that the culture of design was drawn ever closer to the culture of consumption.

designers and design discourse   In the

previous chapter the recent changes in the organization and commercial context of design practice were explained. It concluded by arguing that on the
one hand these conditions of production meant that designers were involved
in a constant positioning and repositioning of themselves in response to these
changing conditions and that on the other, their practice increasingly pushed
them towards a more complex relationship with the culture of consumption.
In both these cases an amalgamation of creative and strategic skills was at
play.

This complexity leads us to the possibility that a solely production-
based account of design is insufficient and the objects of its production must
be interpreted through the interaction of information and values between the
realms of production, consumption and the designers themselves. Thus
under each of these headings we can identify different causative elements we
might take into consideration in creating an account of design objects,
images and spaces.

Scholarship and journalism in fields which relate to design have predominantly tended to isolate one approach from an other, concentrating
either on the business practices of design, the authorship of the designer or
the reception of design goods and services by consumers. Chapter 1 began to
suggest, however, that the conditions of disorganized capitalism imply that
the culture of design integrates these categories so that their interaction
becomes increasingly vibrant. The rest of this chapter is devoted to exploring
the professional and cultural construction of the designer and subsequently
the variances between these and the representation, self-representation and
actual practice of designers. The discourses of professionalization, marginality and authorship need to be addressed in order to understand the relationships between designers, their clients and their public. The chapter concludes
by looking at some attempts to provide updated discursive fields in the face
of new contexts and practices of design.

definitions of design   The meaning of the word 'design' is much contested. The debate concerning its origins is unlikely to be resolved given the breadth of interpretations that the word takes. John Walker reminds us that, 'it can refer to a process (the act or practice of designing); or to the result of that process (a design, sketch, plan or model); or to the products manufactured with the aid of a design (design goods); or to the look or over-all pattern of a product ("I like the design of that dress")' (1989: 23). It has therefore accumulated several different uses. Meanings of design are many and shift according to the context in which the word is used.

Some critics seek a consciously open definition of design. In his cult book *Design for the Real World* (1972), Victor Papanek began with the words,

> All men [sic] are designers. All that we do, almost all the time, is design, for design is basic to all human activity. The planning and patterning of any act toward a desired, foreseeable end constitutes the design process. Any attempt to separate design to make it a thing by itself, works counter to the fact that design is the primary underlying matrix of life. (1972: 3)

Papanek takes an agitational standpoint, attempting therefore to denude design of any separateness. 'All men are designers', he tells us.By contrast with Papanek's proclamation, much of the history of design may be read as the history of individuals and groups who have striven to separate design from other commercial and cultural practices. In doing so they have attempted to identify themselves and their practice as something which bestows things, pictures, words and places with 'added value'. Design becomes the range of goods, spaces and services that are shaped by the intervention of professional designers. It no longer refers to the countless objects which are formed and consumed within everyday life and which do not, of themselves, carry that level of cultural capital.

The linkage to Bourdieu's notion of cultural capital (1984: 12) here is important. Put most briefly (Bourdieu's theories will be explored in more detail in subsequent chapters), cultural capital refers to one's ability to make distinctions between cultivated and vulgar taste. This notion effectively pushes design into a reflexive mode whereby its value becomes self-consciously recognized. Design thus links the economic to the cultural. Indeed, design emanates from the discourses of a culturally dynamic sector of society, an avant-garde metropolitan bourgeoisie. In his discussion of Veblen and Bourdieu, Hayward (1998) articulates the role of the avant-garde in a 'symbolic struggle' to 'step ahead' as cultural goods slip from left to right, from the 'cutting edge' into the mainstream. As such, varying degrees of *designerlyness* are inscribed into its practice.

The study of design history is embedded into institutions which mostly support the reproduction of this meaning. It is mostly taught in art and design colleges as a support to practice-based courses. Unusually it may be mobilized to challenge dominant practices of design through, for instance, feminist or ecologically inspired critiques. More often, however, it acts to reinforce very specific and indeed restrictive understandings of what design is and how it should be carried out. Much of the history and criticism of design therefore falls within a specific formal canon, thereby giving it a refined language to legitimate itself and a self-perpetuating logic which identifies 'good design' as against 'bad design' or 'kitsch'. It therefore conspires to maintain the highly reflexive, self-conscious nature of design. Chaney puts this forcefully:

> Designers' use of a language of style to ironically evoke or play with other contexts of use makes style a reflexive medium: a way of talking about itself and a way of talking about modernity. The logic of a process in which the self-consciousness or reflexivity of design grows more important is that the goods of economic exchange begin to lose any foundation in intrinsic value or function. . . . It seems that an inevitable consequence of a reflexivity of production is that style comes to supersede substance.
>
> (Chaney 1996: 150)

Perhaps judged in the context of a plethora of postmodern critiques, there is a creeping pessimism in his words here. The suggestion is that the manoeuvrings of contemporary design require it to abandon all hope and purpose in addressing real human needs; that it becomes an end in itself, the mere producer of 'desires', possibly losing all relevance to its public.

And thus the object and its mediation become one. The way by which an object is communicated to its public – as a *design* object – in turn becomes its primary value and subsequently the object itself becomes part of that communication. Equally, this is how a designed product works within a brand ethos. The object carries an emblematic status as an image. This may be part of the late-twentieth-century shift in design whereby the product has increasingly aspired to the graphic, or as Lash and Urry put it, 'What is increasingly produced are not material objects, but *signs*' (1994: 4).

the professionalization debate   In the same way that we have seen the practice of design under continual revision, so the definition of design is constantly and self-consciously being constructed, but also de-centred, dispersed and disorganized. An historical overview of the development of the word design as a practice is useful in exploring the tension between the establishment of design as a 'value added' activity and its intrinsic disembedding mechanisms.

Walker (1989: 23) draws our attention to the Renaissance use of the '*disegno*' which literally meant drawing. During this period drawing was the tool employed in the planning, conceptualizing phase that preceded the making of paintings, sculptures and so forth. Thus the practice of *disegno* involved intellectual thought and effectively separated conception and execution. A division of labour in the studios of artists did exist: apprentices would execute some of the more menial tasks such as the preparation of the canvas and even the painting of backgrounds, leaving, for instance, the 'master' to paint faces and details. While, then, this division of labour did not go so far as to completely separate mental and manual tasks, it none the less inferred that a hierarchy existed between the planning and the making aspects of cultural production. This notion of *disegno* coincides with what Balcioglu (1994) terms the 'first phase' of design of the Renaissance and Enlightenment. During these periods, he argues, design had a more open, widely used definition connected to purposes, aims and intentions.

It is clear that the word has stood at the fulcrum of a struggle for professional recognition. In discussing the origins of typography – a subset of design in general – Robin Kinross (1992) argues that it comes into being as it is brought into consciousness through language. He locates its origins in the Enlightenment via an early treatise on typography, Joseph Moxon's *Mechanick exercises* (1683–4). Kinross cites the following words:

> By a typographer, I do not mean a printer, as he is vulgarly accounted, any more than Dr Dee means a carpenter or mason to be an architect: but by a typographer, I mean such a one, who by his own judgement, from solid reasoning within himself, can either perform, or direct others to perform from the beginning to the end, all the handy-works and physical operations relating to typographie.
>
> (Moxon cited in Kinross 1992: 15)

This fascinating passage indicates a struggle to position the typographer against the more 'vulgar' practice of the printer. It marks a step in the profession of design to delineate itself from that of a trade. Notably, in order to fix an identity, Moxon begins by describing what typography is *not*.

During the 'second phase' of the nineteenth century, this discussion of word usage becomes further refined and effectively causes the term design to lose some of its potential power. The debate in Britain revolved around an awareness of the misleading parallel between the English word design and the French word *dessin*. While the French 'Ecoles de Dessin' were exclusively directed towards the teaching of drawing – using the word *dessin* in its literal sense – from the mid-nineteenth century the British 'Schools of Design' were dedicated to a broader curriculum to promote visual innovation for manufactured articles. It is not surprising that henceforward, mid-nineteenth-century reformers such as Henry Cole replaced the word 'design' with 'industrial art', 'decorative art' or 'applied art' to avoid its reductionist connotations and express greater practical and professional complexity. It also allowed the 'designers' to momentarily hijack the word 'art' to lend further status to their activities.

There was a serious disadvantage to this linguistic manoeuvring. 'Applied art' suggested that the profession was involved in the superficial addition of aesthetic measures to objects, rather than in the creation of the article itself. The 'third phase' of the early twentieth century saw the retrieval of the word 'design' in order to separate it out again from art. Thus some individuals, in particular W.R. Lethaby who was founder of the Design and Industries Association in 1915, struggled to keep the word 'art' at bay. Meanwhile, the Americans Walter Dorwin Teague, Raymond Loewy, Norman Bel Geddes and Henry Dreyfuss were calling themselves industrial designers from the late 1920s, and it was mostly their influence which helped to re-establish the use of the word design in Britain (Balcioglu 1994).

professionalization and differentiation The word 'design', then, is intimately bound up in an historical process of the professionalization of its practice. It was important that it was recognized as a pursuit which required specific education and training and could thus meet certain expected standards of knowledge, intellect and skill. As we have seen, it did this by aligning itself with other intellectualized disciplines such as fine art and differentiating itself from other trades such as printing.

This professionalizing process has involved the proliferation of institutions dedicated to the promotion of various aspects of design and the systematizing or safeguarding of its practice. In the United Kingdom, as in many countries, some of these have been state-funded organizations instigated by designers yet highly responsive to the greater demands of government policy. These various design centres have therefore frequently altered in their aims and organization as government policies have changed (Whitely 1991; Julier 1995). Changes in the institutional representation of the industry have also come about as the result of shifts in design practice itself. Thus, for instance, with the rise of exhibition and museum design in the 1980s came a series of calls to establish an association for designers specializing in that field. This in turn would consolidate that discipline as a profession and help to identify its particularities, distinguishing not merely as an extension of graphic or interior design.

The effectiveness of these institutions in securing professional status for designers has been variable. From 1992 to 1994, the Design Council facilitated the award of the British Standards Institution 5750 mark to design consultancies. This awarded an 'objective' recognition of their qualities in management, client service and efficiency. Thus, the institution of the Design Council was acting to establish professional standards in design. Take-up of this procedure among design consultancies was mixed, some seeing the British Standards system as far too simplistic for application in the design industry (see, for example, Letters to *Design Week* 23 October 1992). Equally, the issue of 'free pitching' which arose in the late 1980s, showed that design practice in a market economy could also evade professional regulation. Free pitching involves a situation where a prospective client invites several consultancies to put forward design proposals for a scheme; out of this just one consultancy would be invited to complete the design project and collect a fee. In this system, consultancies risked spending time and resources for no financial return, if they did not win the pitch. If the design industry had had a single institutional representative, then a blanket agreement among designers regarding the acceptability of this approach may have been arrived at. But with a proliferation of representative bodies, a consensus could not be achieved. Furthermore, free pitching might be resisted in buoyant times, but when there is a struggle to find clients, consultancies may not be so choosy. In whichever case, regulation, as design commentator Jeremy Myerson noted, 'points up the folly of trying to engrave regulation on tablets of stone for a business as fluid and fast-changing as this one is' (Myerson 1990).

Fluctuating client demand and the design industry's own lack of institutional cohesion have meant that it has been largely unable to establish its own professional norms. This has been met by a pressure from below in terms of 'design entryism'. Briefly put, while other professions such as law, architecture or accountancy have norms and systems of conduct which are both established by the state and their own institutional arrangements – educational and professional bodies in other words – design has no such normative systems. There is no minimum standard of attainment of training required for individuals to call themselves designers and practise commercially. This pressure from below has been exacerbated in recent years by the development of digital technologies. For instance, Desk Top Publishing programs provide easy-to-use templates for designing to different formats, thus obviating the need for a specialist to do the layout. New technologies have allowed a partial 'democratization' of design through allowing access to its tools: tasks which were once the preserve of trained specialists now become almost menial. Neither is there an agreed fee system for design services. The only known instance of such a situation was generated under Martial Law in Poland in the mid-1980s as a way of regulating entrepreneurial designers, and was short-lived and ineffective (Crowley et al. 1992: 87). This means that a rife system of fee undercutting is possible. In a climate lacking any professional and educational norms the 'outer edges' of design practice – either the highly conceptual ends of design consultancy bordering on other professions or the low end of print design and production – are vulnerable to entryism by non-design specialists. In these circumstances there is even greater demand for the designer to identify his or her services as professional and specialist.

The problems of professionalization are not restricted to the design industry. American sociologist Nathan Glazer (discussed in Schön 1991: Ch. 2) identified an historical split between what he called 'major' and 'minor' professions which are held in tension. Major professions have 'normative curricula' in their training in that there are agreed national standards in their content and assessment. They are also professionally regulated with standard agreed working procedures and norms of commercial conduct. They also often have an agreed, but not fixed, structure of pay. In architecture in Britain, for instance, these features are developed and administered by the Royal Institute of British Architects. Meanwhile, the 'minor' professions, such as design, exhibit diverse curricula, are not professionally regulated, and their pay structures are largely market-driven. In many cases the minor profession historically has referred to a major profession for its research paradigms and its norms and procedures. At the same time the minor occupation has been engaged in a struggle to build its own discursive structures, to free itself of dominance and develop its own professional culture.

One might argue that the design industry has historically been held as a minor profession to architecture. Certainly this was the case in the late nineteenth and early twentieth centuries. However, in more recent years, its points of professional reference have been more diverse. We have seen in the first chapter how the design industry has taken many cues in its management from advertising, marketing and management consultancy. Furthermore, while in the modern age, some other 'minor' professions such as nursing are essential to social well-being, design's necessity has been a harder case to argue.

In historical terms design has been a 'minor' profession. As a social class, designers belong to what Pierre Bourdieu calls the 'new petite bourgeoisie' (1984). For Bourdieu this class includes 'all the occupations involving presentation and representation' (1984: 359) and which are involved in the 'symbolic work of producing needs' (1984: 365). Jobs in advertising and sales would fit this description, but so would public-sector occupations such as in social and health care such as marriage guidance, sex therapists, dieticians and vocational guidance where the need for these services has to be argued in order to *create* their jobs. Bourdieu also notes that certain sectors of this new petite bourgeoisie, such as in media, advertising and design, by working as 'cultural intermediaries' are taste-creators. Their own preferences tend to be in marginal culture such as jazz, cinema and painting of the avant-garde.

As adherents to this 'new petite bourgoisie', designers only half-heartedly aspire to a *conservative* professional status. Attempts by consultancies to create fixed strategies have been tempered by a desire to maintain a more 'creative' drive, unfettered by procedures and hierarchies. There is something of a self-marginalization going on here that runs through design's educational and commercial system. In their sociological analysis of British art and design school culture, Frith and Horne (1987) note that, unlike other subjects in higher education, art does not lay emphasis on academic qualifications (e.g. GCSEs, A levels) for its entry requirements. Instead, much emphasis is laid on the student's portfolio and interview as evidence of their creative potential; beyond the basic skills of drawing and visualization, greater emphasis is layed on personality attributes in the selection process. Once the student is enrolled, the relative lack of strict timetabling, the provision of personal studio space instead of classrooms, the emphasis on individual creativity alongside the cultivation of a group, studio-based atmosphere conspire to produce a working practice, 'which assumes the status of lifestyle' (Frith and Horne 1987: 28). As such the art school ethos separates itself from other educational cultures and actively resists incorporation into the mainstream. Successive governments have attempted, and failed, to make art and design education more vocational, more 'responsive' to the needs of industry. Instead, the art school experience continues, largely, to promote a Romantic, marginal vision of itself, celebrating, 'the critical edge marginality allows, turning it into a sales technique, a source of celebrity' (Frith and Horne 1987: 30). Thus the art and design education system is a sociologically determined recipe for the manufacture of Bourdieu's 'new petite bourgeoisie'.

It is important to reinforce here that designers draw on this system to differentiate themselves from other professions and educations, to identify and distinguish themselves and their skills. But they are also involved in constant manoeuvrings to differentiate themselves from each other. This differentiating system draws on myths of individuated creativity inherited from art education in particular, and fine art culture in general. I self-consciously use 'art' instead of 'art and design' for in the first place, the design student's first contact in post-school art and design education is in the more generalized art and design foundation studies. Here the majority of tutors come from a fine art background and draw on individual (largely male) artist myths as a motivating factor (Clegg and Mayfield 1999). Furthermore, as we shall see in the next section, the system of design curatorship, publication and thus stardom draws predominantly on a fine art tradition of representation. In both these cases the search for and production of novelty and difference are important.

Differentiation is also necessary for the commercial survival of design consultancies: after all, they are competing with each other in order to achieve market share. Ultimately this results in design consultancies who position themselves as brands rather as if they were products or services in a competitive market (Barnard 2000). This may be done through their reputation for thoroughness, efficiency and cost-effectiveness, their experience, breadth and depth of knowledge, but they may also use their creative profile. They have to be recognized as taste-makers. One of the techniques towards this aim is to 'curate themselves' through the production of catalogues, books and exhibitions about their own work. Similarly, Wally Olins suggested in an article entitled 'Getting new business' in 1981 that an effective design consultant should ensure that they published articles 'in influential publications like *Management Today* or *The Director*' (Olins quoted in Baker 1989: 276). Consultancies might also develop their own slogans (such as Elmwood Design's 'There Is No Finish Line') or mission statements as part of this self-identification process or highlight a specialism within their own 'corporate' approach to designing. So, for instance, in 1998 design consultancy The Partners began to promote itself as a consultancy which offers 'Third Brain Thinking', mixing the logical (left brain) with the intuitive (right brain). They claimed that designers are adept at combining these two characteristics and subsequently developed this 'third brain' concept for recruitment and teambuilding consultancy for clients (Valentine 1998). Meanwhile, design consultants Michael Wolff and Piers Schmidt developed 'The Fourth Room', aimed at using creative design principles to help companies plan future strategy (Thackray 1999). In doing so, designers and design consultants are not only curating themselves, but effectively writing their own histories: *historicizing* themselves.

historicity and modernism in design discourse

Much of the history of design has been written and disseminated to effectively support this system of professionalization and differentiation. Many of the earlier design history texts focused on the successive attempts at public recognition of design as both a profession and a product (e.g. Carrington 1976) and this turns the narrative into a discourse of 'pioneering modern design heroes' in the face of a largely uninformed public. Part of the point of many of these texts was, then, to *inform* them and build a respectable status for their profession. This has privileged a particular process and product in design: the account of design has been progressively separated from the reality of its practice.

Central to the historiography of design has been the emplacement and refutation of modernism. This dates back to Nikolaus Pevsner's *Pioneers of the Modern Movement: From William Morris to Walter Gropius* first published in 1936. It traced a linear, progressive perception of design history, a steady development of architectural style, based on the work and aspirations of individual architects and designers, from the historicism of William Morris and the Arts and Crafts movement to the 'machine aesthetic' of Walter Gropius and the Modern Movement. In this book Pevsner established the canon of 'form follows function' as the governing design ideology of the twentieth century. His view no doubt reflects the dominance of German art and architectural history wherein, as Gropius himself professed, architecture is the leading edge in the development of design.

Pevsner's text is essentially teleological in that it strives to explain everything in terms of an historical inevitability. This again is derived from Pevsner's Germanic training. A Pevsnerean account therefore requires a selective, straightline approach to history. Clearly his text privileges modernism as the apotheosis of design: the narrative builds towards its conclusion at the Bauhaus where the resolution of conflicts between art and industry are resolved. As Heskett remarks, '*Pioneers* imposed a linear interpretation upon an age that was diverse and plural in nature, taking part of a complex picture and representing it as the only significant element' (1986: 7). It should be noted that Pevsner was not neutral in this account: he was an editorial member of *Architectural Review*, a journal largely dominated by the modernist canon from the 1930s. Interestingly, as if to reinforce the design = modernism equation, the book was published from 1949 as *Pioneers of Modern Design* rather than *Pioneers of the Modern Movement*.

While many subsequent texts rework Pevsner's narrative through different routes, the structure remains the same. Sigfried Gideon's *Mechanization Takes Command: A Contribution to Anonymous History* published in 1948 eschew's Pevsner's 'great designers' view to foreground the history of industry, technology and social customs. None the less, the notion of progress towards a maturity guides the narrative. Likewise Reyner Banham's *Theory and Design in the First Machine Age* of 1960 reworks notions of functionalism, but still discusses the same objects, people and lineage as Pevsner.

This system supports what John Walker calls 'the canon of design', whereby, 'the baton of genius or avant-garde innovation passes from the hand of one great designer to the next in an endless chain of achievement'

(Walker 1989: 63). Meanwhile, Richard Buchanan (1998b: 260) reminds us of the vast void between the aspirations of some reforming designers and the activities of the consuming public: the acres of publications on William Morris, the Bauhaus and so on, do not explain that public taste often went in quite the opposite direction! For example, while the design of tea-sets was a frequent design exercise for modernists (see Julier 1998), it does not explain why the world's biggest selling product of this type was Harold Hadcroft's distinctly historicist 'Old Country Roses' – featuring floral patterns and a neo-Roccoco form – which has sold 100 million pieces since its introduction in 1962 (Woodham 1997: 217).

The representation of design has been dominated by the achievements of individuals, in the first place, secondly by the aesthetics and ideology of modernism and thirdly, via specific objects of a certain type. Product design in general only accounted for 8 per cent of design business in 1995–6 (Consultancy Survey 1996) and yet it has dominated the pages of design history books and the minds of design historians alike. Moreover, this narrow account is in itself dominated by the discussion of furniture design.

The cabinet or bureau was a standard exercise of the nineteenth century, when furniture was the preserve of cabinet-makers. In the twentieth century the chair has taken its place: it has assumed an educational and emblematic status. The design of a chair's success can be judged both by the volume of production and sales and also by its 'publishability'. A highly successful chair, which returns to the designer a 1.5 per cent royalty commission can ensure a steady income to a studio. Furthermore, a chair may be readily turned into a two-dimensional photograph for publication in magazines. Indeed a designer has admitted to me that he photographs his chair prototypes to see what they look like 'on the page'. Another product designer has agreed that he only does furniture to achieve some public profile for himself in order to get his name around. Designers use objects to ensure and mark their place in the 'canon of design'.

Certain events and locations conspire to support this system. The various international furniture fairs such as at Valencia, Cologne and, in particular, Milan, provide an opportunity to reinforce a star system of designers rather like the film festivals of Cannes and the Oscar awards. Each of these events include design awards, the presentation of new designer products and are heavily marketed to design journalists. The system resonates into design curatorship. The Vitra Design Museum opened in 1990 is exclusively dedicated to exhibiting the furniture of 'name' designers. Significantly the museum's collection of over 1,200 chairs included few examples of industrially produced office chairs which form the major part of global chair production. Instead it was mostly devoted to more experimental forms which are manufactured on a small scale. London's Design Museum has mostly featured monographic shows, and, which furthermore, support a modernistic conception of design: itself supported by the heavily retro-modernist 'white cube' of the building's architecture. Finally, the design shelves of high street bookstores are dominated by glossy monographs which reinforce this curatorship. One bestselling publication, is an exhibition catalogue entitled *Pioneers of Modern Furniture* (Fischer Fine Art 1991), picking up on the Pevsnerean tradition. For its mediators, for its writers, journalists and curators, design comes to mean modernism, or even, modernist furniture. Thus in her round-up of a year's style, Abrahams (1998: 52) suggests that, 'the public are finally coming to appreciate the value of good design'. Her examples of 'good design' were all pieces of furniture which exist in the modernist pedigree of Charles Eames and Robin Day.

In all these cases the object of design is progressively reified. In other words, all aspects of the design, production and distribution are concentrated in the object as if they exist *in* it. The material form stands in for these invisible processes. Acknowledgement or analysis of these need not be explained otherwise. This reductionism in turn builds myths of design history by stripping, 'its subject matter to an unproblematic, self-evident entity (Design) in a form that also reduces its historical specificity and variety to as near zero as possible' (Dilnot 1984: 7). Interestingly, a favourite motif in monographic design books and exhibition catalogues is to place the photograph of the object alongside a curriculum vitae of the designer. Subsequently, all one is left with is the designer's career situated within the historical 'canon of design' as a way of legitimating the present.

Thus the system of design publishing is exploited for the designer's own ends. More broadly, this form of self-representation can be called 'historicity': the designer is building on the way history is written in order to provide a discursive framework for and legitimate his or her own activities. Victor Burgin has called this, 'history-writing as underwriting' (Burgin quoted in Blauvelt 1994: 209). Historicity is a term used most lucidly by the French sociologist Alain Touraine. He uses it to define, 'the set of cultural models a society uses to produce its norms and its domains of knowledge, production and ethics' (Touraine 1995: 368). Thus it is concerned with, 'the creation of historical experience, and not of a position in historical evolution' (1994: 369). It is therefore subjective and open to contestation.

Meanwhile, Poyner (1999: 7) argues that graphic design is either excluded from the history or 'gets a limited walk-on part'. Where graphic design has been represented, again this has been according to Pevsnerean model. So, for example, Meggs's history of graphic design (1983) concentrates on the influences and styles of individuals, building a narrative tending towards the development of modernism and its dismantling in postmodernity. This process of history writing serves to separate graphic design out as a profession as against its 'vernacular' activity carried out by anonymous contributors (Blauvelt 1994). It also provides a self-legitimatizing structure for individuals to take up a moral position. For example, a letter from a graphic designer published in *Design Week* complained of, 'design's very breath of life . . . suffocated by perpetual mediocrity and highly questionable work' (Argent 1998). This dispondent correspondent then went on to cite the work of 'design-greats' Paul Rand and Abram Games as inspiration for the revival of its 'integrity'.

Classical approaches to design history and discourse are thus restricted and restrictive in approach and the objects of its study. Walker raises the rhetorical question as to why design historians don't study military weapons, police equipment or sexual aids – surely three great domains of user investment in a planned product (Walker 1989: 33). Furthermore, as we have seen in the previous chapter, the vast majority of designers are involved in the planning and implementation of communications. Design is about concepts, relationships, ideas and processes. It is also a collaborative venture which is supremely intradisciplinary in that it unites specialists in two- and three-dimensional communication, visual and material culture, and it is interdisciplinary in that it brings different professional domains together. As Victor Margolin notes, 'Design history . . . has not had much success in engaging with current practice. These issues involve new technologies, innovative collaborative efforts among design professionals, a concern with the impact of complex products on users and the relations between the design of material objects and immaterial processes' (1995: 20).

second modernity versus design management   It is interesting to note how the most virulent critiques of the way design history has been written – ostensibly by British design historians – have come from American critics (see Dilnot 1984; Blauvelt 1994; Margolin 1995; Buchanan 1998b; all cited above in this chapter). It seems that they are sharply sensitized to the tensions between theoretical positions and practical action in design.

There is a manifest contradiction between the realpolitik of the design profession and some of the discourses which are mustered to explain and legitimate itself. On the one hand there is the complex, multidisciplinary industry, accustomed to teamwork, stylistic and operational flexibility and active in a broad range of domains of use and exchange. On the other hand, individual biography focusing on the designer's creativity and the Modernist canon as a benchmark of ethical and formal development predominate in the articulation of historical experience. This may explain how the same design critic can write, along with others, in the academic *Design Management Journal* about the need to develop a design education system which eschewed individual creative genius in favour of nurturing teamwork and collaboration (Morris et al. 1998) while in the professional weekly magazine *Design Week* he gives a top ten of the century's best designers, apparently seeking homage to just those values rejected in the earlier article (Myerson 1999).

During the 1980s some critics close to the design profession attempted to revise the 'canon of design' approach in the context of theoretical and commercial developments of that decade. In Britain an example of this was the publication of *Design after Modernism: Beyond the Object* (Thackara 1988) which amalgamated a wide range of essays dealing with technological and social changes and their impact on modernity, the city, questions of functionalism, manufacturing systems and design practice. It opened up a range of issues which the Pevsneristic reading was not equipped to consider. Perhaps given the breadth of subjects covered and writers contributing, this publication did not reach a consistent position. None the less the book clearly honoured the diversity of practices and positions available in design by this date.

At the same time in Italy a focused group of designer-cum-commentators developed a stridently coherent ideological stance and expressed in a refined and sometimes impenetrable language which championed a second modernity in the void left by the retreat of modernism. This was most thoroughly articulated by Andrea Branzi (1984; 1988; 1989; 1993). In his published texts, Branzi acknowledges the end of the era of modernism as a unifying system of ideology, technology and aesthetics. None the less, he does not relinquish the idea of modernity altogether but, rather, he envisages its transposition into an 'ecology of the artificial'. In this 'Second Modernity', Branzi embraces the attributes of a postindustrial society – that flexibility, differentation but also industrial internationalism will prevail. This productive system provides a basis for the exercise of a 'new tribalism', an 'ensemble of linguistic families' (1989: 38) in which cultural preferences – and thus tastes in design – are independent of ideological and national structures. The outcome is a, 'new functionality of objects, that has to correspond to uncontrollable parameters of poetry, psychology and spiritualism'. Furthermore, he champions the Italian *Nuovo Design* (discussed in more detail in Chapter 4 and of which he was a practitioner) which was based on small-scale production of goods with new technologies as emblematic of an appropriate response to this demand (1993: 127).

No doubt Branzi was attempting to develop a discursive field for design which acknowledged the ideological, industrial and commercial shifts of the late twentieth century and which was not shackled by the need for any 'homage to modernism'. His American critics point out that while he identifies new criteria for designing, both in production systems and consumer demands, his proposals for a design to meet these are rooted in a Eurocentrism and at that it is laced with a paternalistic bent (McDonough

1993: 129; Buchanan 1998a: 6). Flexible specialization, supported by information networks may well cater for diversity of taste but Branzi, they opine, still posits a design response from a position of high cultural goods. Buchanan points up how Branzi describes his second modernity, 'as an artificial system based neither on the principle of necessity nor on the principle of the identity but on a set of conventional cultural values that somehow make it possible for us to go on making choices and designing' (Branzi 1988: 71 and quoted in Buchanan 1998a: 5). Both McDonough and Buchanan are therefore wary of Branzi's position, interpreting the 'us' in Branzi's statement as 'we designers'. To put it bluntly, the view is that market segmentation and diversity is okay as long as it falls within the taste parameters of a particular, refined aesthetic sensibility: you can have any shape kitchen implement you like as long as it comes from the catalogue of a north Italian manufacturer.

Given the criticisms of (British) design history already noted, it is interesting that Branzi's critics also come from a self-consciously declared American position. Both Buchanan and McDonough regard modernism as somewhat alien to the American conception and practice of design. Their objections are founded in a conception of the culture of design as being a differentiating and responsive activity in which overarching theorems are untenable. McDonough speaks of, 'design's lack of theory, its vulgar link to real people's lives', and concludes that, 'Design is, almost by default, too vast, too fragmented, too chaotic a system for benign management, for organized reform' (1993: 131).

While these American commentators come from a broad range of opinion and backgrounds, they do seem to promote a more pragmatic vision of design. Buchanan (1998a: 10) in particular draws the debate away from Branzi's linkage of culture as an expression of ideology to reintroduce it as an activity, as cultivation. He is therefore interested in the processes of design as a search for understanding and values. As such he emphasizes that, 'the history of design in the twentieth century is not merely the history of products or of *personal styles of expression* or even *of broad cultural ideas*. It is also the history of the *character and disciplines of design thinking as they are formed through encounters with new problems*' (Buchanan 1998a: 13; his italics). In this way he sees design as being engaged in rethinking the nature of products in the context of action.

Buchanan is not necessarily specific about what he sees as 'products', stating that they can incorporate communicative symbols and images as well as physical objects (Buchanan 1998a: 13), but he also goes on to consider design in its role as shaping systems, environments, ideas and values. In this mature state it may be involved in the external presentation of goods and services to the public, but also in the internal systems that manage their development and distribution. He is thus shifting the debate from material form to immaterial processes, from design as a purveyor of objects to the shaping of structures and relationships.

There are some resonances with Buchanan's argument in Ezio Manzini's elaboration of the concept of 'dematerialization'. Manzini (1992; 1998) explores ways by which material goods may be supported or even substituted by immaterial systems (hence dematerialization). He proposes information-products (typified, for example, by internet-based entertainment), results-products (where their efficiency is measured by the 'absence' of other material products), community-products (for example, collective kitchens organized in the form of clubs) and duration-products (where, for instance, the manufacturer plays a role in the recycling or disposal of products) as strategies for integrated products and services (Manzini 1998: 50–7).

Manzini's position is blatantly forward looking and contains a strong dose of social and environmental agency. It is also tempered by an extensive understanding of materials and information technologies. By comparison, the rhetorics of much American design discourse, at least as evidenced in the *Design Management Journal*, are driven by pragmatic desires to maximize market share and profit. But in common with Manzini, there is a clear enthusiasm to move beyond the object to consider a range of interrelated communicative and material relationships. In the former case this might be expressed in terms of ensuring brand authority, loyalty or engagement through the careful ensembling of marketing, design and advertising. In the latter Manzini demands intervention, 'on the strategies that determine the social and environmental quality of the changing world' (1998: 57). In whichever case, design is not just regarded as a profession or an historical result, but is seen as something which requires management. Its effectiveness is judged more in achieving the most appropriate combination and use of different disciplines and the best relationship with end-users. This contrasts obliquely with a discourse which invests its values solely in the formal characteristics of the object.

conclusion   While much of designers' work has been concerned with the prosaic rigours of running a business, on a larger level, some of their energies have been directed at establishing their occupation as a profession. In doing so they have reflexively constructed an image of themselves and the design they produce for public consumption. The 'Pevsnerist' writing of design history has partially supported this system in giving primacy to the individual designer in the shaping of goods and in the privileging of particular forms and types of design over others. The reception, use and consumption of design is afforded little attention in these accounts, even though, again, we have seen that design practice is intimately bound up in an understanding of its audience and market.

As we saw in Chapter 1, the production of design, however, involves a more complex system of alliances between groups of professionals and is directed at a much wider range of goods, services and spaces than some popular accounts recognize. In the face of these changes some attempts have been made to develop alternative frameworks for considering design. These may attempt to update and adjust traditional conceptions to a contemporary reality of modern manufacture, distribution and social pluralism. Alternatively, discussion has shifted away from material objects to a more integrative view of design which in turn may challenge the designer's role.

the consumption of design

While the major-ity of popular accounts of design remain unashamedly designer-centric, many critics and historians have sought alternative approaches to the sub-ject. In the first instance, they have been critical of the methodological and theoretical stance taken by Pevsnerist approaches, keen to challenge the tyrannies of modernism and point up alternative practices and approaches to design.

Some design historians have stepped outside the predominantly North-West European and American contexts to demonstrate that a straightfor-ward application of modernism is not universally viable (e.g. Sparke 1988; Julier 1991; Boym 1992). Others have carried out detailed exploration of the activities of designers as part of a wider corporate culture, thus placing design more within a business history context (e.g. Heskett 1989).

More powerfully, design historians have moved entirely away from a design and production approach towards foregrounding the role of the con-sumer in the biography of objects. Their interest has been in the taste, social customs and the role of objects and spaces in the forging of human relation-ships and self-identity. This approach has often been fuelled by a political drive to challenge the complacency of designers and design students in believing that their's is the only account. After all, the majority of design his-tory has been taught in practice-based art and design departments, often to provide an alternative narrative to the day-to-day experience of the studio education. Thus they impart a recognition that no matter how much the designer tries, he or she cannot fully control the processes by which the pub-lic read, interpret or even straightforwardly use the objects, images and spaces they shape. As Adrian Forty points out, there is a paradox here in that designers are both in command of what they do but at the same time they are the agents of ideology, subcontracters of a bigger system. He believes that there is no answer to this, only that, 'both conditions invariably co-exist, however uncomfortably, in the work of design' (1986: 242).

Meanwhile, some design historians have evermore vigorously applied themselves to studying consumption to the point that critics such as Richard Buchanan (1998b), whose chief interest is in the processes of design, wonders whether they are in fact hostile to practice. Much of this chapter is aimed at arguing that a singularly consumption-driven approach would miss much of the interest and complexity of contemporary design culture.

In order to open up the discussion concerning the consumption of design, historians have drawn from a wide range of theoretical discourses which have been developed in cultural studies, social anthopology, sociology and cultural geography: a veritable 'spaghetti junction of intersecting disciplines, methodologies, politics' (Slater 1997: 2). These have largely focused on the qualitative analysis of consuming: how objects, images and spaces are valued, thought about or, more straightforwardly, used by their public rather than on the quantitative aspects of size and structure of markets. In their theoretical underpinning they share a range of key thinkers who have developed a series of distinctive positions on the nature of consumption.

the culture of consumption   As we have seen with the term 'design', so consumption is a broad concept which invariably requires qualification. Consuming entails the using or using-up of something. It may involve the pleasures or un-pleasures of having an artefact or it can be concerned with the acts prior to ownership: gathering product information, browsing, shopping and acquisition. Looking, listening, smelling or touching are also acts of consuming. It may also involve the consumption of time, as in the case of some leisure experiences or in the rental of goods. The various acts of consumption are experienced in a variety of ways, locations and moments.

Such prosaic moments of consumption express, knowingly or not, a wider set of cultural and ideological systems. At an immediate level consumption is concerned with the struggle to control the visual, spatial and material fabric of everyday life. Consumer culture, then, concerns the larger picture which acquisition and use represent, the values and systems which are reproduced and articulated through consuming.

Some ground rules as to how we might view the general character consumer culture in the West are usefully established by Slater (1997: Ch. 1). First, consumption is intrisically a cultural process. While it requires economic exchange it also involves the exercise of taste as part of a self-identifying act. Consumer culture includes the balance between a quest for achieving meaningful ways of life and the resources available to be able to do this. It is therefore about 'having' rather than 'being'. As such it is also the dominant value of Western society.

Secondly, consumption entails an exercise of private, personal choice within the market: the emphasis is on the acquisition and experience of goods and services which are not produced by the consumer him- or herself.

It is also universal and impersonal in that in principle goods and services are not produced to individual commission, rather they are produced to an imagined and unknown consumer. Access to goods is only limited by the ability to pay for them. It is open to anyone with the money.

Thirdly, if consuming involves making choices, then consumer culture is identified as a culture of freedom and individualism. Thus consuming is declared as the exercise of private will, free of public intervention. Slater argues that it is also a private act which is consigned to personal pleasure rather than public good. In this highly individualistic mode it may even contradict notions of social order, solidarity and authority.

Fourthly, consumer culture is founded on the constant expansion of demand. Indeed economic organization is fuelled by an insatiable desire to produce more wealth, acquisitive power and thus more consumption. Thus society must be highly rational and disciplined in order to deliver this but at the same time it must foster irrational passions and desires in order to promote consumption. For some thinkers the tension between the two characterizes the crossover from modernity (rational) to postmodernity (irrational) in contemporary society.

Fifthly, in this post-traditional society, consumption becomes the leading device through which individuals construct their identities. Whereas in pre-modern society identity and status were largely given and modes of consumption were subordinate to these, modern concepts of individualism require that the goods one acquires and displays momentarily define one's identity. As the order of society is unstable, however, so is the relationship between consumption and identity. Thus the meanings of appearances, the codes by which we read identities, are constantly changing.

Finally, consumer culture incorporates virulent mechanisms for the production and representation of commodities as signs. They are increasingly mediated – through advertising, packaging, shop display etc. – and become aestheticized. Furthermore, increasing amounts and types of commodities are not material goods but representations (computer software, for example) and experiences (such as certain forms of leisure) – they are 'dematerialized' products. In view of this, there is a new flexibility in the relations between consumption, communication and meaning. Contemporary economics, commerce and politics are therefore driven by 'sign-values' – what things look like and how that image is interpreted. Culture, Slater concludes, takes up a leading position in the modern exercise of power.

design and consumer culture   The above summary of consumer culture is useful for the observer of design in that it establishes a basis with which we can begin to compare specific contexts and modes of consumption and situate the discourses of selected objects therein. By considering specific design examples, Slater's outline requires some qualification.

First, his reduction of consumption to an anonymous act – that goods are not produced to individual commission – is generally the case although we must be mindful of examples where goods and services are designed for customization. Bicycles, computer software and financial packages are often adapted to a user's specific requirements so that the consumer plays an active role in their shaping. Production and consumption thus overlap to form what Toffler (1980) called the 'prosumer'.

Secondly, Slater's emphasis on consumption as a private, politically-passive act ignores the reality that individuals also engage in a public realm with consumption. Much of material culture studies have been dominated by investigations of the private domains of consumption and the private individual. However, more public spaces are powerful loci for the articulation of both public and private modes of consumption. Where the public domain has been considered, it has mostly been within the framework of the commodification of that experience: shopping as a form of spectacle and expedition into modernity (e.g. Corrigan 1997); museums and expositions as the organization and classification of material culture for public consumption (e.g. Vergo 1989); heritage industries (e.g. Urry 1990) and the 'consuming' of public services (e.g. Keat et al. 1994).

By placing the consideration of consumption into a public realm, interesting questions are raised concerning the crossovers between private and public space, commodified and non-commodified goods and services and the personal and the political. For example, voting in local and national political elections may be guided by preferences as to how councils and governments spend the money they gather through taxation. Tourism and leisure involves the consumption of some non-commodified services – such as museums run by volunteers – in a public or semi-public environment. Private consumption may also be directly guided by ideological beliefs which are articulated in a public way: the boycotting of goods from repressive regimes or which have a highly negative environmental impact illustrate this direct link between political will and consumption. More loosely, private patterns of consumption may be informed by a wider public identity concerning the aesthetic and utilitarian dimensions of the places we inhabit and use. Thus, a poor public transport system may cause higher private car ownership. Consumption is not exclusively about the acquisition of individualized goods and services, then. It involves the interconnection of a range of actions through a chain of sites and times (Jackson and Thrift 1995).

Thirdly Slater, at least initially, builds a dualism between a rational society of production and irrational individualistic consumption. To characterize consumption as 'irrational' certainly pays due regard to the role of desire, however this shouldn't be overplayed. Many, if not most, acts of everyday consumption are highly rational. They are based on the stringent calculation of need and value-for-money. Design, may subsequently play to a rational/irrational split in consuming and may in turn blur or confuse the distinctions between the two. Some goods may be made from cheaper materials but still aspire to luxurious ambition in their form (as we shall see in Chapter 4); leisure spaces may be highly rationalized, promising their efficient use, yet give the impression of endless leisure time (as we shall see in Chapter 7).

passive or sovereign consumers?   As an organizing principle, then, consumer culture is *the* culture of the post-traditional age. However, to get beyond the macro-context, to investigate the fluxes, disjunctures and contradictions within it, the design and mediation of objects, spaces and images requires detailed attention. Circulating around all features of consumer culture is the tension between individual autonomy and consumption's wider role in promoting economic competition. On the one hand, consumption may be used as an expression of personal freedom and power; on the other it concerns the manipulation of needs and wants by dominant institutions.

The idea that consumption might be a vehicle for the pacification, coercion and manipulation of the masses stems from a position taken up by members of the so-called Frankfurt School. Writing from the 1920s to the 1960s, they deliberately avoided romantic notions of creativity and individuality in the production of cultural artefacts and pursued the possibility that it was a coordinated, logical and calculated activity. Theodor Adorno and Max Horkheimer (1979) used the term 'culture industry' to express the similarities between popular entertainment and mass manufacture. They suggested that their production became commodified and distributed just like any other artefact in capitalist society. They were consumed by a mass market which was passive in its uncritical tastes and reception of cultural goods. Thus an audience is duped into believing in the quality of the things they consume as evidence of the successful functioning of the state and its political economy. Equally, as Carr and Fusi (1981) explain, the mass consumption of popular entertainment and goods may be mobilized towards what they called 'the culture of evasion': in the case of Spain during the fascist Francoist dictatorship this involved the saturation of the mass media with low-budget musicals, bullfighting and football which promoted passivity and avoided the remotest chance of the politicization of consumers.

This 'manipulation' theory is extended from entertainment to all goods by J.K. Galbraith (1958; 1967) who argued that the fundamental problem of advanced capitalism is the disposal of its surplus products: as we have seen, in order to grow and survive, capitalism must 'over-produce' in terms of current demand. Thus, needs have to be created (the 'production of consumption') in order to deal with this problem. In design terms, this gives rise to advertising promoting 'false needs', as Vance Packard suggests in *The Hidden Persuaders* (1957). Within this, one might even recall the very nature of the design profession which is required to create a need for its services.

This may explain the strategy of obsolescence in which products have a limited life designed into them, either through their lack of physical durability or their quickly becoming unfashionable. Advertising would help brand loyalty so that consumers would continue to buy within the range of products offered by the same manufacturer. Upon their respective goods becoming obsolete consumers would then climb a 'brand ladder' by buying the next product up the range.

At the opposite end of the scale to these manipulation theories is the notion of 'consumer sovereignty'. This effectively turns the manipulation theory on its head and argues that if corporations are in competition with each other, then they must respond to the expressed preferences of consumers. After all, what is to stop them moving between brands rather than buying into a ladder of same-brand products? Thus within this conception of sovereignty the consumer becomes an ultimate symbol of all other freedoms of Western capitalism. Even the most mundane act of consumption becomes an expression of individual freedom and honour. It is an image which neatly contrasted with the inability of Soviet systems to provide for individual desires from the Cold War until the collapse of socialism in the late 1980s.

Complementary to the concept of consumer sovereignty was enterprise culture which expressed the idea of individuals seeing consumption as an entrepreneurial activity in itself. Thus goods and services such as property and pension plans are appreciated for their ability to generate further capital. Similarly, entrepreneuralism within enterprise culture has a 'go-getting' quality, able to anticipate and exploit market opportunities. Both consumer sovereignty and enterprise culture suggest an heroic individualism which received particular promotion during the neo-liberalist Thatcherite 'designer' decade.

Simultaneously, discussions of consumption as a resistant or empowering act have emerged. Social anthropologist Daniel Miller (1987; 1988) has explored the dynamics of consumption in terms of alienation and de-alienation. His argument is that artefacts are intrinsically alienating: they come with little or no information concerning the conditions of their production and distribution and the consumer holds no social relationship to their producers. Consuming is, as we have seen, an anonymous act. Thus the consumer engages in the de-alienation of these objects through their use and customization to their own needs. Among the examples he uses to support this case is his ethnographic study of kitchens in a North London housing estate. The fitted kitchens came as standardized installations in the flats and Miller therefore looks at how tenants made these 'their own' through making adjustments to them or through their complete replacement. By personalizing their living environment tenants were resisting the tastes handed down to them by their landlord. Through their own aesthetic preferences they were also making highly individualized statements about kinship, gender, memory, gift exchange and personal space. Such studies present the consumer as highly active in determining or creating the social meaning of goods, rather than as the passive receiver of given meanings.

Similarly, Dick Hebdige (1979) in his studies of youth subcultures contends that 'street' music and fashion are involved in the re-appropriation of the material of mass culture through a process of *bricolage*, of do-it-yourself assemblage. Hence punk style took the stereotyped dress codes of mainstream gender roles such as the city gent or the streetwalker and altered and subverted them in ironic, playful or confrontational ways. Clearly Hebdige draws on highly spectacular forms of personal expression but both he and Miller consider consumption in areas where its practice is less bounded by economic pressures. Along with Fiske (1989a; 1989b) and de Certeau (1984) they also open up a space for evaluating the meaning of consumption in 'real', everyday life as a creative, pleasurable activity. It thus becomes a productive process in itself.

As much as the sovereign consumer notion has been generated within neo-liberalist conservative ideologies so, then, it has stood behind academic challenges to the Frankfurt School's conception of a docile mass audience and reinvigorated academic interest in actions of ordinary citizens as creative and empowering.

One must approach the work of Miller, Hebdige, Fiske and de Certeau with a measure of caution, for, as Meikle (1998) points out, they have a tendency to romanticize the subcultures they investigate. Their accounts are often biased against the dominant cultures responsible for the design of commercial products and they do not address the majority of consumption which takes place in the mainstream (Meikle 1998: 197). If their aim is to remobilize a sense of dignity in the everyday, particularly in working-class life, one is left asking why, for instance, they haven't discussed the dress, chants and gestures on the football terraces or the effects of hire-purchase and home-shopping catalogues on taste and consumption patterns.

These writers are important, however, because while design objects – kitchen hardware, fashion, music – are discussed their main concern is to show how these enact social or ideological values. Their approach owes something to the work of Veblen and Bourdieu, whose interest was in the active role of consumption in articulating social relations. Based on observations of the *nouveau riche* of the late-nineteenth century in the USA, Veblen's *Theory of the Leisure Class* (1970 [1899]) was the first major contribution to literature on consumption. He argued that this class displayed their wealth through the conspicuous display of non-utilitarian goods. Basing his theories on an extensive study of Parisian consumers, Bourdieu took a similar standpoint to Veblen in the notion that the culture of consumption was concerned with differentiation and identity: goods take on a symbolic role in this process. The key development Bourdieu makes is in suggesting that people distinguish themselves by the distinctions they make. The ability to make these distinctions is in their 'cultural capital'.

Veblen and Bourdieu both tended to separate consumption away from production. It is, however, a pervasive strategy of contemporary commerce to re-appropriate the character of active consumption. Their theories will be interrogated in more depth in the next chapter where we shall look at the role of producers in articulating the processes of differentiation for consumers.

de-alienation and designing   Interestingly the notion of giving back some active engagement through consumption to the public had been explored in various art and design practices from the 1960s. The verve for *happenings* in artistic practice of the early 1970s often included street performance which encouraged the participation of their audiences. This in turn encouraged them to build their own meanings and understandings of the event. A similar 'letting go' was to be found in the radical proposals of the British architectural group Archigram. Their 'plug-in cities' proposed the use of inflatables and prefabricated modules as architectural elements fulfilling a range of services which could be literally bolted on to a structure in response to consumer demand and changing tastes. Out of these utopian, politically motivated movements came the development of modular furniture which allowed the user to assemble seating, storage and other elements according to their personal preferences (Papanek and Hennessey 1974). Thus part of the design task was given over to the consumer.

Self-assembly, modular furniture obviously re-emerges in a commodified form in mainstream manufacture and retail most obviously in the case of Ikea. As the world's largest furniture chain-store Ikea successfully established a brand identity based around the retail of particular design values deriving from its Swedish background. Among these was the promotion of flat-pack furniture which, as they explained to their customers, through their catalogues and in-store announcements, allowed them to reduce costs in shipping and therefore make their goods cheaper. They also argued that the greater ease of transport of such items made them more environmentally responsible. By making these issues clear to customers, Ikea were effectively inviting them to become privileged participants in their corporate vision. This narrative of participation in a 'democratic' corporate vision was reinforced through their advertising such as the 'chuck out your chintz' TV advertising campaign devised by the St Luke's agency in 1997–8. It featured women ridding themselves of oppressive Victorian taste and heading for the libertarian halls of Ikea in a parody of political emancipatory movements. Ikea was being offered through this advert as the reasonable, democratic alternative to belong to. Thus 'freedom' of consumption is conditional on and conditioned by shopping at Ikea.

The Ikea case is a sophisticated example of a crucial challenge which designers and marketers engage with. In effect, among their jobs is the *de-alienation* of alienating artefacts. This means that they mediate the gap between production, in its crude form as the system for the origination and creation of goods and services, and consumption, as the user's engagement with them. The integration of design, marketing and advertising allows for a sophisticated construction of meanings to be supplied with the object and to be identified with it. Thus both the physical content of goods and their interpretation are considered within the production process. Simultaneously or alternatively, the consumer builds his or her own hermeneutical engagement independently of the producer. The designer, in combination with other professionals, must take decisions regarding the degrees and mechanisms of de-alienation. The designer can entirely hand over the object to be received 'as it is', to allow the consumer to build their own meanings or none at all. Or he or she can carefully construct an 'aesthetic illusion' around the product.

This dialogue between the producer and the consumer may not necessarily require complex marketing mechanisms. It may originate in the content of the product itself. A designer might develop ways by which the use of an article involves the building of a relationship with it. An example of this is in photocopier design carried out by King-Miranda for Olivetti during the 1980s (Barbacetto 1987). In designing their operating interfaces, they explored the incorporation of pictograms which required the user to adopt and master its own visual language. While these pictograms were derived from archetypal forms, the learning of the photocopier's language still required an intimate interaction with it. As a relationship with the product was built up then so its alienating character, particularly in a new technology as it was then, receded. In the light of this example, Barbacetto explains that, 'Design is destined to incorporate . . . the cultural contents of the relationship between men and technology' (1987: 101).

the aesthetic illusion   Consuming goods or services may pass through several different stages. After all, we have seen that it may involve several sensorial activities along an extended continuum of time and in various locations. The object itself may thus undergo gradual but continuous transformation in its significance, passing from future desire, to present achievement to memory.

An extreme view would consider all things as commodities at all times, that they always are exchangeable and have value as such. Conversely, Igor Kopytoff (1986) argues that in fact objects can pass from a commodified to a de-commodified status. Thus something might be bought but then given an individualized identity which cannot be subsequently exchanged. Corrigan (1997: 36) uses the example of the cat to illustrate this: a cat might be bought in a pet-store where it is a commodity but then becomes singularized as a family pet and is unlikely to be re-commodified. Kopytoff claims that things can take on biographies whereby their status and meaning change according to different contexts and, of course, the writer of that biography. 'An eventful biography of a thing', he goes on, 'becomes the story of the various singularizations of it, of classifications and reclassifications in an uncertain world of categories whose importance shifts with every minor change in context' (1986: 90).

Some attempts to understand the shifting meaning of objects through time stem from a reading of Karl Marx's *Capital: Volume One* (1957 [1867]), in particular his discussion of the commodity. In Marxist terms, the commodity is the object in the realm of the market. Exchange-value is the value of the commodity in the market, while use-value is the actual value something has outside the market. Once in the marketplace, commodities circulate independently of the labour that produced them; they are effectively alienated from the human conditions of their production and that labour is not visible. Whereas in feudal and communal contexts social relations were directly reproduced by the exhange of goods, in capitalism the products of labour are separated out from the relations of labour. After all, under capitalism, objects are placed into the marketplace where the consumer is unknown just as the consumer is unlikely to know the producer or much about the systems of their production. The division of labour further ensures this anonymity. As a result, social relations through labour are supplanted by relations between things; commodities *stand in* for those relations and only relate to each other or in relation to money which abstractly represents all commodities. This process leads to what Marx called 'commodity fetishism'. A fetish is something which is believed to have a supernatural power. Thus commodities become fetishized in that they are thought to embody the power of human relations (see Figure 3.1). Once the commodity is divorced from its productive base then it is free to take on a range of cultural values about itself. Thus through advertising, display, branding, salesmanship and

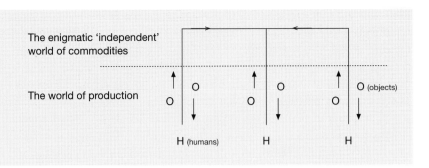

Figure 3.1

Market society

Source: adapted from

Cohen 1979

other forms of mediation, it is conferred with myths which in turn appear to be 'natural' to it. Semiotics is a methodology used to decode these myths and explain how they are constructed.

In this respect mention should be made of the work of Jean Baudrillard. Baudrillard (1988) played a key role in stepping away from the Marxist conception of commodity fetishism being an expression of citizen's alienation from each other as producers. His interest was in the notion that the desire to consume is not directed at specific objects, rather it is a generally produced condition. Instead he suggests that as signs, goods are free to take on any association or meaning as a play of signifiers. This doesn't mean to say that production is unimportant: both production and consumption are caught up in a general system in which each becomes a simulation. This is a radical proposition which requires us to abandon a quest for authenticity.

Considerable attention has been given to the role of advertising in constructing myths around commodities (Williamson 1978; Dyer 1982). Meanwhile, Schudson (1993) argues that advertising is not as important a force as these critics make out and usefully draws our attention to other forms by which product knowledge reaches consumers; these would include word of mouth, mass media other than advertising, direct marketing and promotions. Leiss et al. (1990: 36–9) suggest that advertising is a largely reactive profession which follows market trends and that it is more successful in giving information than actually manipulating consumers into unwittingly buying things they do not want. (The limitations of advertising are discussed further in Chapter 9.) The inference here is that advertising participates in a wider orchestration of values and is not solely responsible for any mythologizing processes. Therefore we have to look to other features in which design intervention is made along the system of provision.

F.W. Haug (1986) presents an argument which forces us to consider the intersection of a variety of visual, textual and material forms in the development of 'commodity aesthetics'. He argues that artefacts in the market have to promise a use-value once they are sold: they have to appear to be useful before they actually are. This 'aesthetic illusion' is established through the appearance of commodities themselves, through the semantic of the product itself. Thus a 'technocracy of sensuality' runs through the origination, shaping and promotion of products and in turn shapes consumer expectations. In part his somewhat apocalyptic text may be linked to the styling of products through the application of a 'second skin'. Cars have to look as well as be fast.

This is important when regarding contemporary product design as part of a brand ethos and also in view of the increasingly sophisticated ways by which the design and marketing of commodities overlap into consumer culture. We shall see in Chapter 5 how the external appearance of products interfaces with their promotion. However, Haug's analysis suggests that commodity aesthetics refers merely to the externally-applied, decorative effects of goods. In this case their performance remains the same while their external semiotic appeal changes (Wernick 1991: 190). The attributes of goods designed for promotion (exchange-value) may also provide the utilitarian content (use-value), however. Where promotion and function converge, for instance, is when chocolate is made to be sweeter, cars to be faster (Fine and Leopold 1993: 27). This is particularly the case in image-based goods such as CD-ROMs, video-games or newspapers and magazines where the look of the thing is intimately bound up in the way they function.

systems of provision   Haug represents an important departure from other theorists in his demand for a vertically-integrated analysis of material and visual culture by linking product form to its mediation to social signification in consumption. To follow this challenge demands that the cultural critic employs a variety of skills. She or he must act as business historian, semiologist, economist, sociologist, ethnographer, anthropologist and above-all, be visually literate. Few consumption theorists (e.g. Featherstone 1991; Corrigan 1997; Campbell 1998) actually approach the objects of consumption. Artefacts, visual or materially-based, are rarely discussed and so we are left with observations which circulate around a void which requires filling.

One commendable exception to this general reluctance to approach the object is Dick Hebdige's classic essay on the Vespa motor scooter (1988: Ch. 4). Hebdige identifies production, mediation and consumption as three key 'moments' in the object's biography. He then skilfully rides it through these, first taking us to the scooter's origination in postwar Italian reconstruction. He then considers the marketing strategies in introducing this new typology in two-wheeled transportation, but also forms of product mediation outside the Piaggio's remit such as owners' clubs and word-of-mouth reputation. Finally he explores questions of gender and sexuality within its accumulated social meanings. In doing so he reveals both the continuities between production and consumption and the mutability of the object – the possibility of different, even conflicting meanings through its various moments. Importantly, however, he does not lose sight of the object; instead he brings together a sense of the Vespa's visceral presence, its various representations and the discourses which accompany these.

Another strength in Hebdige's approach is that he clearly acknowledges the fact that he is dealing with forms of consumption particular to his central object during a given period. Again this is at variance with many texts which approach consumption as if all its forms were the same, as if the conditions of acquisition, use, storage and memory of luxury goods were the same as for, say, staple goods.

An alternative methodology to generalist theories of consumption is proposed by Fine and Leopold (1993; Fine 1995) in their 'systems of provision' approach. They argue that commodities or groups of commodities are structured by a chain or system of provision that unites a particular pattern of production with a particular pattern of consumption. This approach therefore looks for differences rather than generalized similarities between the ways that production and consumption are brought together. They identify distribution, retail and what they interestingly call, 'the cultural reconstruction of the meaning of what is consumed' (Fine and Leopold 1993: 4) as devices for connecting production to consumption.

The mediation of the relationship between product, production and the consumer is paramount to the work of the designer and links back to their work in de-alienating commodities. As Gardner and Sheppard put it, 'The designer is out to achieve what Marx believed was ultimately impossible under capitalism, to bridge that yawning gap between private production and public consumption' (1989: 74). They describe this as the 'holy grail' of the designer in their perpetual attempt to make products 'meaningful' by getting the right fit between production and consumption. It would seem apt to adopt Fine and Leopold's 'systems of provision' approach in the face of this.

As such the designer is involved in controlling the 'flows' of material, visual and textual information of a product. This idea of 'flows' has been promoted by Spanish sociologist Manuel Castells (1996). He argues for a reconfiguration of cultural geography, calling for an analysis of information interchange along networks rather than the discussion of identities within discreet spatial boundaries. Conceptually, there is some resonance in Raymond Williams's notion of 'flows of images' in his discussion of television and cultural form. Williams (1974: 87–9) sought to reconstitute critical analysis of television by challenging us to think of it not as a sequence of individualized moments, but as a flow of image and sound. I wish to generalize the concept so that in design terms, objects are not abstracted from contexts into a reified, modernist canon (the single-piece exhibit, mediated by the expert's caption). Rather, they belong to a never-ending stream of visual and material narratives running in a series of directions. We might begin to think in terms of 'flows of artefacts' both material and visual through a circuit.

circuits of culture   Through their critiques of earlier theorists, some academics have recognized the need for a more complex, but more satisfying, approach to studying the culture of production and consumption. The classic model would be to arrange production, distribution and consumption in a straight line. Johnson (1986) loops this chain back into itself to describe an endless 'circuit of culture' (see Figure 3.2).

Johnson's diagram is useful in a number of ways. First, it suggests a linkage between the public and private domains of consumption, as well as ideological conditions and personal action. Secondly, it emphasizes the interpretative nature of consumption, suggesting that the objects of production become 'texts' which are then 'read'. This reading then feeds into lived cultures, it informs the way that everyday life is articulated which then provides information upon which production then acts. Thus, thirdly, we may begin

Figure 3.2

Richard Johnson's
'circuit of
production and
consumption'

Source: Johnson 1986

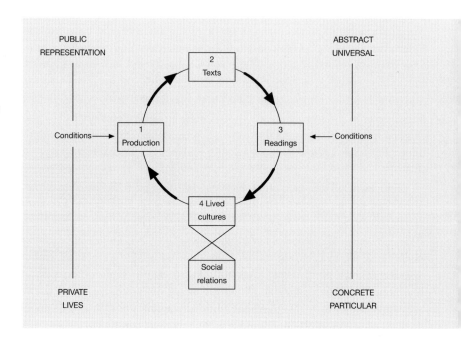

to appreciate design as both articulating and enacting social relations and human action.

Du Gay et al. (1997) push this model further by suggesting that different stages in the circuit all interact with each other (see Figure 3.3). Their text is more specific in terms of the qualities involved in the production and consumption process. They claim that both production and consumption inform social identities, the way that objects are represented and their systems of regulation, meaning the way that norms are established in order that the product is consumed in conformity to specific patterns and meanings. Furthermore, they may be encountered in different formats through this circuit – as primary functional objects, as represented in promotional material, at the point of sale and so on. Their meanings are subject to constant transformation and rewriting by both producing agents (designers, marketers, distributors etc.) and by their consumers. Through their critical and exhaustive study of the Sony Walkman, they continually return to the overlapping and interactions of different nodes in their circuit of culture.

designers and the circuit of culture   Johnson (1986), Fine and Leopold (1993), Jackson and Thrift (1995) and du Gay et al. (1997) all provide models or suggestions for considering the production/consumption relationship which are applicable in different ways to different objects, spaces and images. Rather than assume a universality in this they

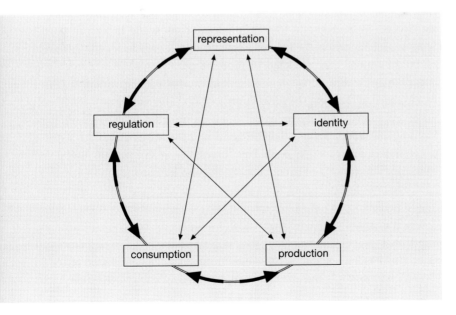

Figure 3.3
Paul du Gay et al.'s
'circuit of culture'
Source: du Gay et al.
1997

honour the diversity of actions and experiences involved between distinct cultural and commercial forms. Thus for instance, so-called Fast Moving Consumer Goods (FMCGs) – goods such as foodstuffs which are subject to repeated repurchase – will be treated differently from consumer durables. Products may be moved through the circuit, or the system of provision, in different patterns and speeds according to the many variables along its route. Certainly design may act as a laxative for this circuit, helping to move goods faster through the system (Reavley 1998). In other words, design promotes an insatiable appetite for newness, variety or 'the next thing'.

As we have seen in Chapter 1, market research for major brands often combines quantitative data through surveys with qualitative research undertaken, for instance, through focus groups. The account planner then develops this information into a detailed brief for designers. As such, he or she is attempting to anticipate consumer expectations as well as develop future desires. The account planner is in a position therefore to orchestrate some measure of the flow throught the circuit of culture.

There are various methods by which design production appropriates the realms of consumption. At one end of this scale, consultancies may employ designers who represent their target market as consumers themselves. In Britain this was particularly the case during the mid-1980s when design consultancies eagerly employed young graduates who had an instinctive feel for trends in the youth market for retail and consumer items (York 1988). It was assumed, effectively, that by designing for themselves they would be designing for their peers. At the other end of the scale, brand and identity specialists will promote complex design systems in order to ensure that all aspects of consumer behaviour are mapped, accounted for and anticipated as part of the design process. Thus while marketing gurus Schmitt and Simonson (1997: 143) lambast open-ended academic discourse on consumption, they are keen to promote models such as a particularly convoluted one devised by design methods and marketing specialist, Peter Bloch aimed at 'Seeking the Ideal Form' (1995). This model networked cultural, situational and psychological domains in order to explore different levels of consumer response. Schmitt and Simonson stated that Bloch's article which outlined this model, 'could be a forerunner to a potentially useful line of research in the area of product aesthetics and identity' (1997: 44).

Despite Schmitt and Simonson's positivistic and somewhat anti-intellectual stance, it must be noted that increasing numbers of designers and design students engage with theoretical discourses in the social sciences and humanities as a way of deepening their critical perspectives on consumer culture. This has led some to some observations that they are better versed in 'French philosophy' than the technical intricacies of design (Kinross 1997: 202)!

writing about things   The rise of interest in consumption has indeed been accompanied, if not prefigured, by an artistic response to the growth of consumer culture. During the 1950s the Independent Group – a collective of artists, critics and architects – and other pop artists explored consumerism, in particular through the impact of American popular culture. The collages and paintings of Richard Hamilton revealed the relationships between product appearance, advertising and sexuality in subtle ways which have led John Walker to describe his work as that of a 'knowing consumer' (1983: 32). His contemporary, the critic Reyner Banham, wrote many lively essays on product design and popular culture such as 'Power Plank' (1996 [1973]), an essay on the semantics of clipboards, and 'The Great Gizmo' (1981 [1965]) on electronic gadgets. His penchant for gizmos and gadgets was expressed in a largely formalistic way; the main concern was for the physical attributes of commodities and his relationship to them as a consumer. Thus his approach was similar to that of an art connoisseur looking at design, except that he vastly extended the border of what the design critic might look at beyond the Modernist canon to all mainstream everyday objects.

Fiction writing opens a pathway by which description and specialist descriptive terms may be celebrated. Nicholson Baker's first novel *The Mezzanine* (1988) follows the journey of an office worker through his lunchhour as he considers the minutiae of his material surroundings: the shape of stapler in relation to locomotive trains; the shift from paper to plastic straws; why one shoelace should break before the other; the labelling of a packaged sandwich as 'Cream Cheese and Sliced Olive' ('why *sliced*?' he asks). Through such obsessive interrogations he links them to memory, showing that, 'our relationship with material things, and our awareness of their gradual but continuous transformations, provide a measure of much of the meaning of our lives' (Meikle 1998: 197). Similarly, David Guterson's detailed explanation of trawler-fishing equipment (1995: 346–7), Slavenka Drakulic's discussion of laundry (1988: 43–54) or William Gibson's description of a 'chunker' (1994: 9) show that articulating the material can provide poetic, beautiful results. In each of these examples the narrative of the novel is momentarily grounded in the visceral reality of the everyday. Likewise, Patrick Suskind's bestseller novel *Perfume* (1987) features a protagonist with extraordinary powers of smell: using this device the reader is navigated through a unique perspective on space and the relationship between sensory perception and place.

conclusion   It is not insignificant that the growing interest shown by sociologists, anthropologists, cultural geographers and historians in matters of visual and material culture and its consumption has emerged in an era where ideological and commercial primacy has increasingly been given over to consumers within systems of liberal democracy and market capitalism. However, given the broad range of academic disciplines with an interest in consumption it is hardly surprising that a wide variety of positions regarding its value, meaning and practices have been adopted. Broadly speaking these may be divided into three camps: to perhaps oversimplify, first, there are those who frame consumption as an essentially docile activity over which producing agents dominate (Frankfurt School, Galbraith, Packard, Haug); secondly, those who adopt, at times, the notion that consuming can be emancipatory or even resistant (Hebdige, Miller, de Certeau, Fiske); and finally, those who view it as neither of these but as an expression which has its own, often spectacular, postmodern logic (Baudrillard, Eco). As subsequent chapters in this book argue, the culture of design conspires to overlap these positions, making consumption both active and passive, meaningful and meaningless at the same time. Consumer empowerment, ironically, may sometimes mean an ability to accept given situations as they are with both distance and engagement. It is perhaps more useful to consider *how* the exchanges of production and consumption take place.

Consumption stands at the intersection of different spheres of everyday life, between the public and the private, the political and the personal, the individual and the social. It represents and articulates these relationships but is also active in reproducing them. Given its ubiquity, the study of consumption need not privilege certain goods and services over others; it promises an open-game where the most prosaic interaction with material and visual culture is laced with significance. Equally, Veblen and later, Bourdieu remind us that we must be aware of the symbolic value that they hold, that despite the promise of democracy of consuming within market capitalism, it may also be an act of differentiation and distinction.

Theoretical explorations of consumption have provided useful conceptual frameworks for the interrogation of the exercise of taste. Some literary and artistic creations develop a lively vocabulary to express the visceral immediacy of our visual and material environment. Both of these pursuits again remind us of the polysemic nature of consuming – that it can mean several things at various levels. None the less, while there may well be levels of interpretation and significance which reside independently of the values which are generated by productive interests, design practice is, though, increasingly concerned with refining and controlling the flows and patterns of meaning which pass from production to consumption. Again this points to the intrinsically reflexive nature of design. Consumer information, both quantitative and qualitative, is filtered, interpreted and recycled in an endless circuit. Different types of goods and services are moved through this circuit at different speeds and each with its distinctive manner. Understanding the exchanges which take place along this continuum requires the mobilization of a range of theoretical frameworks and cognitive skills.

high design

high design   Three slender legs rise from delicate ankles. Bending at an impossibly high knee they sweep back to a fluted, central teardrop form. These aeronautically-profiled, arachnoid supports lift the object heavenward for the admiring gaze. Perfectly fashioned for maximum 'look', this tripod holds aloft the raw nature of the implement's bulbous, phallic head.

It requires both skill and strength to use. The lemon-squeezer gives slightly as one bears down, rhythmically twisting and pushing on the fruit. Your hand is left messy with the detritus of your labour as the lemon disintegrates beneath it. Channelled by the fluting which adorns the head, juices glide lazily down the side to meet at a tip on its underside. From there they stream into a vessel beneath, giving off the glistening flow and satisfying sound of micturition.

Once cleaned up it is then returned to a shelf, a cabinet or its box. There it will sit, poutingly hermaphroditic, insouciantly demanding.

anomalous objects   Besides its strangely transsexual aspect, the Juicy Salif lemon-squeezer exhibits several other 'in-between' characteristics. As a utilitarian kitchen implement, it only half-works. It delivers lemon-juice in an enticing, amusing fashion straight to a glass, but you also get the pips and some pith with it which may then need straining out. For the novice, juice splatters about: it is only after one learns the correct body posture, the optimum conjunction of limbs and the requisite force needed does this problem recede. As if to underline this connoisseurship of function, the instructions supplied with the object include copious advice and detailed drawings on its use and cleaning. They also tell us that upon its first use, a chemical reaction takes place between the lemon-juice and the aluminium, rendering the first squeezing redundant. Equally, the metal discolours, losing its shine.

So is this an object of use or of contemplation? Should it be consigned to the kitchen cabinet or the lounge shelves? Certainly it fits alongside a range of odd kitchen gadgets which are brought out on particular occasions:

Juicy Salif lemon-squeezer. Designed by Philippe Starck. Manufactured by Alessi Spa from 1990

Source: Guy Julier

pasta-mills, artichoke plates, avocado dishes, fresh herb shredders. And the tacit psychomotor skills which are mastered in its use become ritualized acts in the same way that the stirring of a Christmas pudding mixture becomes an annual event. It marks time, repetition and familiarity.

Alternatively, its shininess allies it with a typology of silverware reserved for the cabinet of 'special things'. Since the seventeenth century, the family silverware has functioned in several ways. First, it has had a use-value in being brought out and employed for important occasions such as festive banquets, christenings, weddings. Secondly, it has had exchange-value in that, besides real estate, it has acted as a fixed asset for families, its value on the market being more stable than cash. Selling the family silver then becomes a last resort in times of dire financial circumstances. Thirdly, silverware has symbolic-value in that it is used as gift and heirloom, thus reinforcing kinship. Fourthly, it has sign-value in representing the cultural tastes of its owner.

As its designer remarked of it:

> This is not a very good lemon squeezer: but that's not its only function. I had this idea that when a couple gets married it's the sort of thing they would get as a wedding present. So the new husband's parents come round, he and his father sit in the living room with a beer, watching television, and the new bride and mother-in-law sit in the kitchen to get to know each other better. 'Look what we got as a present', the daughter-in-law will say.
>
> (Starck quoted in Lloyd Morgan 1999: 9)

Retailing at around £45 a piece, the Juicy Salif is absurdly, disproportionately expensive in the same way the silverware of a family of the lower gentry in the seventeenth century was often worth more than their other effects put together. Its exchange-value may appear to far outweigh its use-value. None the less, it's only made of aluminium.

If its visual references combine both male and female bodily attributes then it also reminds one of Buck Rogers style science-fiction imagery of the 1950s (a decade when aluminium in consumer items was coming of age). The teardrop shape of its head is also redolent of the Arabic designs which found their way into late-medieval architectural details, the name 'Juicy Salif' reinforcing this association. Thus it is both popular and 'exotic' in its referents.

Neither male nor female, but both. Useful and useless. Refined and trashy. An object of display and yet it is too damnably singular to fit in with anything else. Perhaps these anomalies are what holds the object's fascination. Lévi-Strauss (1969) argued that in the West, we structure our world around binary opposites as a universal sense-making process, hence male/female, culture/nature, domesticated/wild. Each acts as 'other' to its partner. There are, however, 'anomalous categories': things which transgress the binary divide and as such hold a particular interest and/or disgust. On a lesser level, perhaps, then, the Juicy Salif functions as an anomalous object.

high design   The Juicy Salif lemon-squeezer was designed by Philippe Starck and manufactured by the northern Italian producer of table-ware, Alessi Spa from 1990. It has become emblematic of both its designer and its manufacturer, given a leading role as an image in monographs published on both (see Sweet 1998: 9; Sweet 1999: jacket image; Lloyd Morgan 1999: 8).

Along with perhaps the Alessi-produced Richard Sapper-designed 'Kettle with a Singing Whistle' (1983), the Juicy Salif lemon-squeezer has for some become synomymous with the excesses and pretentions of the 1980s in particular, and design in general. Both have been lambasted for the high ratio of price to functionality. Meanwhile, design 'guru' Sir Terence Conran tells us that, 'it's intriguing, tactile and desirable, and even though it squirts juice all over your shirt, it's fun to use' (cited in Sweet 1998: 36). More soberly, design-buyer Craig Allen suggests that, 'there's more to this than getting juice out of a lemon' (Allen quoted in Russell 1996).

Having seen that the object does not fit comfortably into historical typologies, it is also interesting to consider how it fits in with contemporary hierarchies of design. At one end of the scale we might establish 'anonymous design' as a category wherein objects, spaces and images are conceived and shaped by professional designers or people from other backgrounds taking on a designer's role, but, crucially, the etiquette of designer is not formally recognized. Pencils and zippers may be examples of 'anonymous design' which have been subject to painstaking, if not obsessional historical research (see Friedel 1994; Petroski 1996). At the other end of this scale we find 'high design' where conscious designer intervention and authorship, along with the price-tag, play a large role in establishing the cultural and aesthetic credentials of an artefact.

Design critic Peter Dormer (1990) provides a useful discussion of 'high design'. He divides the concept into two categories: *heavenly goods*, being objects designed for the rich to buy; and *tokens*, objects bought by the 'wish-they-were-rich'. Heavenly objects combine astonishing high performance with exclusivity. However, there is always a limit to degree of performance that most products can be taken to: industrial design and manufacturers in the contemporary age deliver goods which cannot be bettered, unlike 100 years ago. Beyond a certain, relatively low price, the rich cannot buy a better performing camera or home kettle than the wider public. Thus, Dormer, argues, exclusivity has to be invented by the inclusion of unnecessary details ('with knobs on'). Precious metals, unusual leathers or exotic timbers may be incorporated into the product to boost this quality. As in the case of the Aston Martin Lagonda motor car, it may be unnecessarily hand-built in an age when computer-controlled manufacturing may give a much higher standard of workmanship: 'The power to have the exclusive rights to another person's labour is appealing because the possession of someone else's time is an absolute. All the other aspects of an object can be copied and mass produced and, horror of horrors, popularized' (Dormer 1990: 124).

There are other devices in design origination, branding and distribution by which heavenly goods maintain their exclusivity. For example the car manufacturer Porsche also has a separate design company which collaborates with lighting, furniture and accessories manufacturers to develop products for the seriously rich; thus the Porsche design brand is 'lent' to other products. While producers of luggage and accessories such as Louis Vuitton have historically maintained an exclusive status, in recent years companies such as Land Rover and Rolls-Royce have moved into this market, transferring the brand value of their core product into other objects which in turn act as advertisements as much for the corporation as for the owner's status. This is known as 'brand-stretching'. Finally, sophisticated retailers such as Dunhill or Harvey Nichols may reinforce the values of heavenly goods by turning shopping into an exercise of socio-economic differentiation.

However, as we slip away from the material qualities of heavenly goods, and consider their mediation, we begin to overlap with the realm of token goods for they are scenarios of participation of the 'would-be-rich'. Token goods provide imitations or intimations of life as the seriously pecunious and represent a much bigger industry. They are affordable for the professional classes with disposable income or access to credit but maintain an aura of discernment.

The places where token goods may be bought nestle within the habitat of the very rich. (I have bought two Juicy Salifs, one for research purposes from Oggetti and the other as an expensive tongue-in-cheek wedding present from the Conran Shop. Both these outlets are in London's Chelsea.) Shopping for these goods becomes a form of tourism as you venture into the territory of exclusivity to claim a token souvenir of that momentary experience.

Alternatively, since the 1980s we have witnessed a partial de-differentiation between museum curatorship and retail and, indeed, between high art and the high street (Lash and Urry 1994: 272; Whitely 1994; Urry 1995: 151; Zukin 1995: Ch. 4). Museums which display modern design, such as the Museum of Modern Art in New York or the Design Museum in London also have a nice shop attached. You can peruse the exhibits and then go to the museum shop and then 'buy a relic, a token of what cannot be yours' (Dormer 1990: 117). Likewise, designer objects are displayed in shops as museum pieces. Lees (1997: 79) notes that Alessi retail sites invariably display a single example of each product, suggesting their uniqueness and preciousness, just as museum objects have traditionally been curated. In other outlets such as Harrods or John Lewis, the Alessi range is displayed together in the same way that museums often maintain 'families' of objects. Smaller museums, Lees notes, with reduced space and funds will invariably use Alessi products as 'a shorthand for describing 1980s design and post-modernism'. Thus Alessi, in cooperation with museums and retailers, are able to effect an interchange around their objects: they achieve 'museum status' while being affordable and buyable.

'design classics'   Within this process, the term 'design classic' has emerged as a way of labelling products which sum up the best of their time but equally whose appeal surpass their immediate historical context. This is a problematic term, not least because there are certain objects which may offer the best design solution to a functional and aesthetic problem which may not last as a problem. This is particularly the case in the design of corporate identity, capital goods or certain technologies which respond to immediate economic and cultural circumstances which subsequently change and render them obsolete (there is unlikely to be a classic telex-machine design, for instance). Conversely, then, the 'design classic' label privileges certain functional goods over others. Basic activities like sitting, lounging or eating remain unchanged: chairs, chaises longues or tableware more readily receive the 'design classic' accolade.

Certainly there are cases of a brand receiving the 'design classic' status. The most obvious of these would be Coca-Cola which appears with monotonous frequency as such in books on branding (Murray 1998). The inference in much of the discourse of the 'design classic', as evident in Sudjic (1985), is that there is something intrinsic to the artefact itself which gives it that status. In the same way we have seen that objects are subject to commodity fetishism – that the social conditions of their production are magically imbued in them – so then 'design classic' augments the reificatory processes. Thus we must remember that in the case of Coca-Cola, the corporation itself has energetically marketed its brand as historical by featuring the earlier bottle shape on the side of its cans, but less subtly through exhibitions and catalogues tracing the development and applications of its brand identity. In this way the company legitimates itself, reproducing its own myths in order to be both historical and contemporary – timeless, in other words – and thus a 'design classic'. Again the process may work in the other direction. In 1990 London's Design Museum exhibited a 'Flexo' lamp as an example of vernacular Spanish design to coincide with a season of Iberian events. By 1995, the retailers Habitat were selling the lamp, telling the consumer via a label stuck on its base that it was 'a classic of Spanish design' and that there was one on 'permanent display at the Design Museum in London'.

As part of this historicizing process since the late 1970s several international furniture companies, including Aram, B.D. Ediciones de Diseño, Cassina, Knoll and Santa & Cole, have re-edited historical pieces by 'hero-designers' such as Antoni Gaudì, Le Corbusier and Marcel Breuer. This inserts the corporations into the canon of design by aligning them with pro-claimed historical figures. Subsequent new products draw their status from this circumstance. Likewise, Alessi began to manufacture historical designs such as Marianne Brandt's 1925 teaset from the early 1980s. Unsurprisingly the Juicy Salif later gets described as an object which, 'pushed design to new limits and instantly became a cult classic' (Sweet 1998).

Objects become the token goods of high design through association within a complicated system of mediation and distribution. In an essay entitled 'The Work of Art in the Age of Mechanical Reproduction' Walter Benjamin (1970 [1936]) argued that the development of systems for the serial production of images such as colour printing has not devalued the original; rather it has bestowed greater importance and aura on it (which explains why despite the huge growth of art-book publishing, the public still flocks to galleries). Since the 1980s, the distinctions between the design object as curated in the museum and the design object as displayed through retail have been blurred; acquisition of the mass-produced artefact is a way to borrow back some of the aura of the original.

mediating production   The object analysis delivered at the beginning of this chapter is contentious, based on the restrictions of the author's personal experience of it. Clearly responses to it will vary according to differing socio-economic and cultural backgrounds. However, further consideration of the circumstances of its production suggest that its readings are indeed restricted or pre-empted by its manufacturer, Alessi Spa, and its designer, Philippe Starck.

Alessi moved from being a manufacturer of 'anonymous design' household products to incorporating designer goods into its catalogue in the 1980s. An event which marked this step was its Tea and Coffee Piazza project in which it invited world famous architects such as Hans Hollein, Robert Venturi and Michael Graves to each design a set which went into limited production of 99 pieces each in 1983. The designers' individual processes were published in a book edited by Alessi itself (1983) which served to reinforce the 'greatness' of the authors, and by association the manufacturers, involved.

Alessi is an extraordinarily media-friendly company. To promote the brand image and its products Alessi uses Di Palma Associati for its public relations, one of Italy's foremost publicity agencies which specializes in the promotion of design. It produces and distributes a plethora of gift mailings, press releases and publications which get readily reproduced in design journals (Lees 1997: 81).

Since the Tea and Coffee Piazza project Alessi has published several book-length discussions of its own work which give both basic product information concerning size, weight, materials and so on of its goods, but also often turgid postmodern deconstructional essays on the 'meanings' of its products (e.g. Gabra-Liddell 1994). There is an interesting irony in the way that the analysis is derived from the theories of poststructuralism are mustered to deliver a pre-packaged meaning for the consumer. Poststructuralism contends that meanings of textual, visual or material artefacts are multiple according to the consumer's position rendering authorship effectively dead. In the instance of the Alessi publications, the strategies of pluralism and multiplicity of meaning are re-appropriated into the producer's ownership. Interpretation is self-generated, articulated and disseminated as a pre-emptive strike on the consumer before he or she makes his or her own mind up.

This not only legitimates the otherwise banal nature of many of Alessi's products by giving them intellectual status, it is a form of rationalization. By publishing the designers' development sketches, photographs of consultants on the factory floor and finally employing a philosopher or sociologist to write on the significance of all this in the modern age, we can see where the money we spend on their products is going. The brand image of Alessi as wacky, honest, thoughtful and committed to high production and design values is reinforced while at the same time the consumer is drawn into its corporate culture.

consuming postmodern high design: Veblen and Bourdieu
As we have seen, buying tokens such as the Juicy Salif may be an act in the performance of *design* tourism: it is the souvenir bought at the end of a day's cultural sightseeing. Connoisseurship and a measure of privilege are both mobilized in the process of purchase. The link between leisure, consumption and social distinction was elaborated by Thorstein Veblen (1970 [1899]) and later developed by Pierre Bourdieu (1984).

Veblen first defined leisure as time consumed non-productively rather than the space outside paid employment; after all, many household activities such as washing, cleaning and cooking are not considered to be leisure activities. Leisure is created from a sense of the unworthiness of productive work – for some there is no need to work all the time, and for a privileged few there is no need to work at all. Leisure then becomes evidence of one's pecuniary ability to afford not to work. Out of this basis he coined three key concepts: conspicuous consumption, conspicuous leisure and conspicuous waste. Conspicuous consumption involves the possession of goods which in turn demonstrates one's leisure time and economic status to both acquire them (in terms of shopping and choosing them) and to appreciate them (in terms of understanding their cultural value). This inherently involves a degree of conspicuous leisure in that the consumption of goods, and leisure activities one must add, means that one is seen to be using time non-productively but also that one is employing others towards non-productive ends. Thus shopping, tourism and hobbies all involve the labour of others such as shop assistants, waitresses or gamekeepers in supporting non-productively used time. The final piece of this matrix entails the conspicuous waste of goods and services. The artefacts and activities of conspicuous consumption do not fulfil a utilitarian purpose, but often they *emulate* utility. The rich do not need to hunt or fish in order to feed themselves, but they do like to play at it; necessity is turned into sport.

The Juicy Salif clearly fufils all three of these criteria of conspicuosity. We have seen how it has been marketed and placed in a way to ensure its consumer status. We have seen how its lack of efficiency compared with more standard models encourages its contemplation and use in a somewhat non-productive manner: it doesn't squeeze lemons very well and mastering its use may be considered a 'waste of time'. It is interesting to note how much of the Alessi promotional material emphasizes the craft ethics of the company and the incorporation of craftsmanship into manufacture; thus the labour of others is obviously secured for the consumer. Finally, the object while being an object of display, none the less proposed a utilitarian purpose as a kitchen gadget.

Interestingly, the tension between the banal conspicuosity and the potential use of such high design objects is expressed in an Alessi publication. In 1996 its research centre published *L'oggetto dell'equilibrio* (the balanced object) as an updated Alessi manifesto. Speaking of the 'unbalanced object' which the company seeks to avoid, Bruno Pasini described as:

> an object which refuses to 'soften' in the passage from the showcase to the home; an object so highly charged with personality that it cannot be personalised. It is an object whose identity becomes confounded with its advertising, which doesn't age yet falls out of fashion. It is often merely an imitation of something truly functional: an object that doesn't invite use, but whose similarity to one that does serves as an alibi of its decorative essence. . . . From the second half of the 1980s onwards these objects have crowded our stores, our magazines, our homes: indistinguishable, narcissistic, self-aggrandising, pretentious, unjustifiably authoritative: objects which wear you out just looking at them, which you're afraid to touch, which fail to suggest their own purpose.
>
> (Pasini quoted in Lees 1997: 87)

As Lees observes, Pasini could as easily be talking about Alessi's own products, or even the Juicy Salif.

Bourdieu's seminal study was developed from a highly systematic quantitative analysis of the real-life tastes and pursuits of a broad range of French consumers. He adopted a starting point which said that social relations first and foremost are cultural rather than economic. In other words, what we have, and what we do in our leisure, defines us in class terms more accurately than the jobs we are employed in.

Bourdieu's interest was not exclusively in *what* people acquired or did, but *how* they made distinctions between different types of cultural goods. Thus distinction was a key concept: it denotes both the process of identifying differences as well as the way by which goods and their meanings are used to achieve difference. Within this Bourdieu draws up clear categorizations of high-brow, middle-brow and low-brow culture. The process of distinction requires what he called 'cultural capital', this being one's measure of that ability to distinguish between the cultivated and the vulgar. Finally, he employs the idea of the habitus as an umbrella concept, drawing together individual action and social relations through the exercise of taste and cultural capital. In design terms, the habitus is a useful concept – though it is often confused with 'lifestyle' – for it demands the consideration of non-explicit activities in everyday life. It refers to habitual, customary activities, such as squeezing a lemon; it binds these to the body, showing that the processes of distinction and cultural capital are acted out. Thus the bodily pose adopted when squeezing that lemon, the ease or self-consciousness felt in undertaking this task, are expressions of our breeding.

As a broad basis for his systems of distinction Bourdieu drew on Kant's notion of the aesthetic as the taste of the dominant class and contrasted this with an anti-Kantian aesthetic (see Figure 4.1). The Kantian aesthetic differs from Veblen's emphasis on a strongly conspicuous form of consumption by suggesting that it is more detached and that, indeed, the overt display in itself is considered to be vulgar by those of 'high cultural capital'. Their interest, then, is in cultural goods which are 'difficult' to appreciate and which do not promise immediate pleasure. Consumption, in these terms, is an educated, informed practice. Conversely, the anti-Kantian aesthetic is more highly conspicuous and promises a more immediate, sensual pleasure.

There are several problems with Bourdieu's methodology and conclusions. First, his survey was carried out in a way almost identical to quantitative marketing surveys; thus he missed out on much of the looser, qualitative experience of consumption which interviews or focus groups may provide. Secondly, then, he set himself the task of grafting his data onto pre-

Kantian aesthetic	Anti-Kantian aesthetic
Higher cultural capital	Lower cultural capital
Elite culture	Popular culture
Cultivated, abstracted appropriation	Immediate pleasure
Mind-centred (understanding)	Body-centred (sensuality)
Representation as convention, esoteric, formal	Representation as naturalistic
Subtle, detached, inconspicuous form of display readable only by those sufficiently cultivated or civilized	Overt display of wealth and consumption readable by anyone
Preferred photos: cabbages and car crash	Preferred photos: sunset and first communion

Figure 4.1
Kantian and anti-Kantian aesthetics
Source: Corrigan 1997

established social groupings: working class, bourgeois, upper class and so on. This meant that other possible groupings are ignored – gender is not discussed, for instance. There is a tendency to stereotype consumption behaviour of groupings, thus working-class taste is presented as based in the 'choice of the necessary' and is somehow 'unclouded by ideology' (Slater 1997: 163). In this version, the working classes are perceived as an authentic humanity, fulfilling a particularly Romantic vision. By extension, the tastes of other classes are more elaborated, self-conscious and positional.

Miller suggests that an alternative approach to studying the relationship of consumption and social groupings might be found in studying the divisions which pertain to 'object domains' (Miller 1987: 158). Alternatively, then, groups are clustered around particular forms of consumption and stylistic tastes which may be identified. The study of the goods themselves provides evidence of the significance of the social divisions between them. In turn, as Miller admits, if one is to interrogate goods to this end, one cannot separate production and consumption, as Bourdieu (1984: 230) assumed.

To return to Alessi objects, then, it is clear that many of them intentionally combine attributes both of elite culture and popular culture. In Bourdieu's terms they blur the line between a Kantian and an anti-Kantian aesthetic. Thus the contribution of American architect Robert Venturi to the Tea and Coffee Piazza project resulted in a teapot which combined the proportions of classical architecture in form with an overtly kitsch graphic element in decoration. At one level, there is a cultural commentary concerning the way in which urban fabric incorporates both the serious and the banal, from spectacular buildings to poster boardings. On another level, Venturi is providing an object which requires a degree of specialist understanding to appreciate – some knowledge or experience of classical architecture would help in 'reading' the object – but at the same time, the teaset has an immediately sensuous appeal. Likewise, the Juicy Salif by very dint of its poor utilitarian performance forces one to stand back from it and think about it as an aesthetic object. Having demanded a distanced, intellectual engagement it then delivers a set of banal referents in its form. In this way, the Alessi objects oscillate between different categorizations. Their polysemy – the possibility of their occupying different, changing and contradictory meanings – is the one theme they hold in common.

This polysemy, however, is not unlimited. The objects do not promise an endless set of readings. They are carefully orchestrated through a series of movements which may indeed give the impression of a limitless freedom to derive personal significances, but which in reality are constantly self-referential.

historicity   It is perhaps useful at this point to place the Alessi objects in the context of Italian Postmodernism in order to pinpoint the 'historical baggage' they come with. Modern Italian design came of age in the period of reconstruction immediately following the Second World War. For many of its protagonists it was ideologically focused on the home as a site for the personal, moral and social reconstruction following the failure of fascism. The design and production of modern furniture and, in particular, the 'lighting object' (highly sculptural illumination drawn from an abstractionist aesthetic) established international recognition for the new Italian material culture. Meanwhile, the gap between the practical demands of mass social housing of the postwar period and the idealized Italian home widened. Designers were caught between their ideological ambitions of providing affordable design goods for a mass market and a combination of high production costs, even for plastics-based objects at the time, a growing middle class and the lure of international recognition as mediated by lifestyle magazines such as *Abitare*, *Casa Vogue* and *Interni*. Modern design, in other words, became appropriated into, 'a predetermined "culture of the home", associated with a particular middle-class, consumerist life-style . . . turning all Italian objects . . . into highly desirable, élitist artefacts' (Sparke 1990: 194).

Given this tension, avant-garde designers – in particular Ettore Sottsass – sought to destabilize the canon of high design. The anti-design movement grew up as part of the general crisis of the late 1960s, typified by worker strikes and student protests. Radicals among the Italian design fraternity turned their attention to the development of micro-environments rather than perpetuating object fetishism. Within this project designers re-appropriated the imagery of mass culture into pieces so that they became a form of meta-design – design about design. Thus, for example, Sottsass designed the 'Mickey Mouse' table which was produced by Bonacina in 1972. By featuring the graphic imagery and form of the Disney character he returns the 'message' of the table to the fact that, like Mickey Mouse, it is a mass-produced object for global consumption. The potential aura of the object, then, is deconstructed for you. The Postmodern collapsing of distinctions between high and low culture is undertaken, however, with a political point to it. None the less, this enthusiasm for democratization of design in many of the projects undertaken by radicals in the 1970s ultimately found their way into the high-design galleries of the 1980s. Equally the Alessi objects reside in this tradition of Italian high design: witty, ironic, charged with theoretical intention and which harbour self-effacing luxury.

modern designers/modern consumers   The oscillation of the designer between radical intention and reactionary outcome, between discomfort with the conditions of high-design production and compliance with its consumption is somewhat characteristic of Italian design discourse, but not exclusive to it. Indeed, it may even be a condition of European design stardom of the late twentieth century.

Of this mould, Philippe Starck is perhaps the most known. Like Alessi, he has been highly media and public friendly. Like Raymond Loewy, an earlier French designer, he has a media personality that is wholly Gallic: he claims to drink only champagne and even wears a beret. His personal contradictions are well cultivated: he speaks a highly educated French but dresses grubbily; he speaks with intelligence and self-effacing irony. His press interviews have been consistent and well-turned-out for instant media reproduction; public lectures become energetic, theatrical performances. Monographs and articles often feature as many photographs of Starck – usually in witty poses – as the objects he designs. No doubt he is a designer of considerable talent. He is noted for combining a prolific output – by 1986 he was modestly telling interviewers that he had 97 projects on the go – with a sincere design rigour and understanding of technical problem-solving (Aldersey-Williams 1987). His designs span from the interiors for exclusive clubs, through furniture to foodstuffs and fashion. The apparent ease and speed with which he applies himself to such various projects – he claims to design chairs inside 15 minutes – completes the image of flamboyance and decadence.

In 1997 he announced that he would give up designing altogether in order to devote his time to non-partisan political, socially-orientated causes. This collapsing of the house around him and walking away from it was an ultimate utterance in a career made up of smaller gestures. He told a professional journal in 1986, 'I have not one single theory. I have no ideas about aesthetics, and I don't give a damn' (Starck quote in Aldersey-Williams 1987: 51). A decade later he was telling another, 'There is no place for the deified products of the past decade. . . . All those fashion victims are so pathetic – they come home at night and have an apartment full of fashion items made by designers for designers but not for the public', completing this tirade later with, 'I don't have any aesthetic assumptions. The Starck style in the market is a waste of time' (Starck quoted in Capella 1997: 56).

This punk 'gesture towards a nowhere' resonates in the Juicy Salif. The beautifully dysfunctional lemon-squeezer offers a paradigmatic objectification of this attitude. As Miller tells us, 'Objectification describes the inevitable process by which all expression, conscious or unconscious, social or individual, takes specific form. It is only through the giving of form that something can be conceived of" (1987: 81). Thus the cultural baggage of designerly euphoria, its achievements, excesses and wastages converge in the

Juicy Salif. In this context, the Starck signature conspires to brand the object. Indeed, one commentator has suggested that Starck may be the last great 'Designer Hero', but that he is also a brand (Hollington 1998).

It is perhaps less the individual biographical details which generate some of the object's meanings as the way in which they are marshalled up and presented to a consuming public. Whether Starck's self-presentation is genuine or a mere pose in order to generate media, and thus public interest in him, is not a useful question. What is at stake here, is that there is a coherence between the object and its production, designer and consumption.

This coherence exists within a highly refined and reflexive network of producers and consumers. Starck's accusation concerning, 'items made by designers for designers' is telling. By briefly returning to Bourdieu, we are reminded of his so-called 'new petit bourgeois' class many of whom are employed in creative professions and whose tastes lie in cultural goods of the avant-garde. He identifies their task as 'cultural intermediaries' in that they broker modern ideas and aesthetics, both in the work they do, and in the way they consume. Thus the acquisition of high design is a necessary component in the particular system of distinction to which this class adheres. Specific objects and designers subsequently become a shorthand for the knowledge and values inherent in this system. There is, in Bourdieu's words, 'a correspondence between goods production and taste production' (1984: 230).

designers, risk and reflexivity   This process of destabilizing convention within the parameters of the market is apparent in some other design objects and processes. In certain quarters of graphic design a similar self-destructive attitude has mediated its high design and designers to their public. Since the early 1980s a highly localized strain of high design has emerged within graphics clustered around a handful of specific individuals.

Interestingly this discourse has emerged mostly within the discipline of typography. Typography has historically achieved a dominant professional and academic status in relation to other specialized disciplines within graphic design as a whole. Unlike illustration which draws much of its working procedures and stylistic norms from fine art, or packaging design which draws from advertising and branding, typography has developed a stronger academic tradition of its own. Several key texts, such as those by German typographer Jan Tschichold, established ground-rules as paradigmatic reference points for its practice and debate. Several scholarly journals such as *Typos* and *Visible Language* have existed to disseminate research in typography as well as maintain its intellectual legitimacy.

In addition, to this scholarly activity, typographers have developed their own historical canon of designer-heroes. A key text which helped to establish this canon, echoing Pevsner's seminal title, is Spencer's *Pioneers of Modern Typography* (1969). The educational and working processes of typography also promote a star-system. In the same way that the chair has been a standard exercise as well as a way of creating design which becomes emblematic of the designer so, traditionally, typographers have applied themselves to the origination of typefaces to perform a similar role. Like the chair, the typeface design has not necessarily addressed a specific utilitarian outcome. In the same way that the chair may be specified by other designers – it may be chosen to complete an interior design – so other graphic designers will employ specific typefaces. What furniture is to industrial design, typography has, at least until recently, been to graphics.

Through a combination of scholarly discourse and popular publication, then, typography in particular and graphic design in general has produced its own celebrity system. Among these one might name Malcolm Garrett, Peter Saville, Neville Brody, Erik Spiekermann, Rudy Van der Lans, April Greiman, Dave Carson and the design groups 8vO and Tomato. Among these, in London Neville Brody, in partnership with critic Jon Wozencroft, founded the Fuse project in 1991 which published typefaces on CD-ROM by well-known, cutting-edge and almost exclusively male designers. It also established an annual conference to extend its discussion. A similar print-based project had been headed by Rudy Van der Lans in California under the title of *Emigré* from 1982.

While it is difficult to generalize about their graphic style, with perhaps the exception of Erik Spiekermann, all of these have adopted a highly expressive typography. In this mode, the letterform is not merely seen as a vehicle to mediate something else – that is, the sound of a word – but becomes a medium of expression in itself. Through the 1990s many of them pushed the limits of typography by deconstructing both the historically accumulated rules of legibility in both layout and typeform. The Fuse project in particular set out to consider and even challenge the applicability and use of typography in a post-print world, sometimes to the point that the legibility of typefaces was considered not an issue.

These designers have all published their work widely; of them *The Graphic Language of Neville Brody* (Wozencroft 1987) and *The End of Print: Graphic Works of Dave Carson* (Blackwell 1995) became cult works for the 1980s and 1990s respectively. And as if to reinforce the 'constant reinvention' narrative of design, each of these publications had sequels added to them in 1994 and 1997 respectively in order to update followers. These have functioned as catalogue raisonnés of Brody's and Carson's work but are also design artefacts in themselves.

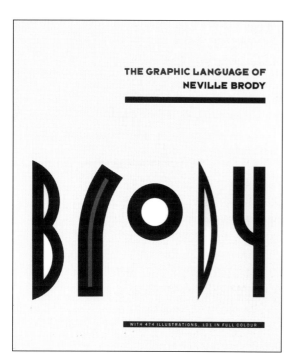

THE GRAPHIC LANGUAGE OF
NEVILLE BRODY

BroDy

WITH 474 ILLUSTRATIONS, 101 IN FULL COLOUR

Cover of *The
Graphic Language
of Neville Brody*
1987

Source: Melville Brody

While much of their content is in the reproduction of highly commercial graphic design projects, such as magazine layouts and advertising campaigns, it is distilled and refined into the book which subsequently becomes a high-design artefact. By editing their own oeuvre and repackaging it, their authorship is given precedence over the original client's importance as the design commissioners. Furthermore, by taking designs away from their original function, their formalistic values become foregrounded over their effectiveness in shaping the editorial content of a magazine or in selling a product. The artistry of a typeface or a layout become the content. Through this process the patina of low culture is packaged into high design. This demonstrates that while Veblen assumed that all taste would filter on a 'trickle down' basis, from upper to middle classes, there can also be a 'trickle up' dynamic, from subcultural roots into the ambience of high graphics.

Such publications have mostly been bought by other designers and design students. As such, a simulacrum of risk, art-lifestyle, but also of negation is being communicated to the world of the design student by representatives of the profession to which they aspire. We have seen in Chapter 2 how students and professionals in design celebrate the marginality of their own practice. The following quotation, drawn from a design magazine article about Tomato, a London-based collective that worked across several communications platforms, may be read as typical of the 'attitude' which accompanies this process:

clients include Coca-Cola, Ibm, Levi's, Nike, Pepsi, Sony and Thomson ... Tomato first 'happened' in February 1991, when a group of graphic desgners and an ambient-rock-techno band, Underworld, began working together out of the London flat of a music business manager. . . . The members of the all-male group (with one female assistant) dress casually, make constant jibes at each other and are impossible to pin down. . . . 'The name Tomato means nothing', Warwicker told me over coffee in the East Village. 'You can put lots of meanings into it but there are none. A bit like our work really.' . . . Tomato provides a look that appeals to

Generation X: fast cuts, layered imagery and distinctive blurred flickering and danc-

ing typography. . . . Freedom is a movement, as the Nike slogan goes, and the mem-

bers of Tomato are ferocious devotees. . . . 'We're not easily employable.'

(Hall 1996: 78)

So how are we to begin to theorize this?

First, while the surface of much of the work of Tomato (and indeed Carson, Van der Lans and later Brody) seems to be expressing an un-meaning it still exists within a framework of meaning-production. The indi-vidual words and letters may be dislocated and impenetrable in the way they are distorted and layered. But there is a confluence in the narratives regard-

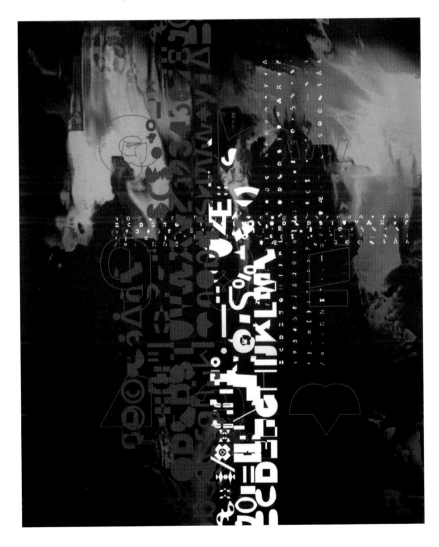

F Code image
designed for Fuse 6
by Neville Brody
1993 as seen in The
Graphic Language
of Neville Brody 2
Source: Neville Brody

ing the designers themselves. We have learnt that Tomato, 'are not easily employable'. We are reminded frequently that Dave Carson does not have a formal training in graphics, but was a surfing champion and failed secondary school teacher (Blackwell 1997). Indeed, Emily King (1995) points out that both the Fuse team and Carson's 'End of Print' thesis may refer to the replacement of paper-based communication with digitization but can also suggest that there is nothing left to say.

This apocalyptic nihilism as a principle of modernity becomes their core theme. If, according to the sociologist Ulrich Beck, one of society's key contemporary features is that rather than being economically positivistic or technologically determinist, it possesses the ability to calculate positions on the basis of varying data. It is, broadly speaking, self-conscious wherein 'modernization . . . is becoming its own theme' (Beck 1992: 11). Likewise, designers may calculate avant-gardist positions for themselves within the parameters of the market. Their Romanticism is reflexively constructed.

Secondly, this process allows for other forms of risk to be inhabited. Beck (1992) and Giddens (1991) both identify risk as a key concept in reflexive modernization. Giddens identifies a progression from a state in which hazards were incidental and intrinsic to experience to a society in which the calculation of risk parameters is a determining influence on activity (Giddens 1991: Ch. 4). According to Beck, these risks are not so much recognized physically but, 'mediated on principle through argument' (Beck 1992: 27). Many of the newer risks (nuclear or chemical contaminations, pollutants in foodstuffs, diseases of civilization, bankruptcy, repossessions) completely escape human powers of direct perception. In terms of design practice, risk becomes aestheticized, reflexive and often deliberate. It has become firmly entrenched into the rhetoric of high design whether in its objects or in their mediation. Thus 'cutting edge', 'experimental' and 'intuitive' have become familiar descriptive terms among designers, design students and design writers of the 1990s. This attitude finds its way into mainstream design practice too. Jeremy Myerson has noted how designers can seldom resist claiming a job to be a 'breakthrough and a radical departure'. He adds, 'I can't imagine a firm of solicitors completing a conveyance and saying "we really subverted the context with that one" ' (Myerson quoted in Whitely 1993: 43).

This may have been carried out in direct challenge to modernist notions of legibility in graphic design. This is done through the disintegration of the modernist canons of Tschichold and Morison to incorporate multi-layering of images and type, collisions of typefaces and multidirectional text reading which seem to invent their own private visual languages. This may be a deliberate ironic subversion or designed to entice the reader into a form of 'decoding'. As Ian Cartlidge said in 1991, 'If the type is laid out in an intriguing, playful and entertaining way, the reader may be immediately stimulated and then begin to break down the type until the message is received' (Cartlidge quoted in Poyner 1991: 34).

This entertainment of negation and denial smacks of a punk inheritance. While talking of punk aesthetics, Hebdige develops Julia Kristeva's notion of, 'positioning in language'. In the punk context this is acheived through refusal, 'to cohere around a readily identifiable set of central values. It cohered, instead, elliptically through a chain of conspicuous absences.' It gestured, 'towards a "nowhere" and actively sought to remain silent, illegible' (Hebdige 1979: 120).

If 'punk will never die' then it is in this realm of babble, denial, conspicuous absence, illegibility. At a wider level of popular culture this is evidenced in the denial of authorship through sampling, blending and layering in dance music. Origins and authenticity are even obscured through distortions such as scratching or modifying the tempo. To the traditional musicologist, techno music is impenetrable. Questions of theme, development, recapitulation are irrelevant. And likewise in graphics. Structure, grid, referents, rhythms and the space on the page are distorted, dislocated, compressed, destroyed, made 'dangerous'. We may term this, 'an art of danger . . . <within> . . . a politics of safety', to rephrase Mark Cousins (Cousins 1994: 423).

conclusion   Cultural creation in high design is mediated through language. We have seen how the Alessi/Starck brands are carefully orchestrated through a variety of channels, each reinforcing the other. The denial of utility in these and the high graphics of Carson et al. is self-referential. The form alludes to the conditions of consumption – commodified yet purporting to unmarketability. The form also draws on a central theme of design production – risk, or more accurately, its minimization. This is high design's apparent radicalism within the structure of deeply conservative institutions.

consumer goods   In each photograph an object floats in the half-light, its dark background stretching to an endless space. It could be a power-tool, a palm-top computer, or some medical equipment. Any utility is stripped away by the picture – the product is reduced to a tasteful conjunction of surfaces, textures and tones. At the front of the picture-plane a point on the artefact's surface catches the glare of the studio-lights. It is close to us, in our space, touchable. And yet, it is isolated on the page. The only one. Unique. Special.

images   Within the design profession a minor subspecialism exists in the photography and presentation of new products. Design consultancies or their clients commission skilled photographers to create images of the objects they have designed. These are processed into high quality transparencies which are in turn handed on to journalists and critics for inclusion in the pages of their magazines or books. Otherwise, they are used in their own promotional brochures or websites.

We saw in the last chapter how retailers will display goods to make them appear like museum objects by showing them individually in their shops. In product design a language of representation has evolved which partially fulfils the same ends. By picturing the product on its own it becomes that singular object of desire rather than one of many identical mass-produced commodities. We are asked to appreciate it as it is, without the interference of other products to compare it to, its packaging or other users. The loss of these contexts and its actual physical presence is compensated for by playing up the colour and textural qualities in the image.

This form of representation has some resonances in the still-lifes of Dutch seventeenth-century oil painting. Berger (1972: Ch. 5) makes a persuasive argument that oil painting was employed because it reproduced as faithfully as was then possible the 'thingness' of things; but in the same token by the act of that reproduction, by presenting ordinary objects on canvas in a frame, they were bestowed a feeling of aura.

An image of a product designed by Josep Lluscà and supplied by the International Design Press Agency, Barcelona

Source: International Design Press Agency

87

Three hundred years later, pop artists on both sides of the Atlantic explored the effects of this representation of products. In New York, Andy Warhol's silk-screens of soup cans or detergent boxes deconstructed the aura which advertising was intending to give them. By reproducing multiple images of the same product Warhol reminds us not of their uniqueness, but of their seemingly unending serial reproduction in the capitalist system. Meanwhile, as with many British pop artists, Richard Hamilton was interested in the representation of commodities. From 1957 he developed a series of paintings which explored the surface forms of products both as they were and as they were mediated through advertising. His painting entitled '$he' impressionistically described the forms of domestic products such as toasters, vacuum cleaners and fridges. In doing so he revealed both their stylistic similarities and the linkage between the exterior form of consumer goods and their representation in advertising. To underline this point, he drew allusions between the exterior surface of smooth curves in these products and mainstream representations of female bodies. The connection between product to be looked at but also sold and consumed and mass media representations of women is reinforced in the title: $he. Thus Hamilton was interested in what Haug (1986) later called the 'aesthetic illusion' of products: the promise of their use-value – in this case as flashy, sexy objects of desire – conveyed in their image and in their status of exchange-value. His in-

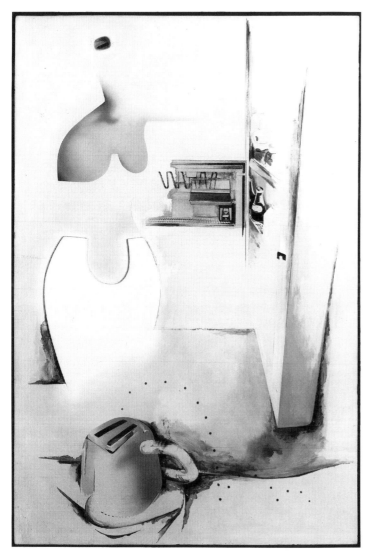

Richard Hamilton's $he, 1958–61. Oil, cellulose on panel 122×81cm

Source: Tate Gallery, London; DACS.

vestigation was into the 'second skin' of the styling of consumer goods and the values this carried.

Interestingly, Hamilton was working on this painting as Roland Barthes's seminal book *Mythologies* (1983 [1957]) was first published. This collection of short essays explored the social and ideological significance of everyday objects and events ranging from 'Steak and Chips' to 'Striptease'. Through these case studies he showed a variety of ways by which Western society sustains, sells and identifies itself while at the same time obscuring its own truth. Like Hamilton, his interest was in exploring what values lay beneath the surface of objects, beyond their external image. His discussion of the Citröen D.S. car, for example, exhibits the same fascination with the literal exterior of the product. Here he draws attention to the perfection of its smooth surfaces to the point that this automobile takes on a magical or even religious aura.

surfaces   Warhol, Hamilton and Barthes all concentrate on the external design values of products. None of them is concerned with their actual performance. They are, in effect, approaching the objects as graphic communication – as adverts of themselves. It is noteworthy that both Hamilton and Warhol worked in graphic design as well as fine art. They were also working at a time when colour photography was becoming increasingly cheaper to reproduce in magazines. Thanks to the development of photolithography in the postwar years, advertisers and magazine editors began to replace illustration and accompanying copy with colour photographs of modern products. Furthermore, developments in manufacture and materials gave increasing prominence to the 'external skin' of objects. The so-called 'Detroit styling' of American cars which fascinated Richard Hamilton so much was made possible by the development of chroming and steel rolling in the postwar period. Similarly plastics had been in use since the mid-1800s, but it wasn't until the postwar period that we find their widespread acceptance in consumer items. For instance, the first all-plastic chair was developed by Kartell in Italy in 1961 but was not marketed widely until 1967. It is notable that this was a children's chair, conceived as both seating and a play object; as such it was aimed at a less conservative market than that of 'mainstream' consumers.

Subsequently, more than any other material, the use of plastics has revolutionized the way designers and their public perceive consumer goods. The advantages of plastics, such as cheapness, lightness and ability to mimic other materials also go some way to explaining a century's resistance to public acceptance. In the English language, 'plasticky' is readily connected to 'rubbishy'. Dormer (1990: 63–4) has pointed out that among many other features, plastic fails to age gracefully, unlike, say, wood or leather. Rather it is prone to discoloration and scuffing. It either looks brand-new or ready to be thrown away. It also shatters or cracks on extreme impact making it impossible to repair. Equally it can only be recycled or reused by experts. Apart from fibre-glass, most plastics are unlikely to be found in the workshop of a do-it-yourself fanatic. Thus a set of values are attached to this material and are thrown into relief by contrast with other more 'traditional' materials.

This line of thought is also pursued by the design theorist Ezio Manzini. In his book *The Material of Invention* (1986) Manzini points out that the majority of twentieth-century design has concerned itself with the structure of objects. Thus, for instance, in using tubular steel, Modernist designers such as Marcel Breuer were able to reveal the physical framework – the skeleton – which supported the sitter. With plastic, the outer skin shows nothing of its internal physics, the make-up of its polymers. We are only presented with a two-dimensional surface. Its light, smooth and shiny aspect effectively *dematerializes* the object.

The commercial and cultural values of plastic lend itself ideally, then, to its use as an outer casing. In terms of many domestic consumer items such as radios or hairdryers it clothes internal workings, and perhaps only indirectly tells us something about the functioning of that object. Elsewhere, it is used to mimick graphic imagery. Thus in children's toys, it is often used for cartoon characters. The loss of a sense of internal structure is compensated for in plastic by the adoption of vivid colours or suggestive shape. Not only is plastic a material of invention, but it is also a material of *representation*. In this context Robin Kinross's statement that, 'product design increasingly aspires to the graphic' (Kinross quoted in Huygen 1989: 90) is particularly apt.

DC-01 vacuum cleaner, designed by James Dyson 1989–92, manufactured by Dyson Appliances Ltd

Source: Guy Julier

doing the Dyson   Many consumer goods offer paradigmatic examples of this late-twentieth-century shift from structure to surface in product design language. Among these, the Dyson DC-01 vacuum cleaner provides a rich array of features which allow us to interrogate this effect. Discussion of this product has primarily focused on the originality of its invention and the problems its designer James Dyson encountered in taking the device to manufacture and market, including a monographic exhibition held at the Design Museum in London in 1996 entitled 'Doing the Dyson'. But no matter how engaging these aspects are, they detract from a full appreciation of the innovations to be found in the vacuum cleaner's semantics – in the way that product communicates its function and value.

The Dyson DC-01 vacuum cleaner is centred around the creation of a mini 'dual cyclone' (hence DC-01) and some understanding of how this works is necessary in order to understand its ramifications in terms of product styling. Vacuum cleaners work on the basis of a fan which in pushing out a stream of air, creates a vacuum; in turn this sets up an equally powerful suction which draws air carrying dust particles and debris into the cleaner. Traditionally, this incoming air is filtered by a paper bag. Air inflates the bag and then filters out through pores in the fabric of the bag and back into the room, leaving the dirt behind. As these pores clog up, however, this system loses its sucking power. The alternative cyclone approach does away with a bag. Instead, the air is pushed into the wider, internal end of a cone. As the air works its way to the point of the cone, it speeds up – in the case of the DC-01, this is from 20 mph to 924 mph. The heavier dust then flies outwards to the edges of the cyclone and the centrifugal force which is created gives each particle increased mass. It then easily drops out of the bottom, smaller end of the cone to be collected in a cylinder into which it fits. Meanwhile, the lighter air finds the quicker and easier route out by rushing back up the centre of the cone. This process is repeated in a slower cyclone which also makes up the outer casing and picks up the larger debris. By providing an alternative to the need for a bag, the dual cyclone avoids clogging and therefore much greater efficiency in suction. Thus the central theme of the traditional vacuum cleaner, the bag, is replaced by another device.

Some historical knowledge of vacuum cleaner design is useful at this point. Following the vacuum cleaner's invention in 1901, the bag of traditional upright models was housed in a zip-up sack suspended from the handle. When the cleaner was switched on it would then inflate, making the physical effect of air being sucked in immediately visible. The conjunction of 'spine', in its column, and 'lung', in its bag gave it an anthropoidal character, its lung inflating as it 'drew breath'. Additionally, one could remove a cover on the base to see the motor band driving the fan. Thus its functioning could be directly viewed.

In the early 1960s, General Electric in the USA brought out its Dial-A-Matic (known in the UK as the Convertible), the first hard-bodied upright vacuum cleaner. By encasing the bag in moulded plastic, the workings of the appliance were increasingly covered up in subsequent models. Air being sucked in and blown out, the rotation of the fan and the inflation of the bag were increasingly hidden away. The streamlined styling of its exterior skin meant that its actual performance was only visible indirectly by seeing how much cleaner the floor appeared to be.

The DC-01 gives back a sense of performance, but only indirectly. As with later versions of upright cleaners, apart from the brushes underneath the base, there are no moving parts to be seen. The effect of the cyclone is visible as dust and debris whizzes round inside the transparent cylinder. But the creation and functioning of the declared 100 per cent suction is communicated, by a large measure, through visual association. The idea of a cyclone as the central theme of the product introduces the mental image of spirals of air, or in the case of the dust in the cylinder, concentric circles. This sets the principal motif for the product styling. From the top of the handle to the design of the plug, then, some 356 full- or part-circular lines are described in the object. The wheels, for instance, feature three concentric circles on their inside and a small 'mudguard' set at an angle, to suggest dynamic energy as well as echo the idea of streaming into the cylinder at a tangent – the optimum angle for setting up the real cyclone. Clearly some of these circles perform a real utilitarian purpose. The spiral casing of the hose allows it to be stretched. But when stowed away in the upright position, it bunches up to create a staccato stack of rings which are carried through to the circular motifs in the handle.

A range of secondary associations also emerge through careful examination of the product. In the handle itself, we find an allusion to cooling fins which do not perform any utilitarian purpose as such. There isn't any heat conduction through the plastic. Instead, they set up other associations with, perhaps, industrial machinery, motor transport or aeroplanes. The silver-speckled grey colouring of most of the vacuum cleaner makes a further connection to aeronautics while the yellow detailing is redolent of heavy plant machinery. The appliance is noisy. The motor thunders along accompanied by a satisfying rush of air being sucked in and pushed out. It has two basic pitches which again suggest air travel. One is when pushing it along: a deep, industrial vibration created partly by the rotation of the brushes (take-off). The other when standing upright is a higher, more airy sound (landing). Through the air travel reference, connotations of efficiency, work, movement and progress spin out from the cyclone theme, to be communicated 'on the outside' of the machine, as it were.

To stretch the machine–aesthetic association further, the typography used in Dyson products is derived from one originally designed at the

German modernist design school, the Bauhaus. In the early 1930s Herbert Bayer developed Universal as a typeface for use in publicity. The suppression of upper-case letters and the letterform's basis in circles rather than ovals was thought to make it easy to read at a distance. The Dyson logotype picks up on the circle theme once again and for those with specialist knowledge of design history, an historicist association is made with the Bauhaus movement which promoted modernist ideals of visual and functional efficiency, fitness-for-purpose and other such 'no-nonsense virtues'.

product semantics   The analysis made above of the Dyson Cyclone DC-01 vacuum cleaner is loosely semiological. We looked at the shapes, colours, textures and sounds of the product and considered how these created content and meaning for it. In this way we identified the link-ages between the thing itself (in semiological terms, the sign), what it indicated (the signifier) and what it represented (the signified). Thus, for instance, we saw how the repeated circular shapes on the handle looked like (or in semiology-speak *denoted*) cooling fins. The idea of cooling fins used to draw off excess heat would indicate an attachment to a high-powered engine perhaps of a motor-bike or an aeroplane. This in turn *connotes* mobility, speed or even modernity itself. These connotations, then, are derived from mythical meanings in society, hence the connection between a particular shape incorporated into the handle and the product as evidence of

Details of DC-01 vacuum cleaner

Source: Guy Julier

our modern, efficient age. Again, this is how Haug's 'aesthetic illusion' is at work: the form indirectly tells us how well the product is going to perform. As its designer, James Dyson himself states, 'Good design, generated out of the function of the thing, will explain why it is better, and why it should be bought. If it looks "the business" . . . then it will present the impression of its own effectiveness' (Dyson 1998: 206).

The rich layering of visual suggestions which are made in the design language of the object derives from a branch of industrial design known as product semantics, a term first used by Krippendorf and Butter in 1984. In short, this method may best be described as, 'designing by association'. Designers will ascertain what emotional values they want the consumer to attach to the product. They then develop forms which instigate the associations to, hopefully, inculcate those feelings.

Obviously there is always the danger of slippage between the meanings the producer intends and those which the consumer interprets. In the case of the Dyson Cyclone the interpretation I have given includes some of its designer's ambitions for the product but also extends them. Dyson explains that the silvery-grey colour, made up of an almost transparent plastic with aluminium flecks incorporated into it, gave it a 'NASA look'. The yellow alludes to warning signs on building sites but also to the stripes of wasps and tigers, adding to a message of the machine as predator. The ribs on the front of the handle were included first as a lightweight way of making that point stronger and secondly to visually smooth the transition from the body to the handle. The suggestion of 'fin-cooling, a high-tech, motorbikey look' was what Dyson calls 'a design byproduct' (Dyson 1998: 199–200). Thus its principal designer claims that the semantic appeal is secondary to the resolution of engineering problems.

A second question which advocates of product semantics must confront is whether or not consumers actually want the associations they design into consumer goods. For example, design critic Hugh Aldersey-Williams complains of how graphics are arbitrarily and garishly applied to sailboards or ski-equipment to connote belonging to some kind of subcultural group through their ownership. Not wishing this enforced lifestyle association he would rather erase the graphics from his own ski-gear (Aldersey-Williams 1993: 142).

The development of product semantics from the early 1980s has led to some ambition and optimism as to its use. Some designers have considered its potential in ascertaining objective ways of designing emotional content into products. In South Korea, Hsiao and Chen (1997) developed a semantic and shape grammar-based approach to individual features of office chair design. They explored the semantic values of various forms abstracted from the basic typology of the office chair by marrying particular primary shapes with their associated emotional effects. From this they then produced a computer program which pieced together separate formal components according to the emotional characteristics they wished to imbue in the object.

In The Netherlands, Muller and Pasman (1996) followed a similar path. They sought to classify certain formal and associational features of chair design in order to provide frames of reference for the designer. They used three broad classifications which encompassed design considerations for products. These were 'Prototype', meaning the utilitarian requirements, 'Solution type' which referred to available and possible formal characteristics governed, for instance, by the parameters of production and materials; finally, they included 'Behavioural-typical features' which took into account consumer experience and preferences and come closest to thinking about the semantics of consumer goods. Subsets within this last category were 'socio-cultural styles' such as 'professional or recreational' and 'progressive and conventional', 'historical styles' such as gothic or classicist and 'style articulation' using bipolar adjectives such as 'controlled and impulsive'. From these categorizations, they wrote a computer program which would then provide on-screen product images of chairs which had already been designed and corresponded to the matrix of design qualities required. This, they claimed, would then provide designers with a 'bandwidth' of visual reference points to then work from and an immediate designerly set of precedents to refer to.

Both the above cases allow for genuine, considered interrogation of the possible cultural resonances which can be designed into products. However, they are both based on the rigorous classification of visual, material and linguistic qualities which are not necessarily fixed or stable. They rely on subjective definitions of concepts such as 'progressive and conventional' and their visual or material counterparts. Does it necessarily follow that one form is 'progressive' when it may be deemed 'conventional' to someone else? Classification often tells one more about the predilections of the classifier than the status of the things classified.

mood boards   By creating a 'map' of various forms which respond to the range of demands made by a client in a brief the designer is able to sketch out and structure a context for subsequent product development. Muller and Pasman (1996) are attempting to provide a more sophisticated, but utimately more precarious method for undertaking this task. In professional practice this is more often done by the use of 'mood boards'. These involve the arrangement and presentation of images of related products, logotypes, environments or other design material onto blank sheets in order to construct an artefactual and associational context for the thing being designed. The designer's own drawings and photographs or samples of mate-

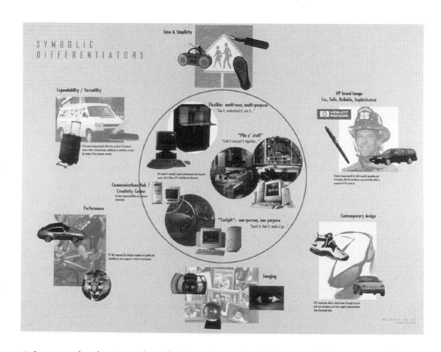

rials may also be introduced. Sometimes the designer might even produce a three-dimensional 'mood environment' or collection of artefacts. This is then used to fix an idea of the relationship of the object of enquiry to other artefacts for both the designer and the client. Whereas drawings, plans and models relate directly to the product under development, the mood board is entirely conceptual.

As such the mood board is a device used to communicate values at various stages in the development of a design project. Thus it might be used early on to clarify market information or the designer's intentions for him- or herself, or the client. It might involve a reflective component in assessing the impact of a design's development. Or it might be used to support a final client presentation. In this format, it provides a visual bridge between the linguistically-based data of a client's brief or market research and the visual and material outcome of the finished product. Invariably the designer is not just classifying and creating a frame of reference for his or her direction through form alone, however. Human activities and comparative brands may also appear on the mood board. This means that the identity of a product is located in relation to other cultural and commercial identities which locates the product as a marketing proposition. As such it may also be produced as a visual map. Equally, as designer Steve Heron (1999) affirms, it can be used to explore the ordinary context of use for a product – how it fits in with the clutter of everyday life.

The mood board is, in fact, used throughout a number of design disciplines: to explore the ambience of a retail environment; to distinguish separate features of an exhibition space or in conjunction with a storyboard for a multimedia presentation. It can then mediate between designer and client, but also express and explore values which lie outside the drawing board or the CAD program. Design methods writer Tom Mitchell warns of the way by which working with forms on paper or on screen can divorce the designer from the day-to-day reality of the finished product in use (Mitchell 1988). At its best, then, the mood board can bridge the gap in the design process between object as planned on the drawing board and the client's conception of the end-user.

Furthermore, this visual interpretation may be finally 'talked up' at client presentations. Clients and designers negotiate a shared understanding of the meaning of a drawing, a 'mood board' or a prototype or model through discussion. Thus even in the private relationship of designer to client, meaning is not necessarily stable, and requires an intense exchange between the verbal and visual (Tomes et al. 1998).

This 'mood board' scenario, then, is strangely at odds with the final photographic presentation of products in design media and consultancy brochures as discussed at the beginning of this chapter: the first presents a contextual network of meanings around the product; the second reduces it to a singular, silent, reified form. The relationship between the two formats – one concerned with meaning, the other with pure form – strikes at the heart of problems in product semantics in particular, and the interpretation of lifestyles in general.

lifestyles and design ethnography   In 1957, the pop artist Richard Hamilton produced a collage for the Independent Group exhibition at London's Institute of Contemporary Arts which was called 'This is Tomorrow'. The collage, intended to be incorporated into the exhibition publicity was entitled, 'Just What Is It That Makes Today's Homes So Different, So Appealing?'. Drawn principally from cut-outs of magazine ads, the collage presents a construction of a 'state-of-the-art' interior complete with modern domestic appliances and furnishings. A number of different discussions are available in this image: the media construction of the body, gender and domesticity, attitudes to the relationship of nature and technology. But overall, this represents a witty invocation of an ad-man's idea of lifestyle. After all, as Independent Group colleague Reyner Banham noted, the 1950s saw the emergence of brand image, consumer research and motivation research (the science of establishing the 'real' or subconscious reasons for buying one product or another) in advertising and design (Banham 1981

[1865]: Ch. 2.4) – all components which engage with consumer lifestyles. By extension, the collage could almost be read as a designer's mood board. Certainly, the title of the piece ('Just What Is It . . .?') smacks of an open blue-skies design brief put before a consultancy.

Hamilton's collage also illustrates the idea that consumer groups may be clustered around object domains rather than being categorized simply by class or demography. This idea resonates with Miller's suggestion, mentioned in the previous chapter, that rather than accepting given class identifications, as Bourdieu had, social groupings are clustered around particular forms of consumption (Miller 1987: 158). As such they may be more fragmented, segmented and fluid. Goods and the way they are arranged, displayed, worn or used become symbolic markers of lifestyle not just to reflect social position, but to enact cultural distinction. Discussion of consumer culture and lifestyle in sociology and cultural studies has largely focused on this symbolic role of goods (e.g. Hebdige 1988; Featherstone 1991; Lury 1996). The emphasis has been on how they are used to say something about an individual's or a group's relationship to other style groupings or their own, and thus their own social standing. Celia Lury calls this 'positional consumption' (1996: Ch. 2).

Sometimes mood boards can look dangerously like clichéd storylines for an ad campaign rather than a genuine attempt to explore user-needs and desires. Often, the images of individual objects within the scenario are themselves lifted from magazines, advertisements or trade photographs, thus adding to this effect. By arranging a set of products onto a flat surface, designers order and classify them into a specific circumstance. In presenting them in a two-dimensional world, much of their status as objects of use is lost as they are turned into imagery. This process may promote a viewpoint of consumption as being purely 'positional'. Furthermore, mood boards may often tell us more about the designers' self-idealization or habitus than the real needs and desires of their end-users.

The use of mood boards may also reinforce what Grant McCracken (1990: Ch. 8) described as the 'Diderot effect'. He describes this as, 'a force that encourages the individual to maintain a cultural consistency in his/her compliment of consumer goods' (1990: 123). This may operate in maintaining consistency in the 'family' of goods a consumer assembles and to exclude inconsistencies; it might force, by the acquisition of something, the individual to adopt an entirely new ensemble of lifestyle accoutrements; it may be that consumers deliberately buy goods which do not complement each other in order to consciously disturb the Diderot effect. So where designers make mood boards look more like the pages of a store catalogue they conspire to assume levels of complementarity in the assemblage of goods that make up the lifeworlds of their end-users. Again, this may ignore the highly personal, seemingly irrational approaches that people harbour in their own value systems with regards the choices they make in the consumption of goods (see Csikszentmihalyi 1991).

Alternatively, then, by the late 1990s, some product designers were using ethnographic research in order to get beyond the restrictions experienced when undertaking market research from a corporate environment perspective and to view human behaviour and interaction with consumer goods *in situ*. Design ethnographers Salvador, Bell and Anderson (1999: 37) argue that individuals will adopt the strict parameters of corporate cultures when they leave home for work; this, consciously or unconsciously, will always feed into and affect the way they conceive of products to be used back in domestic life; market observation and analysis is also affected by the 'corporate effect'. By engaging in participant observation with end-users in their own environments and becoming part-time anthropologists – or 'deep hanging out' as they also term it – they may discover patterns, customs and attitudes to consuming which focus groups or market surveys do not reveal. This may be particularly useful when considering how global product concepts or brands fit in with or may be adapted to local contexts. The final stage in this process is where the anthropological activity is articulated into descriptive data or narratives about their subjects and then becomes ethnography. At this point the designer draws back from immersive, participatory involvement (in anthropological terms, the 'emic' element) and sits outside the scene, as a detached observer (the 'etic' constituent) (Tso 1999: 72). Their description of events may then be communicated through mood boards or visual maps.

This approach suggests that designing products is not exclusively about positional goods for positional consumption. By reducing the design-thinking down to details of texture, colour or semantic association and exploring their relationship to human behaviour, designers are exploring consumer goods, not as they might appear to others, but their patina, quirks, ticks and irrationalities that they perform in the everyday lives of their users.

Lifestyle trends research therefore provides useful data from which designers can work. It is small wonder, then, that many design consultancies incorporated specialists in this area into their practices in the 1990s. For example, the American consultancy Design Continuum listed three key areas they build into the design process, being, knowledge, product and brand. Within their knowledge building services they included 'Consumer understanding', encompassing 'direct observational research' and 'professional immersion and noticing' (role-play in other words) and 'Context analysis' through, for instance, 'cultural assessment', 'archetypal profiling' and 'segment opportunity mapping' (Design Continuum 1999). In 1998, retail and leisure consultants Fitch bought the Paris-based Peclers, a styling agency specializing in forecasting future trends in fashion. They also developed their '4D' approach, being, 'Discover. Define. Design. Deliver' (Fitch 1999). The first two of these refer to the gathering of market intelligence and its articulation into design briefs for clients.

Whatever jargon consultancies use to explain their offer to potential clients, the point is that it evidences the fact that design consultancies may not only exist at the interface between producer and consumer but may move downstream to carry out consumer market research and upstream to provide strategic product management for clients. Scenario planning, including the use of mood boards to articulate lifestyle perceptions, is one tool used in this process.

While quantitative data regarding lifestyle preferences may be mustered through market surveys, the partnership of ethnography and design may yield innovatory results. A well-known example of this is in Sony's development of portable televisions. The American company General Electric had conducted a survey by judging people's responses to mock-up televisions to estimate demand for a small portable TV, the conclusion of which was that the, 'people do not place a high value on portability of the television set' (General Electric quoted in Lorenz 1986: 34). By contrast, Sony looked at people's behavioural patterns at home and the number and type of TV channels available. Using this data they anticipated that a portable TV would actually suit changes in these patterns. Following the success of their portable TV, they then went on to do precisely the same with the video cassette recorder, the Walkman personal stereo and the Watchman flat-tube TV. Thus, lifestyle research for design consultancy becomes a form of cultural analysis, ethnography or design criticism in itself.

back to the workshop   But how is all this research for design translated into actual artefacts? The incorporation of lifestyle trends research into a design consultancy may be consolidated in order to promote its professional standing with clients. But ultimately, this data has to be used towards the shaping of material objects. Clearly, visual mapping aids the synthesis of data into formal characteristics. In the course of drawing or pasting-up images for this the material qualities of weight, density and surface texture are lost: again the emphasis leads towards the exterior, graphic qualities. Designers may therefore brainstorm with conjunctions of objects in their quest to achieve the optimum form. For example, multinational product design consultancy IDEO keeps a box in each of the company's six major offices in San Francisco, Palo Alto, Grand Rapids, Chicago, Boston and London. Each box contains five drawers holding 200-odd objects which are tagged and numbered. There are related websites on a company intranet which then give further materials information including their manufacturer and previous use in other products. Designers rummage through the compartments and play with the items, which include tiny batteries or miniature switches, in quests for inspiration (McGrane 1999).

There are times, however, when designers may be exclusively absorbed in technical and formal development in the workshop and where the intuitive manipulation of forms without the intellectual baggage of research data takes precedence. James Dyson devotes much of his autobiography to explaining the many hours spent in workshops manipulating mock-ups of his cyclonic vacuum system, emphasizing the 'hand and heart' aspects of designing. Indeed, many consultants will claim that despite the increased conceptual complexity of the job, there is still an artesanal element to design (Hollington 1999a).

Writer and designer David Pye made a useful distinction between different modes of craft and design practice. One is 'workmanship of risk' where the exact formal qualities of an object are not determined before its production – a situation normally allied with craft making. The other is 'workmanship of certainty' where the finished outcome is preconceived and which we would identify in most product and interaction design (see Dormer 1990: 144–5). There are artesanal moments in much product design where 'workmanship of risk' exists; but it forms just one of several stages in an overall research process. Ultimately, precision and certainty dominate in the development of consumer goods. This is due not only to the importance of synthesizing front-end consumer research, but also the various restrictions of production tooling. The belief of nineteenth-century reformer John Ruskin that the best design was the product of the faculties of head, heart and hand accurately describes the demands made of modern designers (see Frayling 1999).

product semantics and flexible manufacture Product semantics emerged in the early 1980s for a number of historically specific reasons. One was due to the growth of microchip technology for products which allowed for the miniaturization of the internal workings of many electronic goods. Henceforth, the form of such products did not have to be so tightly determined by their internal workings. But it was also derived from a theoretical discourse on both sides of the Atlantic which was perhaps overoptimistic in its practicable ends but reflected wider ideological and commercial shifts of that decade.

At the Cranbrook Academy of Art in Illinois, USA, Michael McCoy and his students explored the potential of product semantics to the hilt during the 1980s. Many of their projects explored visual languages for information technology hardware and consumer electronics. This led them to consider the kinds of software they processed. Thus in designing a CD player, students Kevin Fitzgerald and Scott Makela considered hip-house and 'house music' and the way they collaged excerpts of music together. By extension they saw this as metaphor for the street lifestyle where these genres grew up and where appropriation was necessary for survival. These 'street' themes were then introduced into their design so that the CD player featured welded-steel speaker horns and body constructed of the wood used in baseball bats. McCoy claims that this process means, 'that designers are moving closer to their audiences, the people who use the technology. They are trying to understand and empathize with a particular culture and needs' (1993: 136). It must be remembered, however, that Cranbrook was working as an educational laboratory for ideas, and that while these proposals did much to challenge hitherto accepted norms in design language, in the so-called 'real world' their products would probably only appeal to niche markets. The flexibility of manufacture required to realize these designs would push them into a 'high-design' category.

In Italy, the Memphis projects of Milanese designers from 1980 were concerned with the ironic, playful and colourful re-rendering of the exterior of household products. The practitioners and theorists of this 'new Italian design' were closely bound up in the family-run workshop networks of Northern Italy. The dominance of small-sized neo-artesanal industries allowed for the steady flow of batch production objects of desire to turn the theoretical ambitions of Milanese designers into material artefacts. Thus a close link between a semantically informed design approach and its ready translation into products could be forged: just as language is flexible, so could its manufacture be. In this climate, leading designer and commentator Andrea Branzi was able to extol the virtues of a 'New Handicrafts' as the basis of a 'Second Modernity' (Branzi 1984). According to Branzi's argument, product design could return from its wilderness years as a department of alienated corporate capital to a workshop of ideas and their making. This, in many respects, was a revindication of the Arts and Crafts ideals of a hundred years earlier.

During the early 1980s, this euphoria was matched by an emergent discussion on flexibility in the political economy of the West which was evenly matched in its optimism by both right- and left-wing observers. Within this, the example of the so-called 'Third Italy' was frequently invoked by progressive writers on economic sociology (e.g. Berger and Piore 1980; Sabel 1982). The notion of small manufacturing businesses innovating both luxury and high-technology products for an international market was seductive. In the workshops of the Veneto and Emilia-Romagna, artesans developed and batch produced either exclusive fashionware and furnishings or capital goods such as machinery, tooling or specialized equipment. Here, then, was William Morris's ideal of the amalgamation of intellectual and manual labour made real (Sabel 1982: 220–31). And what is more, their products kept apace with fluctuations in market demand. For extollers of consumer sovereignty, then, the flexible manufacturing system, like that of the Third Italy, complemented and exonerated the dominance of a market-driven political economy. It provided ample proof of the correspondence of enterprise culture and consumerism in the 1980s (Block 1990; Jessop et al. 1991). Seen in this light, Branzi's socialist-driven intentions – his so-called 'radical design' – may, in fact, be seen to unwittingly conspire with the economic ambitions of neo-liberal proponents of the free market system.

The flexible manufacturing system which Branzi and his cohort drew on is just one form of it, however. It was probably apt for short-run high-design products but also capital goods and certain components – short-run specialized, capital intensive products in other words. But for mainstream consumer goods, this could not provide sufficient scale in research and development or the cost savings in manufacture that large corporations could offer.

Much of the engineering demands required in even the most straight-forward products draws on significant capital and human resources in their development. James Dyson talks of having developed 5,127 prototypes for the cyclone system over three years (Dyson 1998: 121). In 1996 the in-house design department of Hewlett Packard numbered 27 professionals in all. This was made up of six industrial designers who took care of product aesthetics and human factors, sixteen mechanical design engineers responsible for the components that make up the product, five tool designers whose job was to add and modify features in order to facilitate component manufacture and two plastics process engineers who provided specialist knowledge as to the behaviour of plastics in their various states of formation (Wood and Ullman 1996: 202).

Generally speaking, new product development absorbs around 15 per cent of the production budget, but commits 80 per cent of overall costs (Thackara 1997: 424). Thus while we have seen that the human resource costs may be substantial in the Dyson and Hewlett Packard cases, these are overshadowed by expenditure on tooling up, raw materials and manufacture. In view of this fact, it is vital for companies to achieve the optimum product development before actual expenditure on production 'ramp-up' is made. Furthermore, the resultant high overall costs must be met by high volume sales.

The pressure on designers is not just to achieve the right 'fit' of aesthetic and utilitarian values in a product in order to satisfy the brand requirements of the producer or the lifestyle desires of the consumer and subsequently justifying tooling and manufacturing costs. To these demands, the question of product safety has added to the weight of responsibility on designers. In the UK, for example, the Consumer Protection Act of 1987 made, 'the manufacturer or importer of a product with a design defect liable to compensate a person who suffers damage, without the sufferer having to prove negligence or a contractual relationship' (Abbott and Tyler 1997: 116–17). From 1993, the 'CE' marking in the European Union was established to signify that products conformed to all the various safety controls of the different member states: in other words, it acted like a 'passport' to be allowed free movement within the Community market (Abbott and Tyler 1997: 95). In addition, the EU General Product Safety Directive imposed obligations on producers and others in the chain of supply to place only safe products on the market. Such directives put the responsibilities for product safety and its testing on the producers and suppliers and by extension, back to their designers.

Given these restrictions, it is not surprising that variety and flexibility in certain consumer goods such as electronic hardware and white goods, is, in fact, reasonably limited and does not live up to the ambitions of some proponents of product semantics. There is also a range of associated features outside the flexibility of manufacture: the amount and type of retail space available and the need to cluster products around core brand identities rather than produce fragmented flights of design fantasy both contribute to this effect. A typical scenario, then, is for variety in a product line to be created by establishing a new product and then subsequently adding variations and additions to it.

In terms of the body design of products, computer aided manufacture is limited in delivering flexibility. Van Hinte (1990) argues that its forte is in processing information, with which it can control other machines by switching them on and off according to consumer demands at its most basic. The computer is therefore most influential in carrying out simple operations in manufacture such as in spraying or welding, or controlling variation in punching and drilling tools. By contrast, he reflects, three-dimensional data for moulds takes longer to process digitally than 'real' moulds. Variety as a means of catering to individual consumer desires is achieved less from computer-controlled machinery than by taking a modular approach to designing. This is typical in power-tool systems with a variety of attachments or in bicycle assembly. A glaring example of how product variety could only be expressed in simple details rather than in the main body, is in the Nokia 3210 mobile phone. This product features clip-on fasciae so that the user can customize it – within a narrow menu – to their favourite colour and finish. Otherwise, the hardware is relatively undifferentiated from other models.

In many consumer goods, flexibility of production is achieved through a combination of computerized information systems with relatively low-technology industrial arrangements. A classic and well-known example of this is in Benetton clothing. Its headquarters is in Treviso, northern Italy and eight Benetton family-owned factories in the immediate region carry out design work, grading, marking and cutting. Labour intensive assembly, pressing and embroidery is contracted out to small firms. Below them these firms subcontract to a third tier of very small workshops – often non-unionized, low-wage setups – who carry out more specialized tasks. Benetton tightly controls demand down through these tiers according to market fluctuations. Upstream of the final assembly, the company only sells its products through franchises which bear its name. Each outlet is connected to automated warehouses and regional and world headquarters through a computer network. In this way, the company can receive information on customer demand. Of particular importance is data on shifting tastes in colours. Using information which originates in the retail outlets and is then downloaded through the Benetton network, computer-programmed equipment shifts from one colour order to another. The dyeing process of goods is held off as long as possible so that consumer information can be fed into the production at the last minute (Harrison 1994: 89–95).

'United Colors of Benetton' is not just a slogan which expresses a brand identity, then: it is shorthand to describe the flexible production systems it employs. As a company, Benetton itself is stripped down to its core competencies of design, marketing and assembly. It not only benefits from using information technology and flexible manufacture to close the producer/consumer gap, it is also free to concentrate on interposing itself at a variety of points on the 'circuit of culture' so that its identity in the marketplace may be bolstered via strident and well-known marketing campaigns.

The Benetton example is similar in many respects to the industrial structures of Japanese design-led corporations. Of these Toyota was the pioneer, it having stripped down to core competencies in the 1980s so that it relied on a tiered system of suppliers: 168 in the first tier, 4,700 in the second and with 31,600 suppliers in the third (Harrison 1994: 154). Equally, by the 1990s, 75 per cent of the production at NEC, Panasonic, Mitsubishi and Sony was contracted out (Harrison 1994: 158). This contracting-out organization is a development of the *keiretsu* system, literally meaning 'societies of business', upon which the Japanese manufacturing sector thrives.

Sony was among the innovative Japanese corporations which modified this system in order to facilitate greater flexibility and creativity. In this climate, the Walkman personal stereo system was conceived, not through an orchestrated process of product planning, but, it appears, as the coincidence of a number of ideas and the need of the tape-recorder division within Sony to revitalize its prestige within the corporation (du Gay et al. 1997). The subsequent product and marketing mix was, however, highly organized and has allowed for subsequent developments of the Walkman in order to broaden its consumer appeal as well as reinforce its brand recognition. For instance, the Sony showrooms – located in major global cities such as Tokyo, New York and Paris – are furnished with 'lifestyle settings' such as bedrooms, offices and lounges rather like the 'mood board' scenarios made almost real. Here consumers are encouraged to play with Sony products. Their behaviour and preferences are closely monitored by Sony staff. The showroom thus becomes a laboratory for analysing consumer reactions to different products. This information is then passed on to Sony headquarters which then feeds into subsequent product research and development. As a result of such market research, Sony has gone on to manufacture over seven hundred versions of the Walkman. While maintaining certain basic features in the design, Sony draws on flexible manufacturing systems – either in its own automated technologies or in the way it contracts components production out – in order to reach particular lifestyle segments of the market. By catering to different and progressively changing tastes it is able to spread and reinforce the brand across a wide range of consumers and global markets.

designing global products   The Sony and Benetton examples show that, as Bennett Harrison (1994) argues, it is in fact the large, global corporations who have continued to hold the commercial initiative and economic power in terms of their ability to exploit the fit between detailed consumer information and flexible manufacture. The end of Fordism does not necessarily mean the end of large corporations. As James Woudhuysen states, 'if small firms may be able to go global more easily than in the past, the world still belongs to multinational corporations' (1998: 111).

Product designers have benefited from this situation. Chapter 1 pointed up the vast growth in interior and graphic design sectors since 1980 as Western economies have shifted more in favour of services industries. However, so-called de-industrialization has not meant a decline in product consultancy. Those manufacturing companies in the West who weathered the storm of the early 1990s recession are mostly those which were more predisposed to product innovation. Since 1990 there has also been widespread growth in the number of in-house designers employed by manufacturers and service providers who take a central role in product planning and the commissioning and managing of external design consultants (NDI 1994: 7).

Furthermore, economic globalization creates a situation where design information is passed between different nodes on a global scale. This may be between separate offices of a multinational design company. Thus while large consultancies in the 1980s established offices abroad to tap into local markets, by the late 1990s the traffic was two-way. Since consumption patterns and taste in certain products exist on a global scale, market intelligence and design know-how are constantly passed between the nodes both to keep up with and subsequently intervene in the global flows of information. In 1995, Japan's Ricoh, the photocopier manufacturer, located a design studio in Taiwan. Woudhuysen (1998: 100) lists three advantages for shifting Research, Development and Design (RD&D) offshore: first, the internationalist effect of this move means that such offices develop products which are marketed over a range of countries, thus providing economy of scale and scope; secondly, by linking RD&D in different time zones through information technology networks, firms move Computer Aided Design results between sites on a 24-hour basis so that new products are developed more rapidly; thirdly, RD&D sites can tap into local knowledge on competitors, the market and specialist expertises and share these features globally.

This last point effectively evidences the global–local nexus. It suggests that globalism and locality are not in tension, but are mutually dependent. As Kevin Robins suggests, 'Globalization is frequently seen in terms of the "disembedding" of ways of life from the narrow confines of locality. But, increasingly, we are coming to recognize that it is – parodoxically, it seems – also associated with new dynamics of re-localization' (1997: 28). This means that the global–local nexus involves, 'a pragmatic compromise between the aspiration to expand market spaces and the realities of cultural gravity and resistance' (1997: 30).

product designers and their clients   Product designers increasingly address the demands of representing a client's brand aspirations and creating products for a global marketplace. There are no standard norms as to how this is achieved, however. Just as the nature of design consultancy does not allow for standardization of practices so clients will make different demands of designers depending on their own expertises, product, scope and scale. Here are some examples.

Except for the occasional assistant drafted in to work on specific projects, British designer Julian Brown works entirely alone. Yet his clients include global corporations such as NEC, Sony and Curver. In the development of products, he explores what he calls the 'prime forms' that make up the quintessence of the client's products. Thus in his domestic and office gadgetry for Italian company Rexite, he extended from a design language already laid down by GianCarlo Piretti over a period of 15 years. 'Good design', in his words, 'arises as an evolution both of the client's own development and of its relationship with the designer'. His quest, then, is to discover a client's particular cultural identity and develop products which act as 'attitudinal markers' of that identity. This kind of dialogue, he claims, puts design onto a 'higher plain' than mere problem-solving; it is a level which,

Advantix T700 camera. Designed by Hollington. Produced by Kodak from 2000

Source: Hollington

he claims, 'cannot be calculating' (Brown 1999). This design approach may resonate with 'brand thinking', although the emphasis is more on the client, producer side rather than on complex consumer research.

This notion of striking an 'attitude' with clients as part of the design process is also inscribed into Hollington's approach. This British product and interaction design studio, numbering around 15 employees, is more explicit in taking on and developing a client's brand through products. In mid-1998 they began working with Kodak, in the USA, towards a new range of cameras. The first camera was introduced in mid-2000, an Advanced Photo System (APS), Zoom camera, called Advantix T700. Development work used very specific information regarding camera purchase. Two key features were that traditional film was not going to be entirely replaced by digital photography and that a significant number of leisure cameras are bought prior to vacationing. Using this data, Hollington developed key features of the camera which accentuate these notions. First, these included a rugged, robust exterior with big, easy to use controls; the challenge was to combine this ruggedness – akin to luggage – with the 'precision tool' values expected of a quality camera; to do this they combined soft-feel materials and sculpted forms with instrument-like, crisp, metallic detail; colour/material/finish consultants Barron Gould developed the grey-green colour palette which relates to travel clothing and luggage; secondly, some external design cues which stress the qualities of the APS system, such as the facility to choose picture format (classic, HDTV or panorama) were incorporated; thus the 'CHP' control is moulded in jewel-like opalescent green plastic, is large, and can be seen from the front of the camera, the point-of-purchase viewpoint. Additionally, the range of cameras incorporated a flash housed in a flip-up cover that protects the camera's delicate lens and viewfinder optics and enables the flash to stand well away from the lens and thus help avoid the perennial problem of 'red-eye'. This unique-to-Kodak design feature is also seen as a strong part of the product's brand identity. Hollington's clients call the basic physical layout and shape of the product, 'form factor'. This is elaborated into what is commonly termed 'product design language' through combining the otherwise 'abstract' design considerations such as ergonomics, fitness for purpose, design-for-manufacture with a design idiom which adds to its brand identity (Hollington 1999b).

At times the language used to describe the product designer's work may appear rather more opaque, however. For instance, Richard Seymour of well-known design consultancy Seymour Powell states in an interview,

The X-factor in the product is its essential personality, its desirability quotient, if you like – those intangible, emotional features, over and above function and efficiency.

> . . . We're constantly searching for that elusive iconography, the psychological bridge between consumers as they are and consumers as they'd like to be.
>
> (Seymour quoted in Tomes et al. 1998: 129)

In each of these examples, the designers are establishing common frames of reference with clients, not just in the visual or strategic scenarios they envisage for them, but in the verbal articulation of core ambitions. Language is thus not just a vehicle to mediate and explain ideas, it helps to shape the content of the product and ultimately, its public meaning. It is small wonder that it appears to assume increasing prominence in the design process in an age of branded products, where semantic values are paramount.

Dyson stories   The narratives and themes set up in this dialogue between designer and client focus the design process. They may also be extended outwards to provide content for other interventions to promote the brand. A designer's characterization of a product through identifying a key word or phrase to crystallize their aims may indeed sound like an ad slogan. For example, designers working for J. Walter Thompson on the corporate identity of Delta Airlines came up with, 'Lufthansa with a smile' as a tag-line to centre their development work on – it meant that they wished to communicate their client's brand values as those both of efficiency and friendliness (Richardson 1999). These are for internal use of the client and consultancy, but may find their way into the public realm. The key theme of the Dyson DC-01 was dispensing with the bag through the invention of the cyclone system: Dyson's first advertising campaign used the words, 'Say goodbye to the bag' (Dyson 1998: 231).

Indeed, the Dyson DC-01 and subsequent models provide a tight-fitting case study not only because of the transparency of the product's values, but also because its designer was responsible for its manufacture and subsequent marketing. In this case, the story of its conception, shaping and the efforts made in taking it through manufacture and distribution become an integral element to its brand image.

The notion of 'brand image' is slippery. While the brand identity of a product involves the straightforward attributes given to it by its producer, brand image belongs to both producer and consumer. It refers to those values which are both created and communicated around the product; but these values are also subject to the fluxes of their possible meanings in society. Concurrent events may add to or detract from the public image of a brand. It is not surprising, then, that in the 1990s some design consultancies even joined forces with public relations companies (Richardson 1999). This helps ensure that the brand identity of a product could then be influenced in the public domain through the control of accompanying information.

In the Dyson case, the analysis of brand image is made even more circumspect as in the first place, the company is concerned to distance itself from mainstream marketing systems which promote brand identity. Throughout his autobiography Dyson reminds us that the styling of the vacuum cleaner emerges in the first instance from solving engineering problems and that the strength of its innovations do not need further dressing up through advertising or sales gimmicks. None the less, the Dyson story interfaces with a rich set of cultural discourses which help to shape the brand image. In other words, Dyson the individual, Dyson the manufacturer and Dyson the product have their own mythologies which are both produced and consumed.

As an affable but retiring personality, James Dyson is well-known. He is a genuinely philanthropic entrepreneur who has supported a range of charities and causes. Some of these relate to his own activities, such as his support of London's Design Museum. He has also been a vociferous critic of patenting systems, which due to their high costs, he claims, stifles the enterprise of many small-scale inventors.

The 'Dyson story' has been told through numerous newspaper and lifestyle magazine articles (e.g. *Sushi* 1999). It is also recounted in a small booklet given with each Dyson product, in the Dyson autobiography and on the company website. It is an heroic story of an inventor and designer who developed a range of innovative products for international export. Each product has its own chapter in the story in which a simple design idea is taken from the workshop, through struggles to find backers to their eventual market success. Each successive business venture builds on the last one until the narrative reaches its apotheosis in the realization of the DC-01.

This is a gripping story full of yarns and cliffhanger suspense. It has resonances in a long pedigree of British 'visionary' hero inventors. Many of these have not reaped the rewards of their own innovations: John Hargreaves, inventor of the Spinning Jenny had his idea pirated and died in poverty; Charles Babbage, who built the precursor to the calculator and computer, died a disappointed man; Sir Clive Sinclair is more known for the failure of his C5 electric car than inventing the pocket calculator, a version of the home computer and the digital watch. The Japanese, reportedly, believe that 56 per cent of the world's greatest inventions came from the UK; yet at the same time an estimated £165 billion has been lost from British inventions going overseas (Crace 1999). There are none the less some members of this 'it's crazy but I think it'll work' school who have achieved recognition and even gone on to become national icons. Among these one would include the nineteenth-century engineers Isambard Kingdom Brunel and George Stephenson who, interestingly, is featured on the UK £5 note. Contemporaneous with Dyson, we must acknowledge the 'Bayliss story'. This has a similar narrative of an inventor, Trevor Bayliss, who came up with an idea for a clockwork radio in 1991 but had to work through a series of hurdles, including rejection from the British Design Council before his invention got into production. By 1999, 120,000 Bayliss radios were being manufactured each month. These are stories 'out there', fashioned in the public domain by journalists and TV producers. But it is noteworthy that in his autobiography Dyson cites Brunel and Dan Dare (an equally 'knife-edge' hero of the boys' comic *Marvel* fame) as his two greatest inspirations. Both the Bayliss radio and the Dyson vacuum cleaner objectify these narratives. As mental images, the ratchets and springs in the radio and the chunky aspect of the vacuum cleaner resonate with notions of engineering of a bygone era.

The DC-01 came onto the market in 1993. Historically, this was at the tail-end of Britain's deepest economic recession. Just as the Vespa motor-scooter from 1947 signalled Italy's postwar reconstruction, and the Mini Metro car was supposed to mark an emergence from a decade of labour relations discord in the automobile industry (Johnson 1986; Hebdige 1988) so the Dual Cyclone vacuum cleaner represents a new entrepreneurial sensibility based on design-led innovation. To transpose from Hebdige's argument about the Mini Metro (1988: 82–3), reading the Dyson story involves understanding the 'official' fixing of the product's image (Dyson literature, advertising, packaging, press releases etc.). Whether that reading makes sense and has resonance depends on the reader's prior knowledge of and relationship to external, related factors of ideological issues and cultural codes. Consciously or not, the consumer is presented with not one object, but a series of objects born of different 'moments' in the circuit of culture.

re-doing the Dyson   This chapter has concerned itself primarily with the relationships between representation, design processes and manufacture, marketing and distribution. The discussion has shown how layers of meaning are built around consumer goods. A coalition of the fluid processes of design, market research techniques and flexible manufacture attempts to sustain brands, continually layering meaning while retaining the core product and brand identity. These processes involve cognition both 'inside' and 'outside' the product. In the latter sense, new product development is viewed scientifically, as a commodity with potential exchange value. The majority of this chapter has focused on this foregrounding of the activities of design and production domains interpreting and exploiting consumer markets. But the designer, and indeed the user, also experiences it as a 'thing', as a raw object of use. This final section looks more closely at the Dyson Cyclone in use, in order, perhaps, to retrieve design values which lie beyond the brand and are more firmly embedded in the everyday use of the artefact.

An innovation of the Dyson Cyclone and its less-known forerunners, the G-Force (1985) and the Iona SF7 (1988), was the inclusion of a transparent cylinder. Previous vacuum cleaners had steadfastly hidden the dirt collection away. With the transparent plastic cylinder, the DC-01 proudly displays all dust and debris it sucks up. Being able to see dirt whizzing round in the chamber reinforces the 'cyclone' idea. It also makes a 'feature' of the dirt and allows it to be quantified. Conventional vacuum cleaners physically and visually spirit dirt away. With the transparent cylinder of the Dyson Cyclone, the dirt is held in suspension. This can provoke both shock and disgust as the user sees what was in the carpet, but also satisfaction at seeing that it is now captured. The domestic labour of cleaning is neatly quantified in the level of dust and debris to be seen in the cylinder. On a small level, then, the results of traditionally invisible domestic labour are made visible and measurable.

At the same time, the actual use of the vacuum cleaner might become 'autotelic'. This is a term used by the behavioural scientist Mihaly Csikszentmihalyi (1975) to describe the instrinsic satisfaction of carrying out activities in their own right, rather than towards any goal. Autotelic experience is one of complete involvement in the activity where there is neither boredom with it nor worry about performance. It may require skills and skills development, but clear feedback on actions is given. There is therefore a rational cause-and-effect wherein the results of actions are realistic and predictable. The activity engrosses the participant, blotting out all other external stimuli. It centres the individual entirely in the present, rather than being laden by past knowledge or future expectation. These factors add up to deeply pleasurable, self-confirming experience.

Autotelic activities, or 'flow' as Csikszentmihalyi otherwise calls them, might include dancing, sport, navigating a computer game, or even using a vacuum cleaner. Cleaning may involve domestic drudgery rather than domestic euphoria. But reaching to corners of a room, moving furniture, choosing and assembling hose attachments while lost in the drone of the motor may draw the individual into an intense involvement with an external challenge. This might be the experience of using any vacuum cleaner, but certain design details in the Dyson Cyclone may engender this effect. The apparatus features many points of physical interaction. The cable has to be manually wound back onto the body rather than being sprung. There are no fiddly adjustment buttons. Rather, points of contact – the clips to release the hose and the cylinder, the filter holders, the button to switch it on – are flagged up in yellow against the grey body. The chunky aspect of its general form reinforce this physicality, as does the superior weight of the plastics used. As design observer Peter Lloyd Jones tells us, 'if a person's possessions are to be capable of stimulating lasting intrinsic satisfaction it is clearly desirable that they are designed from the outset not only to provide emotional goals and perceptual challenges which stimulate flow but to be moreover inexhaustible to this kind of contemplation' (1992: 6.9).

conclusion   The Dyson vacuum cleaner is perhaps more unusual than many products in its consistencies between design, manufacture and mediation. This is not least because all these aspects have been centred around the efforts of one design-entrepreneur. While specialist design critics or ordinary users may have genuine criticisms of the product's primary design – its weight, its noisiness, its overplayed styling – the coherent fit of product content and image, in a variety of representational forms, may well explain why it has been cited so frequently as an example of design excellence. James Dyson plays down the roles of branding and marketing to promote the integrity of the product instead. But even this contributes indirectly towards shaping a brand image.

There is no getting away from it. Consumer goods exist both as objects and signs. Design methods, in particular the use of the mood board, often ensure this attitude. The development of plastics has led to design values being concentrated on their exterior surfaces to the extent that they may be as easily considered as graphic symbols as haptic forms. They become semiotically loaded. It is on this exterior surface only that most domestic goods may be subject to specialist treatment so that a variety of consumer tastes can be catered for. Generally speaking, the use of product semantics requires more design certainty than flexibility. Increasingly, they integrate both hard-edged market research and other academic disciplines, such as social psychology and ethnography, into their processes as a way of ensuring this certainty. Research and development costs, tooling up for manufacture and global distribution networks mean that economies of scale mitigate against any return to a romantic notion of small-scale workshops producing almost artesanally-conceived objects for a segmented market, at least, in domestic consumer goods. By contrast, the dominance of multi-national corporations in the global economy makes them the prime clients for product designers, and the demands they face are therefore evermore complex and challenging.

branded places

In the city centre of Leeds a series of new urban furnishings appeared in 1991–2. The date is important, for two reasons. First, it coincides with the Department of Health and Social Security's move of its headquarters from London to Leeds, bringing some 1,500 employees and their families with it. For this metropolitan influx, the city was shifting its image as northern industrial town to major cosmopolitan centre. Secondly, 1992 was the year of full integration of the European Union where internal trade barriers and passport controls would apparently disappear. The EU flag was proudly flown outside the Leeds City Council buildings.

The seats, lighting poles and balustrades were doing more than providing a perch or a leaning-post for weary shoppers, therefore. They seemed to be conspiring to redefine urban identity through their form. They are architectural detailing. But they are also part of a graphic treatment of the cityscape. They are about communication.

So what of their form? They were implemented as the redevelopment of a pedestrianized core of city centre streets to connect a series of covered shopping plazas developed in the late 1980s. In addition to the basic seating and lighting, they included decorative paving, planters and a series of 'gateway' features. As focal points at junctions and places of repose they provided areas for buskers, street hawkers and political activists as well as ordinary shoppers to congregate. They not only served to physically break-up the streetlines and remind us that this was an area which had been claimed back from vehicular circulation; they also provided a scenario for urban spectacle – entertainment as laid on by yet another Andean pan pipe band or the sellers of charity publications and political pamphlets. The multiculturalism, flows, inequalities and disunities of urban living are strangely harmonized in this seemingly modern space.

On first glance, the overall image of this scheme is generally European modern. Powder-coated steel, aluminium tubing and granite provide a textural mix which would be equally at home in Düsseldorf as Rotterdam. The application of coloured, curvilinear decorative effects to some of the ele-

Various views of the Landmark Leeds project, 1991–2. Designers: FaulknerBrowns Source: Guy Julier

'Leeds Look' architecture early 1990s. Quarry House (Department of Social Services) architect: Building Design Partnership (*top*) Leeds Magistrates Court architect: Leeds Design Consultancy. Source: Guy Julier

ments, however, cause some elements to recede into their immediate retailing context. Their slightly freehand signature is redolent of many corporate identity and retail interior schemes developed in the late 1980s.

Architectural critic Ken Powell described this scheme as, 'out of place', 'meretricious', and, 'a disgrace in a city full of fine Victorian craftsmanship' (Powell 1992). In the context of the Leeds City Council's ambitions these criticisms may well be taken as praise. The project was very much the brainchild of the city council's leadership and was, according to another of its critics, not the product of 'the normal process of public consultation' (Leeds Civic Trust quoted in Smales and Whitney 1996: 209). As will be revealed in this chapter, it was precisely the client's, ambition to be 'out of place', to be strident and to leave behind certain associations of being a Victorian city.

Discussion of such schemes does not belong exclusively to the architectural critic, however. Urban design projects suggest change in the conception and experience of city spaces and touch on leisure and urban planning studies. It also belongs to critical geography in that it is about the changing economic and cultural status of cities in a global context. These installations suggest new urban tastes arising from shifting class and employment patterns and may be studied by sociologists. By broadening the net of discursive contexts for such objects we might achieve an enriched vision of them. But we can also find out more about their material and visual significance beyond their superficial forms and functions. We can explore the values and experiences to which the objects are connected and of which they give expression. In turn we can begin to step away from a notion that the identity of urban centres resides solely in the exterior qualities of their architecture and adopt a more diverse approach to this question.

This chapter takes the position that in the developed world urban centres, regions and nations are marketed as brands. While for many centuries their advocates have used various means to compete with each other, it is only recently that this strategy has moved up several gears. It is important to analyse, therefore, the various bases on which this has taken place. In the first instance, a variety of design manifestations are mobilized towards this effect, shifting the discursive territory away from architecture. This in turn implies a different relationship of consumers to the identities of these spaces. Secondly, this system of branding is energized and problematized by shifts in the global flow of capital and labour and the reconfiguration of political and economic power towards cities and regions and away from nation-states.

evaluating place: beyond architectural criticism The Leeds City Council had played a significant role in shaping the architectural contours of the city centre immediately prior to the Landmark Leeds scheme. The inward-looking shopping developments which prefigured the 'Landmark Leeds' project were not built on the same massive scale as seen in Manchester's Arndale Centre or Newcastle's Eldon Square in the 1970s. Large 'signature' developments did not dominate, therefore. Instead, a layering of somewhat chaotically and contradictory planning initiatives dating back to the pre-industrial revolution (Nuttgens 1979) provided an intact heart within which new developments had to function.

During the late 1980s the city planning authority ensured that developers and their architects followed a set of unwritten design principles which came to be known as the 'Leeds Look'. This coincided with an unprecedented growth in office building: in 1987–8 new office development in Leeds rose from an annual 155,000 square feet to 275,000 square feet; by Easter 1989 640,000 square feet were under construction with another 700,000 in the pipeline (Barrick and Thorp 1989). This was partly motivated by a desire not to repeat the perceived planning mistakes of the past by allowing more assertive International Style office blocks to dominate the cityscape. The city's Planning Committee therefore 'tinkered' with those design details over which it had limited jurisdiction, such as the shape of fenestration or the pitch of a roof. Broadly speaking, this meant that new schemes reinterpreted the style of its riverside warehouses. This created a climate in which bold architectural statements would not be accepted and therefore not proffered. A series of prominent buildings were established exhibiting the same exterior usage of red brick, York stone for lintels, sills and other such details, slate roof, and Tuscan towers, pitch-roofs and window openings. These elements were not distinctive of Leeds in the late 1980s – a similar set of features could be found in office building throughout Britain of that period. The higher growth in building and the influence of the city Planning Office none the less conspired to concentrate this style with far greater density than elsewhere.

The 'Leeds Look' term was first coined by Ken Powell in an article entitled 'The offence of the inoffensive' (1989). Commenting on the influence of city planners on architecture, one critic described the city as, 'Leeds: the smotherer of invention' (Kitchen 1990). Meanwhile, another claimed that the, 'brick aesthetic ... seems to have been wrapped around most of the new buildings to prevent planning delays' (Whittaker 1990). These criticisms reveal that while the Planning Office did not overtly set about forging a particular architectural identity for the city, certainly the style elaborates a general aesthetic which was founded in aspects of its commercial heritage, but even this was a generalized typology. None the less both the response of its critics and the activity of its various producers demonstrate that the so-called 'Leeds Look' was, at the time, equating building with urban identity. More precisely, the *exterior* surface of a building, rather than its internal spatial arrangement and functional use, is privileged as the carrier of that identity.

This relationship between the built environment, its planning and design, and the visual consumption of places might be generalized further. Urry argues that novel modes of visual perception in the city were formed in the nineteenth century (1990: 136). Citing Marshall Berman's discussion of the mid-nineteenth-century Paris of Charles Baudelaire, he links new urban forms and their experience by the middle classes through to the growth of photography as a way of seeing. Berman (1983) contends that the rebuild-ing of Paris in the Second Empire under the direction of Raoul Haussmann brought forth a quintessentially modern experience of the city. The creation of wide boulevards was partly to facilitate rapid troop movements. But it also provided sweeping vistas of the cityscape so that each walk included dramatic visual effects. The boulevards became stage sets for an audience of the street-side cafés. The street provided a scenery for the middle-class stroller to see and be seen – the deprived and destitute having been removed from the action altogether. Here, the anonymity of the crowd gave both the security of private life and the stimulation of public action. In this world, the pedestrian (male) visitors – the *flâneur* in Baudelaire's terms – could observe without actually interacting with the objects or people of their gaze.

There is an indirect link, Urry therefore suggests, between this emer-gence of a cityscape designed for looking – both at it and its subjects – and the growth of photography. Just as the *flâneur* visually consumed all city sites, so the tourist photographs each vista on offer. There is the same detach-ment, the same pursuit of the picturesque in all things, the same wandering eye. The equation made between the built environment, the 'ordinary' stroller and photography stresses in each of these their *visual* consumption. Buildings, urban furniture and street layouts are valued solely for their exter-nal appearance; visitors merely look at them and each other within their scenography.

An extension of this attitude is to argue that the external appearance of buildings function like advertisements (Crilley 1993). The public are spec-tators of a two-dimensional presentation of city; the exteriors of buildings act as triumphal displays of its historical, commercial and cultural resources. In their influential book *Learning from Las Vegas* (1972) the influential theorist-practioners Robert Venturi, Denise Scott-Brown and Steven Izenour had encouraged architects to conceive of their buildings as 'billboards', to concentrate on their exterior surfaces in conveying certain messages through the choice of materials, historicist quotation in design details and/or their allusion to other imagery. In turn, Crilley notes, architects learn their imagery from the findings of market research; they speak of 'taste cultures' and 'semiotic groupings' as would advertising executives (1993: 235). Finally, famous architects and artists may be engaged to design buildings and public art works for a city. This acts to publicize its power and enlightened attitude as a patron.

In the light of large-scale redevelopment projects such as Canary Wharf in London this analysis carries considerable weight. Cities whose built environment is significantly marked by the interventions of historically important architects, such as Mackintosh and MacMurdo in Glasgow, use their signatures to market themselves (Laurier 1993). Equally the boulevards and vistas of Paris remain intact for the visitor to re-enact the strolling and viewing in the great city. But what if funds, public demand or conservation laws hinder large-scale redevelopment? What if a city does not possess the advantage of 'great architecture'? What if political or commercial demands require something less overt, of a smaller, more intimate scale? Here, perhaps, a different sensibility in architectural or urban design, but also in the conception of how a city is consumed kicks in.

That this 'Leeds Look' period was soon superseded by the 'Landmark Leeds' initiative demonstrates a significant turn from architecture to design as a key defining feature in the identity of a city. The 'Landmark Leeds' project originated in pressure from shopkeepers and the Leeds Chamber of Trade and Commerce to regenerate the city centre. Despite the significant growth of office space in the city centre, retail and entertainment demand was falling. In the face of growing competition from out-of-town shopping centres and alternative nearby urban centres, the designers of the Landmark Leeds scheme, FaulknerBrowns undertook a wide-ranging study of the city as whole, reviewing transport, green corridors and key city centre sites in order to revitalize its use. Out of this survey the urban furniture scheme emerged as a way of recreating a sense of place in the heart of the city (Davenport 1999). Many design decisions were guided by pressure from the City Council to put in place a scheme as quickly as possible – thus, as is often the case with projects of this scale and complexity, its various features were assembled in a piecemeal fashion.

The project coincided with a vigorous and swift campaign to position the city as a major European centre, an ambition which Leeds was not alone in harbouring. For its particular part, however, the City Council encouraged the establishment of the '24-hour city' notion (again not an entirely original initiative as, for instance, Manchester and Bolton had both adopted the same strategy). This looked to relaxing licensing hours for bars and restaurants in the city centre and supporting the 'night-economy' (Bianchini 1995) of 'after-hours life'. It strove to kindle a continental-European 'café culture' which was vigorously promoted by the local government tourist offices, regional news media and lifestyle magazines. The social life and visual constitution of Leeds could emulate Parisian restaurants, Barcelonese bars or the coffee-houses of Vienna. The identity of the city became design-dense. This effectively decentred its cognition. It shifted from the purely visual consumption of architectural exteriors (the 'Leeds Look') to the more holistic 'experience' of seating, signage, sounds and smells. It was also decentred in that it pursued an identity through assembling and arranging from, 'a kit of dangerously fragile parts' to make itself up as a 'good European city' (Smales 1994: 51). Despite the potential dangers of this 'cut and paste' approach to developing a city identity, it is noteworthy that the more intimate, visceral experiences of eating, drinking, dancing and socializing – and the design hardware that surrounds and encourages these acts – are given greater prominence.

In terms of the management of city centres, in several instances the 1990s saw a clear shift away from foregrounding the architect, or at least repositioning him or her as the orchestrator of a wider range of urban activities. In Leeds, the chief city architect was reappointed as the overseer not just of the quality of individual buildings, but with a remit to manage the cultural use and infrastructure of its urban fabric. In 1999, the city of Hull appointed its first city 'brand manager' whose job was to coordinate all aspects of the city's image, ranging from its public architecture to its information leaflets. Between 1980 and 1984, Oriol Bohigas famously acted as Barcelona's City Council head of architecture and urban planning; he returned to public service at the beginning of the 1990s to take charge of the city's cultural planning.

In a critique of contemporary architectural discourse and practice, Martin Pawley (1998) reveals the dominance of visuality. He argues that criticism has been dominated by art-historical approaches: this is highly selective in what it considers to be of value and that selection is itself based on the discussion of purely formalistic values. In turn, styles are presumed to express the *zeitgeist* of an era (Pawley 1998: 99). Eras themselves are defined by the art historian. Thus a particular style is judged as 'typical' of its period while the art historian is also instrumental in defining these characteristics. By extension this self-referential discussion leads to two key effects on architectural practice. First, it encourages a constant and uncritical replication of features which are assumed to express a particular age. In town centres, for example, where architectural heritage is 'preserved', historical façades are retained while redevelopment will completely alter the interior functioning and spatial arrangement of the building. Secondly, and more importantly, the majority of architects and their critics foreground the external appeal of buildings as the chief, or only feature of value. As we have seen with products, buildings are presented in magazines or brochures via their superficial formal and semantic effects. They are shown as images of themselves.

Pawley suggests that the implications of breaking away from this canon of appreciation and practice are enormous. It would dispense with the fetishization of external form and embrace internal use. In turn this will reveal the real import of buildings:

> In place of the city as the treasure house of civilization, it will expose the city as monstrous squanderer of resources. In place of the building as an investment, it will put forward the building as an expendable container. In place of aesthetic value it will put forward the value of access to networks that annihilate distance, presence and want.
>
> (Pawley 1998: 93)

This suggests that architecture, exists as the support for information exchange (as in computerized office environments), the distribution of material goods (as in warehouses) or the ebbs and flows of everyday life (as in urban furnishing such as the Landmark Leeds scheme).

Urry's analysis gives special prominence to the visual in the (tourist) cognition of places. It is one where *looking* at buildings, people and scenographies is the mainstay of visiting localities. By moving the emphasis away from the visual consumption of architecture, Pawley challenges us to explore alternative ways by which the built environment is experienced.

Other authors have suggested similar reorientations. Novelist Jonathon Raban (1974) provided a portrait of London which explored the city as a place of encounters and events. His 'Soft City' of experiences, sometimes inhumanely violent, sometimes lovingly intimate, contrasted with the 'hard city' of urban planning and architectonics, financial and demographic statistics. Over a decade earlier Jane Jacobs published an autobiographical journal of 24 hours in New York (1961). It affectionately dwells on the daily rituals of urban streetlife – the opening of shops, sweeping of streets, collecting children from school, returning home from work. Marshall Berman eulogizes Jacobs's commitment to the vitality and diversity of urban experience. According to Berman, Jacobs's vision extends Baudelaire's interest in the visual spectacle of the city streets and is evidence of the continuous unfolding of modernity in the urban context (1983: 312–19). However,

Urban design in Barcelona 1980s. Metro signage designed by Josep Ma. Trias, Joan Antoni Blanc and Miguel de Moragas 1981 *top*; waterfront designed by Manuel Solà-Morales 1987 *right*; Parc de l'Espanya Industrial designed by Luis Peña Ganchequi and Francesc Ruis 1985 *above left*; drinking fountain designed by Daniel Nebot and Nancho Lavernia 1986 *bottom left*

Source: Quod; Pedro Mandueño; Isabel Campi; Guy Julier

Jacobs also brings the experience down to a more immediate level. Her cityscape is not one of majestic vistas and building façades to create an heroic stage-set; it is a more chaotic, denser place of social exchange.

This kind of analysis opens out the internal organs of a city for inspection. It claims urban identity to rest not merely on the external appearance of its buildings, in the architectural *look* of a place, but in the everyday attitudes and actions of its inhabitants. Both Jacobs and Raban, perhaps romantically so, suggest an emancipatory individualism in the city experience. They celebrate a triumph of the individual's will to determine their own metropolitan meanings. At the same time, the character of that participation is supposedly shared. Jacobs's and Raban's explorations reveal not just their personal viewpoints, but a collective recognition of the social encounters or auditory rhythms in the city. Localities have their own stories and yarns to tell which in turn communicate something about what one might expect of them. These are what sociologist Rob Shields (1991) terms 'place myths'. Subsequently, designers and marketing experts may appropriate these place myths or even originate them to position a city, region or even a nation against their competitors.

the Barcelona paradigm   Of all examples of the mobilization of design in the public context in order to position and differentiate a city, Barcelona has become paradigmatic. For example, it is cited as source of inspiration for Rotterdam's extensive redesign work in the public domain (Hajer 1993: 64); it was awarded a Royal Institute of British Architects gold medal for recognition as a role model for urban regeneration in 1999. Russ Davenport, project architect for the Landmark Leeds scheme had visited Barcelona several times prior to and during its development. He used images of urban design in Barcelona in his presentation to Leeds City Council clients and encouraged them to travel there in order to see the possibilities for themselves. Seeing what had gone on in Barcelona gave him and his team of designers, 'a lot of confidence as to the possibilities available for an urban design project' (Davenport 1999).

None the less, many of Barcelona's plaudits have ignored the several layers and networks of signification on which its redesign in the 1980s and early 1990s took place. Clearly a major impetus for development was given by the city's hosting of the Olympic Games in 1992. International 'signature' architects such as Arata Isozaki and Norman Foster were engaged to design major buildings, the indoor stadium and the communications tower respectively. The city's architectural heritage of Gaudì, Domènech i Muntaner and Puig i Cadalfach was cleaned up and promoted. Public transport was extended and traffic circulation improved. Four kilometres of seafront were reclaimed and its portside was redeveloped. But much of the redesign of the functional and experiential apparates of the city belongs to initiatives outside this event.

In Barcelona through the 1980s we find the confluence of a number of events which added up to produce a concerted reworking of the city's identity in a European context. During four decades of the right-wing dictatorship of General Franco, the infrastructure of Barcelona and most other Spanish cities was largely neglected. By the time of Franco's death in 1975, its urban fabric was marked by chaotic traffic systems and high levels of pollution, irregular public transportation, and a dearth of public amenities.

The subsequent transition to democracy ushered in the partial decentralization of state power to city councils and regional governments which gave them greatly increased autonomy in their education, transport, public and commercial policies. In Barcelona from 1980 onwards, the socialist city council set about a radical urban regeneration, first of its metro system but also of its parks and plazas. Signage for its public transportation system installed a greater feeling of order and structure to the city chaos; paving projects and new public spaces gave back a sense of dignity to urban life (Buchanan 1986; Julier 1991: Ch. 4).

This emergent design hardware gave material form to some very specific metropolitan and 'nationalist' aspirations. They must be read not just in the context of the urban regeneration of a recently democratized locality and its preparations for a global event but also as part and parcel of a wholesale ideological, cultural, commercial and, hence, *aesthetic* repositioning of a region.

The creation of the autonomous government of Catalonia in 1979 gave way to the establishment of complementary regional–national identities of ruralism and modernity. On the one hand, more conservative notions of tradition and heritage of the Catalan region were embedded in the rural economies; but the autonomous government also sought a position in a dynamic, federalized Europe. The latter required the mobilization of cultural models in order to communicate a notion of an enterprising, flexible, creative and technologically sophisticated workforce and economic infrastructure both internally to its own population and externally to prospective foreign investors (Julier 1996). This push came under the heading of 'normalization' in which both linguistic and cultural 'Catalan-ization' were advanced hand in glove. To be 'normal' meant that Catalonia's own language would be hegemonic and that at the same time, cultural infrastructures and habits of cultural consumption would be comparable to Europe (Fernández 1995). In this context design would be an apt signifier of the cultural sphere.

Branding Barcelona. 'Barcelona més que mai' (Barcelona more than ever) promotion by the Barcelona City Council, art directed by Pepino Garciá, 1984 *below*; Barcelona 1992 Olympic logo designed by Josep Ma. Trias 1988 *opposite* Source: Ajuntament de Barcelona; quod

Taste is therefore linked into the process of identifying a city or region. It communicates its cultural capital. In the Catalan case, this idea was promoted not just in terms of the imposition of modern street furniture or through vigorous regional support of design institutions (Julier 1995) but even when one turned the television on, the equation of Catalan = modern was communicated through visual form. The first official Catalan television channel TV3 brought together a team of young media professionals and graphic designers who shaped its aesthetic. As Catalan design historian Viviana Narotzky has commented:

> With its carefully designed studio sets and animated graphics with minimalist music, its newsreaders' choice of clothes and hairstyles, and its selection of furniture, the visual world it brought into over 50% of Catalan households every day was a designer's world. Using the same didactic insistence with which it was promoting a habit in cultural consumption in Catalan, it normalized a certain type of visual and material environment: 'normal' Catalans spoke Catalan, listened to Philip Glass, dressed smartly and sat in designer chairs. How different were they from other Spaniards! One only needed to switch channels to see the proof.
>
> (Narotzky 1998)

If modern 'cool' was frequently invoked to communicate the European, technocratic style-consciousness of the new Catalonia, then this was frequently balanced by messages of spontaneity and freedom. In many examples of graphic design in the 1980s, painterly gestures in primary colours which echoed the style of Catalan artist Joan Miró were frequently employed. Miró had been associated with anti-Francoist dissent, but the directness of his visual language was now being appropriated to advertise the freedom of the market rather than political emancipation (Satué 1997). This was evident in the 'Barcelona més que mai' (Barcelona more than ever) campaign visualized by Pepino García in 1984, an advertising campaign developed to inculcate civic pride. On a more international scale, Josep Ma. Trias's identity for the Barcelona 1992 Olympic Games released in 1988 similarly expressed local identity. This identity programme was 'explained' through the pages of design magazines (e.g. Trias 1988) and later through the press. Catalans learnt that the logo incorporated 'Mediterraneanism' with its artistic heritage and was

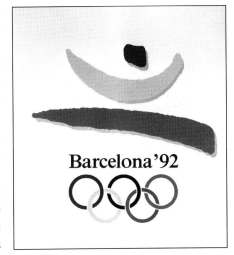

neither an abstract mark nor a figurative representation but both. They were also told that the use of Times Semi-Bold in the typography evoked an antique Roman past. This process of 'telling it like it's meant to be' served not only to repeat certain place-myths as embodied in the graphic work, but also to reinforce the self-consciousness of their use in the public realm.

New design in Barcelona infiltrated all levels of everyday life by the late1980s. The values of modernity, Europeaneity and technology but also locality and creativity were invoked throughout the cityscape. Its significance was underlined by a series of interconnected ideological and cultural features: it contrasted starkly with Spain's immediate past by replacing national isolationism, conservatism and environmental chaos with internationalism, modernity and civic pride; it foregrounded new design as an amenity for a new civil society; it aspired to achieving a confluence between local identity, regional political will and modernity in a transnational context. Design hardware – the city's new bars, public spaces, street graphics – was deployed in an intensely public arena both in itself but also in its constant mediation and reproduction through the media. It served to bolster the emotional software of the city, promoting attitudinal aspirations and unity by linking nationalistic sensibilities, self-identity and place. The consistency of its message in terms of taste and cultural capital gave the appearance of local cohesion.

The Barcelona paradigm must be read not only in terms of the complex network of individuals, agencies and institutions which produced and consumed its new design, but also in the context of global patterns in the redesign and marketing of place. Critical analysis of its developments, and those of many other locations, may be shaped, according to Booth and Boyle (1993: 22–3), by three theoretical approaches. First, a regeneration programme and its attendant cultural policy may be seen as an attempt to cushion the effects of a slippage from an industrial to a postindustrial context. Secondly, it may be a local response to the globalization of capital and the demand to attract international investment. Thirdly, it may be a way of producing an illusion of the cultural capital of urban unity for the benefit and reward of upper- and middle-class commitment to urban living. Let us consider each of these in turn.

cultural economies and regeneration   Between 1977 and 1993, the United States lost about two million of its factory jobs. Britain lost 3.6 million, a decline of 45 per cent over roughly the same period (Ward 1998: 187). Leeds saw a similar manufacturing employment drop from 33 per cent to 17 per cent over this period (LCC 1998). Manufacture as a percentage of gross domestic product dropped in Catalonia from 36.2 per cent to 30.4 per cent between 1986 and 1991 (Martín 1992: 39). In each of these cases, employment structure has come to be dominated by services.

In responding to the shift from an industrial to a postindustrial economy, or more widely, from organized to disorganized capitalism, urban centres engage in the development of cultural policies which are defined in economic terms. It is seen both directly and indirectly as a form of job creation, a way of attracting inward investment and in converting the existing labour force to new modes of employment and bringing in skilled professionals from outside. Culture is bundled up with business services, leisure industries and tourism in an effort to regenerate city-regions and therefore create wealth and employment (Booth and Boyle 1993).

The creation of events, services and attractions in order to regenerate and marketplaces is by now, well documented and discussed (e.g. Bianchini and Parkinson 1993; Kearns and Philo 1993; Ward 1998). These include the establishment of festivals, major sporting and cultural events and the development of museums and other visitor attractions. A commonly reproduced and even caricatured theme, was the development of waterfront or dockland areas. Originating in Boston in the mid-1970s, this approach integrated high-class new housing, visitor attractions such as an arts complex, a major museum or theatre as well as new restaurants and bars.

Boston's regeneration was supported by a high-profile public relations campaign. In a similar vain the 'I ♥ New York' campaign was launched in 1977. In 1983 Glasgow brought out its 'Glasgow's Miles Better' slogan which was followed by a plethora of similar attempts at boosterism by individual cities. Whether it involved substantial building programmes or the consolidation of advertising campaigns, all such manoeuvres are highly design intensive.

In terms of employment, the support of cultural industries in post-industrial cities is not insignificant and was given increasing attention by governmental bodies from the mid-1980s. In the UK, the total number of people directly employed in the cultural sector in 1991 was 650,000, 2.7 per cent of the total workforce. Its gross fiscal value was greater than either the mechanical engineering and the chemical industries (PRI 1996: i). In Leeds, more specifically, the cultural industries were judged to reflect a similar pattern, but were also expected to grow significantly in terms of output and employment (PRI 1996: 12). Individual cities, regions and nations sought strategies to boost this sector.

The cultural industries also came to be appreciated for their symbolic capital in contributing to the self-image of a place and its population as dynamic, creative and entrepreneurial. Zukin (1995: Ch. 4) makes the same argument concerning the high contribution of the cultural sector to the New York economy. Reflecting Bourdieu's notion of 'cultural intermediaries', she observes that they work in a vanguard, trying out and exemplifying new trends both as producers of cultural artefacts and events but also as their consumers. More specifically, she states that:

> We owe the clearest cultural map of structural change not to novelists or literary critics, but to architects and designers. Their products, their social roles as cultural producers, and the organization of consumption in which they intervene create shifting landscapes in the most material sense. As both objects of desire and structural forms, their work . . . directly mediates economic power by both conforming to and structuring norms of market-driven investment, production, and consumption.
>
> (Zukin 1991: 39)

Equally within the Barcelona paradigm during the 1980s, designers were invoked not just as signifiers of modernity, but as energetic exponents of a new enterprise culture. Their internationalism, facility for commercial networking and technological know-how carried a high symbolic value within the city's reassertion on a national and international stage (Julier 1996).

Enterprise culture has to be 'made reasonable' in order to make direct sense to those involved (Keat and Abercrombie 1991: 10). By giving material and visual form to this notion, design and designers, as cultural intermediaries, were appropriated by politicians and journalists in this quest.

The conversion of focused pockets of the cityscape in turn supports this self-image. The new cultural economy of postindustrial cities is invariably located in 'gentrified' zones. Downtown areas which formerly housed warehouses, small-scale workshop units or struggling specialist shops are converted into night-clubs, designer bars and restaurants, private art galleries or craft studios and offices for other participants in the creative industries. Numerous examples exist to illustrate this: The Calls in Leeds; the Born district of Barcelona (catalogued and promoted in Pibernat 1999); Hoxton in London (analysed in Benson 1999 and home to many of the design consultancies discussed in this book!). This concentration services the avant-garde visual and gastronomic tastes of those working in the creative industries. The spaces have a symbolic role too. They reproduce the relatively low capital investment on which creative industries are habitually founded. As befits this sector, they are also liminal: they cross between cultural experience and commercial entrepreneurialism; they extend from the working day into the night economy reinforcing the 24-hour code of 'art is life, life is art'; and as former locations of urban degeneration, their heritage is visually and mythically hard-edged and lowlife yet now harbour the 'higher' ideals of cultural production.

Gastronomic infrastructure for the 'creative quarter' around The Calls. (1) Metze bar/café, (2) The Arts Café and (3) Oporto
Source: Guy Julier

responses to globalization (1): place-making of city-regions through design With de-industrialization, the clear imagery of specific systems of production and particular products which could be associated with locations – Sheffield steel, Staffordshire pottery,

West Midlands light engineering, for example – recedes into memory and museums. This heritage may be retained as a tourist attraction, by way of industrial museums or experience centres, becoming a major industry in its own right (Hewison 1987). However, the link between such initiatives and local history may be more tenuous at times. For example, as part of the regeneration of Leeds, the Leeds Development Authority secured the establishment of the Royal Armouries museum, bringing in investment of £43 million. Aside from being the home of a First World War tank factory, Leeds does not have a history in the manufacture of armaments, unlike, say, Birmingham. Heritage, argues Gregory Ashworth (1990), is a contemporary saleable experience produced by the interpretation of history. It is defined by the consumer not by the raw materials, however; it is, in essence, a function of the market. The presence of the Royal Armouries in Leeds is only legitimated by consumer demand.

Conversely, museum and exhibition designers Event Communications insist that to ensure their success in terms of visitor numbers, it is vital that projects are tied into the local economy and culture (Phelan 1999). In the first instance this reinforces the historical identity of a place and lends greater credence to the attraction itself through that association. When in 1998 they came to design the Dynamic Earth attraction in Edinburgh, these associations had to be quite self-consciously underlined. The experience centre tells the story of evolution which was, needless to say, a global event. However, in its scripting, early connections are made with James Hutton, the eighteenth-century Edinburgh man who conceived the idea of geological time, and Arthur's Seat, the volcanic hill behind the centre. The linkage to Scotland is also forced in a more subliminal way. Scottish actor, John Hannah, is used to narrate film sequences within the exhibition, the scipts of which frequently refer back to Scotland as 'ancient land'. It is hoped, on the part of the designers and clients, Lothian and Edinburgh Enterprise, that by anchoring this sense of place into the experience and continually referring separate elements of it back to its immediate location, visitors will want to go out and discover more about Edinburgh and Scotland. The production process is also important in consolidating the attraction within the local community. A project of this size and complexity generates local interest and involves a large amount of subcontracting to tradespeople (Edwards 1999). It is therefore connected to the locality in very real terms. The development of places of consumption (such as the Dynamic Earth) produces, 'multiple local enthusiasms' (Urry 1995: 2).

However, while the creation of heritage museums and experience centres can have a significant impact in the regeneration and marketing of places, there is clearly a limit to how much heritage many urban centres can take. Other regeneration initiatives are marked by their homogeneity between different cities – the statutory waterfront development, 'continental' café culture, public art schemes, high-profile cultural events – which in turn fosters their sameness.

Meanwhile, the dual shift towards service industries and the globalization of capital means, though, that cities compete evermore vigorously to attract inward investment. In Europe, an estimated 300 smaller cities and regions compete with each other for investment and jobs. Internationally, 40–50 medium-sized cities of populations of more than a million vie with each other; in addition there is the rivalry between London, Frankfurt, New York and Tokyo as world financial centres (Thackara 1997: 129–31).

While improvements in transportation and communication technologies have facilitated the exchange of goods and information across national boundaries, the industrial and commercial agglomeration on cities and their immediate regions (the city-region, in other words) has increased. This is primarily because production and work depend on a dense and complex network of exchanges of information, skills and goods (Scott 1998). It results in focused regions of particular activities such as Silicon Valley in Southern California as a hub of information technology industries or Milan and its hinterland supporting design-intense fashion and furniture development and manufacture.

Separate nodes of activity may be closely interlinked across national boundaries in order to share and exchange their specialisms. The film, animation, advertising and design industries of central London give a very precise example of this effect. Since 1995, they have been served by their own information technology network called Sohonet. It capitalizes on and further facilitates the dense system subcontracting on which the zone thrives. Using fibre-optic cabling, this network allows the rapid movement of video, audio and other data in digital form between interdependent studios. Furthermore, it is linked via transatlantic cabling to the Hollywood film studios. With the time-difference between London and Los Angeles, material such as special effects animation can be worked on in Soho during 'down-time' in California.

Exchange between separate nodes bypasses the parameters of sovereign states. Geographer Allen Scott (1998: Ch. 8) contends that this has important ramifications for the organization of global political power blocs (see Figure 6.1). This emergent political organization emphasizes the strengthening relationship between regions and multination blocs. If design acts at the vanguard of structural change, and indeed produces a 'cultural map' by which these changes can be recognized, then it deserves examination. We have seen how the Landmark Leeds scheme, and parallel developments in the city's cultural economy, aspired beyond the aesthetic borders of

Figure 6.1

Global political

reorganization

Source: after Scott 1998

Level	Example	Commentary
Global	United Nations	Coordinates agreement on global issues of health or environment, but politically weak.
Multi-national blocs	European Union (EU) North American Free Trade Association (NAFTA) Asia-Pacific Economic Cooperation (APEC)	Facilitates intra-bloc exchange. Not politically or economically strong but size allows manageability. Roles as centres of authority and influence will grow.
Sovereign states	Spain United Kingdom	Still has the most potent bases of economic and political power. But regulatory power being passed upwards to supra-national blocs and functions of state passed downwards to regions.
Regions	Catalonia Øresund	Traditionally subordinate to nation-state. But ability to coordinate concentrated social and economic activity means that they will strengthen. Regions have direct, unmediated relationship with multi-national blocs, bypassing sovereign state

the nation-state in order to broadcast itself as a European city. Likewise, Barcelona design short-circuited any notions of 'Spanishness' in order to make the equation of Catalan/modern/European.

Aesthetically speaking, this confirms a notion of what Nederveen Pieterse (1991) termed 'fortress Europe'. Modern European identity has, in his estimation, developed a self-image of itself as 'the cradle of civilization', seat of reason and the inheritor of the Enlightenment. According to Nederveen Pieterse, this ethnocentricism requires a 'barbaric' other, identi-fied in the Islamic world of North Africa and the Middle East that surrounds Europe. Simultaneously if, as Spivak (1988) argues, the developed world – and thus Western Europe – now appropriates postmodernism and pluralism as a core value then the celebration of a supposed culture of diversity also becomes a celebration of the West and the sophistication that this value entails (see also Billig 1995: 155). By contrast, parts of the world outside this set are seen as monocultural, lacking, impoverished and unsophisticated. European modernity, then, incorporates particular sanctioned forms of multiculturalism. It is one that confirms the concept of Europe as a federation of regions, therefore.

responses to globalization (2): the branding of city-regions and nations

More benignly, this reorientation of political and cultural discourse towards regions musters some interesting results. As in the case of Catalonia, European regionalism allows for the retrieval of local identities. But technological and economic change may indeed create new regional identities. Such was the case of Øresund where the building of a bridge linking Copenhagen, Denmark and Malmö, Sweden across the Øresund sound would open up opportunities for the concentration of specific shared or complementary partnerships in a transnational region. The new region brings together Zealand on the Danish side and Scania in Sweden. Steps to their integration originated partly in an historical study of their shared past and cultures (Weibull et al. 1993). Making up a population of 3 million the new region shares expertises in bio-industry, environmental technology, life sciences and food, tourism, trade and distribution as well as information technology, media and communications. The region is therefore constituted less in formal structures of governance – since these reside within their respective nation-states – but in their shared physical environments and human resource bases.

The Øresund Konsortiet, a consortium of organizations involved in the promotion of the region, engaged the London-based design consultancy Wolff Olins to develop a brand identity for it. The ensuing study consolidated an appreciation of the shared features of history, environment and economy. It also identified attitudinal factors to the region's personality – being openness, inclusivity, responsibility and innovation – which flavour the brand. Eventually all these facets are distilled into the Øresund marque. Here two organic shapes and the palette of earth and sky colours represent the coming together of the two areas, but also the shared, 'attitude and visual language of the region' (Øresund Committee 1999) in its natural environment and the human values of its population.

The use of 'attitudinal' factors to identify a city, region or nation is evidence of an emergent tendency by politicians and their design consultants to consider them as brands. Hans Arnold working at Wolff Olins developed a structure for identifying different levels of branding within a region which integrates place factors and human resources. The regional brand was equated with its overall 'attitude'. This is subsequently made up of: 'local brands', which incorporate its various environmental features such as its towns and cities; category brands which describe its competences as evidenced in its economy and educational infrastructure; and, finally, its product or service brands, such as specific leisure attractions which are sold and consumed as part and parcel of the place (Øresund Committee 1999; Vinogradoff 1999). These categories are then distilled into a central idea which provides a short-hand, by way of a slogan or a simple image to communicate its essence.

Co-founder of Wolff Olins, Wally Olins reinforces the notion that governments can control the brand image, and thus the attitudinal markers, of an entire nation. In a report written for a British government think-tank, The Foreign Policy Centre, he stated that,

> Governments can create the mood and lead and co-ordinate the image. . . . All countries communicate all the time. . . . Collectively, all these millions of messages represent an idea of what the nation as a whole is up to, what it feels, what it wants, what it believes in. It should be the task of government – with a very light touch – to set the tone of these messages.
>
> (Olins 1999: 25–6)

Wolff Olins was highly influential in promoting the idea of rebranding places during the late 1990s. In November 1996 it approached BBC2's *Money Programme* with an idea for a programme in which it would develop a brand for Britain. Their research had shown that Britain's image and reputation was damaging the country's ability to compete in world markets. Furthermore, British people had a uniquely poor self-image of their country. They determined 16 key signals and values which, 'encapsulate the essence and personality of a new brand for modern Britain' (Wolff Olins 1999a), these being: Original; Invest in; Made in; Educating; Creative; Leading; Team; Skilled; Discovering; Welcoming; Diverse; Innovative; Strategic; Exporting; Popular; Serving. Their recommendations were that the word 'Great' be taken out of Great Britain, arguing that, 'New Britain will demonstrate greatness without having to say

so'. The visual scheme they proposed to substitute the use of the Union Jack – which had become associated with football hooliganism, imperialism and right-wing politics – would not make particular emphasis on red over blue or vice versa. The brand, they claimed, was 'post-political'.

The resulting television programme, 'Made in UK' was followed by a report produced by the think-tank Demos entitled *Britain^{TM} Renewing our Identity* (1997) and a pamphlet produced by the British Tourist Authority *Branding Britain* (1997). They coincided with the emergence of the 'Cool Britannia' slogan, used liberally by politicians to describe this new Britain. The term 'Cool Britannia' originates in the title of a song by the Bonzo Dog Dooda Band released in 1967, and was re-used both in a headline in *The Sunday Times* and in an ice-cream brand in 1996. In 1997, the British Council commissioned design consultancy Johnson Banks to develop a campaign to promote the 'new Britain' brand abroad. In each of these cases, the drive was to manoeuvre the national image away from historical associations of empire and cultural conservatism towards one of modernity and pluralism.

This 'softening' of national image through brand strategies clearly reflects the shifting status of nations in the new world order. Wolff Olins undertook a similar study to their 'Made in UK' programme for the German television station, ZDF in 1998 in which they developed proposals and sketches for a rebranding of Germany. The recommendations included redesigning the national colours by introducing the European blue in place of black and using a typographic signature of 'DE' to stand for 'Deutschland Europa' (Wolff Olins 1999b). The applications of this in the resultant television programme and an exhibition which opened in Berlin in January 1999 played up such values as tolerance, diversity, non-conformism, creativity and peace, values which are easily generalizable to other European nations. Pluralism, as we have seen, is readily appropriated as a core value in (post)modern fortress Europe.

Images used in the Deutschland Europa exhibition in Berlin as proposals for the rebranding of Germany, designed by Wolff Olins 1999

Source: Wolff Olins

problematizing the branding of place   Unsurprisingly, attempts to create a cohesive brand image for a locality under relatively loose headings such as 'creativity', 'modernity' or 'multiculturalism' are easily problematized. In the first instance, it locates identity less in the unique characteristics of a focused place (if they indeed exist) than in a constellation of transnational shared values. This might immediately result in contestation as to exactly what those shared values might really be. But equally where a localized 'flavour' is placed alongside such brand building, the contradictions between the two are immediately recognizable.

The Barcelona paradigm is powerful not just because of the strength of the sum of individual design interventions deployed in a single context. There was also a tight fit between different components of du Gay et al.'s 'circuit of culture' (1997). Local and global demand was met by design production. Local taste-makers, be they famous architects or TV channels, effectively regulated the nature and scale of design culture. Specific design products satiated notions of self-identity. Looking at the Barcelona paradigm in terms of 'systems of provision', it is clear that the city and its industrial and commercial infrastructure provided a tightly-woven and highly localized channel linking production, distribution and consumption, which was self-supporting, self-legitimating and self-authenticating.

This 'success', however, was not without its critics. Catalan journalist Arcadi Espada noted that the nation-building of the regional autonomous government so effectively reached all areas of everyday life (including its design) that one seemingly could never cease to be a Catalan (1997: 43). He questioned whether the very specific identity of Catalanism was truly inclusive of its population – a sizeable proportion of whom were not of Catalan family background – and whether its claim to inclusivity was met in practice. For Espada, Catalan identity was constantly represented and reproduced through what he called *cultureta* (literally meaning 'small culture'). This placed cultural 'normalization' at the level of the everyday (such as in the design of studio sets on the local TV station) whereby national values and myths of nationhood were more insidiously inculcated.

Espada's argument coincides with what Michael Billig (1995) saw as 'banal nationalism' in action on a wider scale. While in liberal democracies the state could only dictate national values through minimal legislative means, so these were reproduced more effectively at a more domestic level – through language, the attitudes expressed in television soap operas, the commentaries made in sporting events or identities carried by particular food products. Equally, the branding of cities, regions or nations seeks to implement values at a 'banal', nuanced and symbolic level: through the subtle application of a logo to a poster or a product, through the provision of public seating of a particular aesthetic pitch or through inflexions used in copywriting. It seems that attempts to communicate and promote cohesion are brought down to the everyday material and visual features of private and public life. Marxist geographer David Harvey (1989) argues that the kinds of initiatives to define, distinguish and broadcast the cultural capital of cities are merely a gloss. In appealing to bourgeois tastes and aspirations for urban living, it patches over class, racial or ethnic divisions.

This process, within which design culture plays a significant part, may even enhance these fissures. Gentrification may result in traditional communities being displaced – as indeed happened in a limited way around Barcelona's Plaça Real as part of its renovation prior to the 1992 Olympic Games. Sharon Zukin (1991: Ch. 7) presents an equally critical viewpoint. She contends that the new middle classes of global, disorganized capitalism exercise cosmopolitan tastes as a vehicle of their cultural capital. She discusses how this has resulted in a growth of demand for international cuisine since the 1970s. The 'vernacular' of diverse immigrant communities (to New York in her discussion) is thus appropriated and consumed by this class, displacing it from its traditional function in serving its own community. Identities are served up or even themed for this new audience. In doing so, their original vernacular is superseded by a conformity to and coherence with the values of the marketplace.

Coherence, as indeed purveyed by the machinations of design culture in the city, region or nation-state, others argue, can only be momentary, or may only address particular levels of social experience. Global cultural flow of ethnic groups, media, technology, finance and ideologies means that place and identity may be understood in several different dimensions. Their shifting nature and rapid movement continually disrupt the unity of economics, culture and politics. The disjunctures between these five elements are experienced and articulated in different ways, by different people and groupings in different localities (Appadurai 1990).

Movement can also lead to hybridization, as distinct global cultural sections are assembled to present new identities. With the weakening of the nation-state, globalization can result in a growth of various modes of ideological and cultural organization so that groups and individuals may be represented at transnational, international, macro-regional, national, micro-regional, municipal and local levels. This ladder of representation is criss-crossed by functional networks of corporations, international organizations, non-governmental organizations as well as professionals and even, simply, internet users (Nederveen Pieterse 1995).

Cultural coherence may therefore be destabilized by a range of organizations, conflicting flows and activities. And if designers and other cultural producers are mustered to protect that stability, they may as easily attack it.

Commenting on the 'Cool Britannia' phenomenom and its incorporation into the British Tourist Authority marque, cultural critic Robert Hewison wrote that:

> What the Cool Britannia phenomenon does tell us is how symbolic goods – music, movies, food, fashion, art, design, architecture – all of which convey values over and above their value in exchange, have become vital to the moral as well as the material economy. But in the end, symbolic goods have to symbolise something – and that is why the buzzword Britain has become so significant. When our evangelical Prime Minister Tony Blair uses the words Britain or British 53 times in his speech to the Labour Party conference he is not reinforcing our sense of identity, he is betraying a profound anxiety about it . . . it is up to the creators of symbolic goods – the designers, artists and architect readers of *Blueprint* – to scribble all over [the marque], to break in from the margins of an ersatz, marketised identity and reveal just what our collective sense of ourselves could be.
>
> (Hewison 1997: 31)

conclusion   The emergence of disorganized capitalism has effectively denuded many localities of their power to identify themselves through their traditional industrial bases. Instead, cities and regions compete with each other as nodes of information, capital and labour on the basis of the skills and infrastructure they have to offer, but also on their aesthetic profile. The architecture of a location may have a role in this, but is of decreasing significance in relation to the broader evidence of its cultural capital which is to be found in an array of activities drawing on the creative industries. Within this, design therefore provides visual and material cues, but as a practice it also represents a certain 'attitude' pertaining to the human and creative resources of that location. Design and the image that design conveys may at times enmesh itself with other manifestations of the metropolitan *habitus*. This may mean that it is aligned with other qualities of the urban night-time economies of bars, restaurants, clubs or galleries. These are given further resonance by the transformative practice of gentrification, where the traditional and conservative industrial or working-class cityscape is appropriated, moulded and remodelled into the modern and liberal postindustrial or middle-class urbanity. The rhetorics of regeneration are considered to be enough to legitimate these practices. Equally, however, the enthusiasm to arrange all the material, spatial, textual and visual design elements which go together to communicate a brand identity of a location requires such consistency as to make its claim to any unique qualities, by comparison with its competitors, an evermore difficult task. As the message becomes more and more simplified, so it becomes increasingly open to contestation.

branded leisure   [Leisure] spaces appear on first inspection to have escaped the control of the established order, and thus, inasmuch as they are spaces of play, to constitute a vast 'counter space'. This is a complete illusion. The case against leisure is quite simply closed – and the verdict is irreversible: leisure is as alienated and alienating as labour; as much an agent of co-optation as it is itself co-opted; and both an assimilative and an assimilated part of the 'system' (mode of production). Once a conquest of the working class, in the shape of paid days' off, holidays, weekends, and so on, leisure has been transformed into an industry, into a victory of neo-capitalism and an extension of bourgeois hegemony to the whole of space.

(Lefebvre 1994 [1974]: 383)

So wrote the Marxist intellectual activist Henri Lefebvre in his seminal enquiry entitled *The Production of Space*. Originally published in 1974, this text explores the relationship between mental space as conceived and represented, for instance by architects and planners, and the spaces of everyday experience. Thus Lefebvre strove to reconcile the forces that shape the social meanings of places with the human and social activities acted out within them.

Lefebvre raises a number of interesting points in the above extract. First, he suggests that leisure spaces only *appear* to offer opportunities for play, freedom and pleasure as a flip-side to the restraints of ordinary working life. Secondly, they are conceived and shaped to give that appearance whereas in reality they are highly controlled – as controlled as all other spaces. Thirdly, just as work is organized and industrialized, so is leisure. He goes on to list more specific ways by which the control and management of leisure space constrains: it has its own 'rituals and gestures' (such as suntanning); its own 'discursive forms' (what should be said or not); and its own modulations and models (such as chalets and hotels which reproduce family order and private life) (1994: 484). By extension, we might consider the possibility that design conspires to provide and maintain this illusion of emancipatory leisure, and in delivering 'value for money' against time spent, colludes in its commodification.

In the early 1970s, Lefebvre was writing at the tail end of a decade of rampant development of mass tourism, in particular of the cheap package holiday to the Spanish costas. The idea that spaces could be produced specifically for leisure consumption on a vast scale would have been particularly evident in this context. Contemporaneous with *The Production of Space* was *The Golden Hordes* (Turner and Ash 1975), a vitriolic exposé of the environmental and social impact of mass tourism. In Lefebvre's terms, these attractions transform a locality into a space of consumption. But they are also consumed in a variety of ways: they are looked at, and thus consumed visually; they are literally consumed, in that their resources are used up; and they can consume one's identity (Urry 1995: 1–2). The spaces of consumption therefore imply the consumption of space.

Twenty-five years later one can only speculate on what Lefebvre would have made of the range of spaces which have since been designed and produced for leisure. Leisure activities these days are more capital and design intensive than ever. In the UK, annual expenditure on leisure activities rose by 50 per cent between 1992 and 1997. By the end of the 1990s, UK consumers as a whole spent more on leisure and tourism than on food, rent and rates put together (Rees 1998). While the average working week has declined slightly since 1950, leisure sociologist Chris Rojek (1985: 15) argues that the amount of leisure time available has not increased dramatically. In short, many leisure activities entail short bursts of energy, spending and visual consumption. They require fleeting absorption in branded spaces and experiences, as momentary and instantaneous as the flickering images on a television set.

This chapter is devoted to unpicking paradigmatic examples of design for leisure. The fact that it ranges across theme parks, short-break destinations, retail outlets and experience centres demonstrates both their commonalities and differences. Branded leisure demands even greater interdisciplinarity in terms of the various design specializations under discussion. It is necessary to review the leisure centres' software in terms of their promise – mediated through promotion – and the way they interface with other cultural phenomena. Thus, for instance, a promotional video pre-packages the consumption of the 'real' thing in that it provides expectations and narratives to follow when you actually get there. But it also suggests the televisuality of many leisure spaces. With regard to the hardware of the real thing, it is important to consider their layout in terms of planning and landscaping, their architecture and interior design, and their graphics in terms of their signage and identity marques, but also such aesthetic matters as the quality of transactions between employees and consumers. As we shall see, many leisure spaces provide a veritable *gesamtkuntswerke* (total art) of experiences, an entirely baroque splendour of sensations. We must journey through these spaces both open to and aware of their illusory power.

from 'Fordist' to disorganized leisure   Organized mass leisure was instigated by the Industrial Revolution. In the UK the growth of railways provided easy access to tourist destinations of the seaside and spa towns. Subsequently entire industrial towns would close their factories for specific fortnights – known as 'the wakes' – as its workers and their families headed *en masse* for Blackpool, Bridlington or Bognor. The 1844 Railway Act obliged companies to make provision for the 'labouring classes' and within four years over 100,000 people travelled from Manchester to the nearby resort of Blackpool during Whit week. By 1850 this figure had doubled (Urry 1990: 21). Seaside entertainment – music hall, amusement parks, piers – developed to cater for the concentrated demand for pleasure which these visitors brought with them. Just as work was rationalized and regulated by industrialization, so, then, was leisure.

Using their specific attractions, holiday resorts would compete with each other for market share – the length of their piers, the quality of the air – and through 'boosterism'. Advertising campaigns, often carried out by borough councils in conjunction with the rail companies, were mobilized to show off their special qualities. In this way, leisure spaces began to be conceived as brands. Thus, for instance, we find Bridlington marketed as 'Bright, Breezy, Bracing' from the 1910s.

The Butlins holiday camps, established in 1936, were, then, a more tightly orchestrated commercialization under a single brand of what seaside towns had been doing for a century. These provided relatively luxurious facilities with on-site amusements and organized entertainments. They reached their heyday in the 1950s but had gone into sharp decline by the 1980s. Through this period Butlins, and their rivals Pontins, shifted their identities from 'camps' to 'centres', 'villages' or 'holiday worlds'. By the 1980s they moved towards the provision for a more segmented market, offering different specialisms at the various centres. This indicated a move away from the mostly homogeneous, rationalistic holiday locations for an equally homogeneous market towards the creation of more varied and subtly developed leisure brands.

Whereas rationalized leisure inherited from nineteenth-century industrialization took place at specific times of the year and entailed fixed destinations and activities for tourism, the development of the Spanish costas in the 1960s ensured that holidaymaking was a more sporadic affair. By 1980, around 5 million off-the-peg package holidays were sold each year; by 1990 stand out as exceptions to a general conception of leisure involving momentary engagements with cultural goods and environments. Thus the latest film, music recording or sporting fixture is as easily picked up on as relinquished, just as an evening out may take in a range of sites or a night in front of the television may involve continual switching between channels. As such there are no rules which legitimate one form of entertainment over another. A leisure facility might offer a menu of distinctive experiences to choose from, but movement between them is seamless and dedifferentiated.

As locations and the entertainment they offer compete to provide something more distinctive, more semantically loaded, so their originality and 'authenticity' become progressively more packaged. An extreme case of this would be in the production of a 'hyperreality' in which the imitation of an original is so good that it exceeds it to the point that the original no longer matters. This is what the cultural critic Umberto Eco termed 'the absolute fake' (1986: 40) amidst his discussion of Disneyland.

the Disney paradigm   For designers and cultural critics alike, Disneyland represents a paradigmatic extreme of the theming and branding of leisure spaces. As a European visitor to the American Disneyland, Umberto Eco discusses it in terms of its ability to deliver a faked reality which corresponds more lucidly with our daydream demands. Eco focuses mostly on the details of Disneyland: how, for instance, a themed Polynesian restaurant includes a fairly authentic menu and apparently authentic Tahitian waitresses – so convincing that one would expect nothing but Polynesia to be outside it. It isn't that the real equivalent doesn't exist: instead we admire the perfection of the fake. Thus our desire for illusion is stimulated further (1986: 40).

Meanwhile, American sociologist Sharon Zukin takes a broader overview of Disneyland and Disney World. She illustrates how, 'its size and functional interdependence make [it] a viable representation of a real city, built for people from the middle classes that have escaped from cities to the suburbs and exurbs' (1995: 53). It offers a gated, secure environment where the unwanted underclass cannot gain admittance. It is an idealization of urban space: autonomously governed and controlled by corporate management.

The notion of Disney's simulation of an ideal stems from Walt Disney's enthusiasm to materialize his utopian dream for America. Equally, the Project on Disney (1995) skilfully illuminates how its public relations machinery, its layout and detailing and the training of its staff is tightly assembled in order to maintain an unbroken surface so that the visitor may never get behind the scenes, so to speak, and experience anything of it as a producing system. *How* its spectacle is created is a consistently shrouded feature – the magic must not be broken.

Furthermore, Disneyland is packaged for visual consumption. Its early critics argued that it proposed too few rides and too much open space. But this was missing Walt Disney's point. In developing the first Disneyland in Orange County, Southern California, which opened in 1955, Walt Disney rejected the schemes of two architects. Instead, alongside one of his own animators, Herb Ryman, he set about planning it himself (Marling 1997). As a result, Disneyland was more acutely inscribed with the narratives and visuality of Disney of cartoon fame. It promised the security of the idealized vernacular as seen in Snow White or Mickey Mouse. Euro Disney, opened in France in 1992, takes this a step further. Zukin suggests that, 'it was designed as though never seen by the human eye, only by a camera – either a director's movie camera or a tourist's VCR' (1995: 57). It reproduces all those elements of America that European tourists want to see: New York City, the West and even Disneyland itself. In this way, the artifice and object collapse into each other. Disney simulates places and events for the tourist gaze, including itself.

post-tourists   Leisure spaces may be consumed in a variety of ways. Weekend breaks or foreign travel may be undertaken with different expectations of their outcomes for the individual. A distinction may be made, for instance, between the traveller and the tourist (Urry 1990; Rojek 1993). Clearly the Disney paradigm has nothing to do with the traditional identity of the traveller. Travel experience – from backpacking in the Andes to a month's usage of a student rail ticket to criss-cross Europe – involves a measure of self-realization. Hardship may be encountered but the traveller experiences this as a rite of passage, as a maturing process. The journeying involves a series of physical, mental and visual challenges, but the work put into this is rewarded through some form of personal education and growth. By contrast, tourism dispenses with such exertions. The right to leisure has already been gained; pleasure is readily sought. It involves a search for the authentic in unfamiliar territory, either at home or abroad, and the consumption of these sights. This gives rise to the tourist's obsession with photographing things seen in order to capture and authenticate that moment for themselves (Sontag 1978).

Maxine Feifer (1985) suggests, however, that we are now in the age of the 'post-tourist'. Here the quest for 'authenticity' is abandoned. Instead of expecting to see 'real' locals performing folkloric dance as if it were part of their everyday life, the post-tourist knows that such events may be put on precisely for the holiday season. The post-tourist is not disappointed by this:

after all, it is the quality of the show that counts. And if it is a show, it needn't even be seen *in situ*. The post-tourist might enjoy such experiences through other channels: through the television or in a theme park. It is the quality of the experience that counts, not how authentic it might be. The post-tourist is also able to appreciate the irony of this and treat it playfully. If leisure entails divesting oneself of the seriousness and posturing of working life, then the post-tourist is unlikely to make these demands. Furthermore, the post-tourist is accepting of or even delighted by the overlapping of various levels of experience. Souvenir shops, for example, sell kitschy model replicas of an historical site just visited that are appreciated as an integral part of the post-tourist visit as a whole. Various levels of consumption in leisure are therefore dedifferentiated: high and popular culture overlap or even trade places.

If indeed post-tourists are that knowing, if they are prepared to relinquish the pursuit of authenticity in favour of richness of the experience, then this will make them increasingly demanding consumers. In design terms, this pursuit of pleasure has to be catered for in evermore complex and blatant ways. Retail and entertainment design specialist Mark Artus argues that even the Disney paradigm is unable to satisfy this demand. For Artus, Disneyland offers attractions that make reference to something which has already made its mark: a vignette of a movie or the continual loop of a theme tune which may remind the visitor of a favourite film. Visitors, he contends, are looking for a direct sensory experience where they are physically and mentally stimulated and involved in the entertainment brand. Rather optimistically (and revealing the designer's belief that leisure and brand experience can be one and the same thing), he adds that it is, 'at the point of discovery that everything should change for the consumer; the soul and personality of the [leisure] brand should kick in, stroking the senses, encouraging serendipity and promoting anticipation about what might happen, never allowing the narrative to finish but letting it grow through individual interpretation' (Artus 1999).

Designing for post-tourism must therefore involve a strong measure of self-conscious artifice. Situations, events or places may be simulated. At the same time, however, this trickery is deliberately incomplete. There is little point in pretending that the real thing is being delivered. Rather, the designer hopes that the visitor is sufficiently involved in the experience to appreciate its convenience and perfection in its own terms, rather than as the 'absolute fake' as described by Umberto Eco.

Furthermore, the visual and material arrangement of branded leisure spaces need not be as dense or cluttered as suggested within the Disney paradigm. They need not present a postmodernistic arrangement of surfaces for visual consumption in which visitors lose themselves and their own sense of identity. Some leisure spaces are designed with the promise of quite the opposite. They appeal to an appetite for retrieving a sense of personal identity and achieving, albeit momentarily perhaps, self-realization. As such they aim to combine all three notions of travel, tourism and post-tourism. Such is the case of Center Parcs.

naked and nowhere at Center Parcs
Center Parcs is the European market leader in the provision of short break holidays, operating in The Netherlands, Belgium, Britain, France and Germany. It has been in existence for 30 years, its first venture being a small complex of 40 holiday villas and limited sporting facilities in Holland established by sports entrepeneur Piet Derksen in 1968. It is now an international group of 13 Holiday Villages. Their average size is around 100 hectares, the sites being combinations of woodland and water, always located inland. There is an average of 650 villas in each Village; Center Parcs is targeted primarily at the family market and the design and layout of these villas reflect this use. The focus of each Village is a Subtropical Swimming Paradise but they also offer a range of indoor and outdoor sporting and leisure facilities and a selection of themed restauraunts. The Center Parcs concept is commercially very successful: it boasts over 90 per cent occupancy levels throughout the year. In 1997 the company had over three million guests staying in its Villages. As the Center Parcs 1990 Annual Report mission statement put it, simply, the company's mission is, 'the provision of year-round residential leisure'. What kind of leisure experience is constituted within the brand and, subsequently, through design briefs?

The design of Center Parcs forest resorts follows the philosophy of the first development at De Lommerbergen. From this a generic concept and design guidelines have provided an overall model for any Center Parcs development. Factors such as size, density and lay-out relationships are specified. Through this uniformity, principles and standards can be set that allow a consistent basis against which other variables may be measured. Differences in take-up between different Center Parcs resorts may be assessed in terms of regional or national variations in consumer habits, demography, disposable cash and other socio-economic factors. As such, the uniformity of the design helps to provide market feedback.

As Herrmann et al. (2000) argue, the approach taken in the design guidelines for the overall layout of each site is similar in idea to Christopher Alexander's *Pattern Language*, first published in 1977. Alexander developed a design methodology which argued for a correspondence between the patterns of events and the patterns of space. His interest, then, was in the psychological and sensory experience of spaces, and using this as a starting point. Interestingly Alexander's book was published three years after Lefebvre's *The Production of Space* and they reflect common concerns. Alexander opposed a design method based solely on the imposition of geometric criteria and his philosophy provides practical measures for achieving Lefebvre's concern in reconciling mental and physical space. The 253 patterns he proposed range from the towns through to buildings and construction details. These were not to be read as rigid structures for designers to follow but proposed an 'inside out' way of designing whereby the user or consumer experience of space provided the key criterion. Different spaces, and thus different experiences could then be assembled into an orchestrated whole. Individual elements of their design conspire to establish an overall effect. Over twenty years later, this foregrounding of the experience of spaces is highly relevant to the Center Parcs model and indeed relevant to designing for and analysing branded leisure spaces in general.

Two key components emerge in a consideration of the Center Parcs leisure offer and are reflected at all levels of design intervention. The first is that their overall layout and many details create a spatial and temporal dislocation. Visitors thus find themselves 'nowhere' in relation to their everyday conceptions of place and time. They are also nowhere in terms of the idea of being in a Utopia (being the Greek word for nowhere). This links to a second key feature – that of being 'naked' though not in a literal sense. The Center Parcs venues present a highly encultured version of nature which draws on a strong environmentalist theme both in their image and working practices. The woodland resorts are 'naked' in that they are apparently stripped of the normal detritous and complexity of everyday life. Design details continually refer back to this identity. As we saw in the Disney paradigm, theme parks may constantly make references outside themselves. At Center Parcs the thematic clothing of elsewhere is abandoned. Finally, the emphasis on physical activities means that these features become *embodied*. The dislocation from the outside world and the essences of nature – fresh air, greenery, a different pace – are physically consumed.

As part of its marketing, Center Parcs produced a promotional video to accompany its brochures. With the inclusion of a voiceover, background sounds and the camera's ability to rove through the site, this medium is able

Various views of
Center Parcs leisure
centres including
sub-tropical
Swimming Paradise,
villa exterior and
boating lake

Source: Chris Royffe

to take prospective visitors through a 'typical' day there. Thus some of the emotional appeal of the place can be filled in while also setting up a narrative for consumer expectations. The July 1998 version of this video begins with the scene of stressed professional couple in a car, presumably on their way to Center Parcs, mobile phone blaring. Cut to early morning at Center Parcs itself; the couple with young children ride their bicycles gracefully through the woodland. 'It's an island with no sea, a state with no passports, it's Britain, yet it's abroad . . .' the voiceover tells us.

Even if you haven't watched the video before making your booking, the experience of arriving, participating in and departing from Center Parcs ensures one's dislocation from the normal cultural referents of place. Two arrival and departure days ensure that there is regular turnover of temporary communities. Arrival becomes ritualized as clients move through the reception area, redolent of a border crossing with barrier and passport control booth. Vehicles are only brought onto site to unload children and baggage before being left on off-site car parks and without one's car the dislocation begins in earnest. Paths are deliberately laid out to avoid straight lines so that getting from A to B takes much longer than one anticipates. Low-key barriers and the planting of shrubbery dissuade one from taking short cuts. As if to reinforce the messages of being in nature and to therefore slow down, signage implores new arrivals to 'Beware of rabbits crossing the road'.

Vistas are restricted so that one rarely gets glimpses of the outside world. Long views are mostly across water, being either across the main boating lake or small canals and ponds. Over 90 per cent of the villas are placed to overlook water; this enhances the calming effect of the landsape design and establishes a key motif for the Villages. It also adds to the labyrinthine effect on circulation by providing further 'natural' barriers. The villas themselves are arranged in clusters but they do not overlook one another. Rather than effect temporary subcommunities by getting to know their neighbours, then, occupants are encouraged to form a relationship with the Center Parcs Village community as a whole, it seems. The villas them-

Opening sequence
to Center Parcs
promotional video
made by Peter
Hughes Productions,
1998
Source: Center Parcs

selves follow a format designed by Dutch modernist architect Jacob Bakema for the first Village in De Lommerbergen in 1968. They have remained largely unchanged with their vaguely Nordic interiors which so steadfastly resist fashion that they are fashionable in themselves.

Regardless of whether you are in Holland, Belgium, Germany, France or Britain, then, one's visual and material experience of Center Parcs will remain largely the same. As John Urry tells us, localities are constructed for the aesthetic gaze which requires a level of decoding on the visitor's part:

> This . . . strategy requires an ability to locate one's own society and its culture and make aesthetic judgements between different natures, places and societies. Thus it also requires a certain semiotic skill . . . and to know when they are partly ironic.
>
> (1995: 167)

Simultaneously, growing aesthetic cosmopolitanism makes this gaze ever-more demanding. In the Center Parcs case, rather than pump up the sign-value to emphasize a specific cultural location, place is stripped of referents. There is nothing intentionally ironic at Center Parcs, although the artifice of the place or placelessness is clearly visible.

In his intelligent discussion of the use of white space in graphic design, Keith Robertson states that:

> The presence of white space is a symbol of smart, of class, of simplicity, of the essence of refinement. The absence of white space is a symbol of vulgarity, of crassness, of schlock, of bad taste. . . . So the bourgeois aesthetic sought to hide the presentation of wealth behind a diversion of interest into areas supposedly *outside* the economic and necessary . . . [its] expression in material things is one of

Where you take your body...
...to free your mind

disinterest and detachment. Such an aesthetic focuses therefore more on the *form* of doing things rather than the material things themselves.

(1994: 61–2; Robertson's emphasis)

One might easily translate this concept to Center Parcs, except that here we are dealing with green rather than white space. By denuding the visitors of their cars and own homes, by putting them in International Style villas, by making them walk or cycle everywhere and slowly at that, by offering a cultivated patch of nature Center Parcs provide a gated, nowheresvillage as a momentary creation of 'fortress Europe' (Nederveen Pieterse 1991) that only exists within the temporal and spatial boundaries of the weekend and the perimeter fence.

If the environmentalist agenda comes over in the form of Center Parcs, then this is matched in its content. In 1991, Bioscan (UK) Ltd and Landscape Design Associates began a series of rigorous environmental audits for Center Parcs which reviewed village design and layout, including their flora and fauna, waste management and recycling, energy consumption including employment patterns and goods sourcing as well as environmentalism within its corporate planning system. This would consolidate and extend the 'greening' of Center Parcs and its stated benefits would include cost savings, increased profitability, competitive advantage, compliance with environmental legislation particularly in France, Belgium and Germany and in the future in the United States and an enhanced corporate image (Landscape Design Associates/Bioscan 1992). And if the ecological theme is still missed, design consultancy CGI Ingleton Thomas wove it into the design of the corporate identity 'leafbird' logo for Center Parcs in 1996.

These initiatives have subsequently found their way from the brand identity of Center Parcs in the 1990s to their design and management. In the UK just 5 per cent of existing trees are removed to allow for the construction of the villas and main buildings. The landscaping places the emphasis on screening of buildings so that they appear to be *in* nature. The restriction of changeover days to Mondays and Fridays restricts the impact of traffic movements on the locality. In 1994 the Longleat Forest Center Parcs Village was opened in Wiltshire developed in Aucombe Wood, a site designated as an 'Area of Outstanding Natural Beauty' which but for its by now well-publicized environmental strategies would otherwise have been banned.

The low consumption level of the Villages in general is a notion which is also transferred to its temporary residents. The Village centre does include a sports shop (the continentally named 'Sportique'), a gift and toys shop and a confectionery outlet. But the general emphasis is away from Bacchanalian orgies of shopping, and excessive drinking is dissuaded in the guest rule book. Indeed the redesign of the shops, by entertainment and retail design specialists Fitch in the late 1990s, reinforces the Center Parcs brand message rather than refers them to the outside world of shopping malls (Wren 1999). Of the three existing stores at Center Parcs, Fitch created new names for two of them: 'Natural Elements' and 'The Tree House'. Both of these in name and in their interior design elements return the theme to the overall Center Parcs concept of woodland holidays. Within 'Natural Elements' three categories were created, 'Family time', 'My time' and 'Memories', which pick up on subthemes of the Center Parcs 'mood'.

Interior of Center Parcs shops at Eveden, 'Natural Elements' and 'The Tree House', designed by Fitch, 1998

Source: Fitch

While stress is laid on sporting and leisure activities at Center Parcs, the need to exceed personal targets or to compete is played down: the promotional video includes missed archery shots and sailing boats running out of wind. By stripping away the mass cultural detritus of everyday life and eschewing an environment for competition, leisure is returned to the body. Michel Foucault (1977) has provided an extended and reasoned discussion of the relationship of the body to power. To briefly summarize one of his key arguments, Foucault discussed the way that social and economic relations were *embodied*. He contended that a corollary to industrialization was that the body was subservient to it: it was machine-like, routinized and disciplined through the repetition of physical tasks. The working body is made subject to labour. It might therefore follow in leisure that it is shown to be active and liberated. Rojek argues that in leisure it does not necessarily follow that the reverse is true, however. Instead, leisure relations are also those of, 'discipline, training, coding, and control' (Rojek 1985: 156). After all, as we saw with the quotation from Lefebvre at the beginning of this chapter, leisure is as regulating as work. Leisure is pacified as is work.

Conversely, one might approach the body as an instrument of consumption. Generally speaking, in Victorian times the sea was regarded to produce health and sexual attractiveness, hence, the verve for bathing. Progressively through the twentieth century, however, the sun has usurped the sea on this issue. For many white Western Europeans, a tanned body symbolizes health and the economic power to spend time under the sun. This attitude has been extended into a verve for fitness. The period 1992–7 saw a growth of expenditure on health and fitness clubs in the UK by some 60 per cent (Nutley 1998). Whether suntanned, muscular or both, this represents a significant aestheticization of the body. The body is shaped as an object for viewing.

So where does the Center Parcs offer fit into this? One of the Center Parcs slogans is, 'Where you take your body to free your mind'. The corporeal restitution promised by its environment and activities may work to retrieve the individual's and familial values as much as repair mind and body for more labour. Center Parcs provides a refuelling stop for, in Foucault's terms, the placid body. But with its fitness rooms, sunbeds and sportswear store, it also conspires with the consumeristic notion of the 'body beautiful'.

The combination of a utopian creation and environmentalism as a backdrop for the aestheticized body has a twentieth-century historical pedigree. The idea of 'going into the woods' as weekend leisure is historically well established in Northern and Central Europe. More specifically, links have been made between both left- and right-wing political movements, personal purity, nature and, indeed, naturism in the 1920s and early 1930s (van der Will 1990). While one is encouraged, mostly, to keep one's clothes on at Center Parcs, the emphasis on sporting leisure, bodily reconstitution and nature has evolved from this general tradition of weekend nature. The important distinction, however, is that although their forerunners may have gone to commune in the wilderness, visitors to Center Parcs join an ecology which is part given, part created and maintained. Woodland space is inhabited, but it is also carefully planned and managed. As such, it becomes cultivated by technology. And while the Disney strategy conspired to cover up any productive system in its illusion creating, Center Parcs makes frequent reference to itself as both a site of production and consumption. Its promotional video includes several views and scripted moments of employees at work ('for your benefit'). Visitor handbooks include copious information relating to the maintenance of its forestry and animal life.

This strategy creates an interesting link between the notions of 'traveller' and 'post-tourist'. While Center Parcs only very lightly incurs hardship and discomfort in forcing one to leave one's car behind, nevertheless the travel themes of self-realization and personal growth through the experience appear. At the level of the post-tourist and given the enormous commercial success of Center Parcs, its consumers accept that a certain level of artifice is at play and they are willing to go along with it.

As Marshall Berman put it, 'to be modern is to find ourselves in an environment that promises adventure, power, joy, growth, tranformation, disintegration and renewal' (1983: 15), words which could easily come from a Center Parcs brochure. Perhaps Center Parcs isn't the kind of modernity Berman was thinking of, but its techno-ecology suggests that modernity, these days, is in fact about going, albeit very slowly, naked and nowhere.

televisuality and designing leisure experiences

If Disneyland and Center Parcs have one prominent feature in common, then it is that their public must leave their cars behind before making their visit. In his discussion of Disneyland, Umberto Eco remarks that by doing this, visitors give up their ultimate symbol of their individual identity. They therefore give themselves over to the power of the leisure space they enter. Following on from this, he points out how, 'its visitors must behave like its robots. Access to each attraction is regulated by a maze of metal railings which discourages any individual initiative' (1986: 48). The speed of consumption at Disneyland is regulated. Once the visitor has paid that waiting price they then go into an attraction which compresses a series of temporal or spatial phenomena together: the entire history of the US presidents in 15 minutes, a dizzying roller-coaster ride through 'Frontierland'. Alternatively, Center Parcs stretches, rather than compresses, time and space by its twisting paths and frequent water features.

This time and space compression or stretching has resonances in television and cinema (see Harvey 1989: Part III). These media use powerful ways to escape chronology. Through the techniques of slow motion, freeze frames, fast forwarding and rewinding, the passage of time can be compressed, expanded, reversed or frozen. They can also put us, the viewers, in several points in space at the same time by quick cutting or screen dividing. Television sports reporting can put us in several points in the stadium at the same time giving us several viewing-points. It can also give us a range of narrative structures to follow – we follow the game, an individual player or the spectators, but also the commentators' interactions with the match and each other. We also get flashbacks to pre-game interviews or review highlights afterwards. We are watching a narration of both the factual and fictional components of the event. There is the time of the thing told and the time of the thing telling (Metz 1974).

Developments in exhibition and museum design from the mid-1980s have shown a stridently televisual approach to the arrangement of interior spaces. During the 1990s, the number and scale of these attractions rose dramatically as lottery funding was allocated to the creation of new centres or the further development of existing facilities. Millennium Commission projects stepped up this pace further. Notably many of its key figures have come from a background in television production. John Sunderland, chief designer of the Jorvik Viking Centre, the White Cliffs Experience and the Oxford Story previously worked in television as did Cel Phelan, founder of Event Communications, a multidisciplinary consultancy devoted exclusively to museum, exhibition and experience centres. As such they emphasize the need to script the experience of such attractions. One key difference from television scripting is that broadcast requires a linear narration of events (though as we have seen, not necessarily chronological); scripting a museum, exhibition or experience centre is multi-vocal (Janson-Smith 1999). Visitors are of different age groups and engage with the exhibit at a range of levels and so the storytelling of these spaces must work on several different levels at the same time. In this context, it is often necessary that the interior is visually dense, multi-layered and sign-heavy, providing visitors with a choice of routes through which to pick their way. As we will see in the context of many examples of interactive media design in Chapter 8, exhibition design provides both immersion and detachment. On the one hand, visitors are engaged at an immediate level in the sensory experience of the presentation (the time of the thing told) but are also involved in following the narration of the experience (the time of the thing telling).

Designers of some retail and entertainment spaces therefore take on a televisually informed approach to their planning. During the 1980s architect Nigel Coates pioneered this attitude in his design work for the interior spaces of bars and shops. Coates recognized that the function of a building had less to do with its architectonic structure and was more dependent on virtually invisible elements such as electrical cabling and radio waves. By extension, the hardware of a building merely functions as a framework for exchanges of energy and information. His primary interest, then, was in the software of architecture – how it invokes experiences and provides narratives (hence his group was called NATO, meaning Narrative Architecture Today). Part of Coates's philosophy is extended from a notion that television and other mass media events have changed the way we live for good. Citing the influence of Jean Baudrillard, he contends that:

> Instead of progress, we tend to heroicize what is normally hidden, to play up the differences, to encourage a society in a simultaneously primitive and advanced state of flux, in which adopted narratives and roles are able to reactivate the otherwise empty social stage, which television as a phenomenon (but not as a language) appeared to have forced us to abandon.
>
> (Coates 1988: 98)

Architecture, he continues, must face up to and confront this change. His own interior design work went on to incorporate rich textures of images and objects. He claims that, in developing a project, 'drawing has to contain a filmic hypothesis . . . [to identify] . . . key pictures of the action even bigger than the building' (1988: 100).

dedifferentiation/distinction   If the visual and temporal language of television provide structures and forms for the design of some leisure spaces then these centres may become dislocated. In the same way that the images and sounds on a TV screen may come from any global location and be viewed almost anywhere, so experience centres or shopping malls can provide environments which are hermetically sealed away from their immediate locality. A sense of place is replaced by a simulation of elsewhere.

This is acutely noticeable in themed restaurants and shopping malls. In America the theming of such spaces has reached intensive levels and is well discussed (see, for instance, Hess 1993; Gottdiener 1997; Betsky 1999; 2000). These were pioneered by John Jerde at San Diego Horton Plaza and then the Rouse Corporation at Faneuil Hall, Baltimore at Harborplace and New York at South Street Seaport (Betsky 2000). Jerde's Horton Plaza drew from the architectural forms of the Italian Renaissance in order to invent a sense of history and permanence for it while the plan emphasized meandering lines to stimulate a sense of 'wandering through' rather than hieararchy and order. Amidst the cacophony of shops, food courts and cinemas, plazas and cul-de-sacs were incorporated to provide points of social gathering and repose.

As such, shopping is repackaged as a 'retail experience'. Browsing in shopping centres is invariably associated with Charles Baudelaire's *flâneur*. His late-nineteenth-century dandy gravitated to the sidewalk cafés of Paris to consume the visual spectacle of the city. Baudelaire was writing at the time of the growth of department stores which offered not just a range of goods under one roof, but opportunities to meet socially and be entertained by the spectacle of the site. A crucial difference, however, is that Baudelaire's *flâneur* rarely bought anything. Instead, in the late twentieth century retailers hope that perusal will eventually end in a purchase. Thus the 'retail experience' is designed to provide a stimulation to acquire by linking to other mediative forms of the brand value. The patina of the goods, the adverts and the shop interiors all tie together to produce 'similar coded lifestyle values' (Ellwood 1998). The leisure of 'just looking' in the themed shopping mall, of being 'elsewhere', and of then identifying with particular lifestyle forms as mediated within the individual retail units is consummated in the purchase of goods.

The distinction between leisure and retail has become blurred in many cases. Some retail developments have moved towards the provision of leisure activities – so-called 'retail-tainment' – in order to spread their brand offer. The supermarket Tesco Extra at Pitsea in Essex offers a fast-food and take-away area, mooing imitation cows and roller-skating customer services assistants (Rees 1998). Specific brands have also extended into the leisure sphere: the Volkswagen Autostadt in Wolfsberg, Leggoland in Windsor or Cadbury World in Bournville, NikeTown in New York and London all provide visitor attractions which subsequently reinforce product identities. Significantly, investment for the Nike 'brandlands' comes from global advertising budgets rather than capital-revenue. NikeTown interweaves a sportswear store with a museum telling the story of Nike products with visual and architectonic recreations of the Nike brand experience. The last of these is made by reference to the core themes of its marketing strategy. This sportswear company had made a concerted effort to equate their Air trainers with 'rags-to-riches' stories of members of American street youth cultures making it to sporting stardom (Flusty 1997). This narrative is subsequently laced into the design of the brandland through a cacophony of projected images, taped sounds, video walls and stage-set architecture to produce an ersatz and generalized simulation of Bronx streetlife, or its many other global equivalents. Thus advertising, company museum and department store merge into each other. The chief designer of Nike's in-house team who developed the NikeTowns has said that he wants, 'the experience of the shopper from the moment they see the Nike commercial on TV to the point where they are wearing the shoes when they come out of the store to be completely seamless' (Henry Beer quoted in Betsky 2000).

NikeTown in
London, opened
1999, designed by
Building Design
Partnership
Source: David Balfour

Dynamic Earth
experience centre,
Edinburgh, opened
1999.
Architecture by
Michael Hopkins,
exhibition design
and development
by Event
Communications
Source: Event
Communications

This strategy of dedifferentiation between retail and leisure conspires also to blur distinctions between the public and the private. Shopping malls themselves are, of course, both public *and* private spaces. Operated by private companies they employ security guards to exclude unwanted elements – vagrants, buskers, street-hawkers and so on. They are invariably locked up at night. Equally, as museums since the 1980s have received progressively less state financial support, they have become increasingly dependent on sponsorship funding from private corporations.

This presents designers with a difficult challenge as a large part of their job is to *differentiate* the object – to make it distinctive or even unique. There is a limit to the amount of gimmickry which can be mustered to achieve this, however. Designers of more traditional leisure spaces such as parks and museums therefore have to separate themselves out from this highly branded and thematized ambience. At Trentham Gardens near Stoke-on-Trent, Fitch sought to strip away any hint of theming, playing up the historical and environmental qualities of its brand image. As if to emphasize this 'innovation', they trademarked their approach to this project as 'anti-theming™' (Fitch 1999).

At the Dynamic Earth attraction in Edinburgh (introduced in Chapter 6), Event Communications played up its educational content by linking into the national educational curriculum. With architect Michael Hopkins, its value as a public space and resource was also emphasized by opening up its vestibule and surrounding area to general public access. In this way its designers strove to distinguish the attraction from highly branded leisure centres where space is more rigorously privatized and the content is often more tightly tied in to corporate or brand promotion (Phelan 1999). By re-appropriating a notion of public-ness into the project, it seems that the quest to differentiate through design pushes the nature and practice of leisure into newer and perhaps unexpected territory.

conclusion   The development of branded leisure spaces requires painstaking coherence of all design features. This ensures the seamless progression between the brand image as purveyed through marketing strategies through to the actual consumption of their products and services. As such they are tightly scripted as a flow of experiences. This owes something to a televisual approach in their conception, but they also provide multi-linear routes through them. They conspire to compress or expand the cognition of temporal and spatial dimensions within themselves. That said, the consumption of branded leisure spaces does not necessarily entail total immersion in them. Visitors may read them on a variety of levels: they may be highly engaged in the artifice of the occasion to the point of suspending disbelief, but equally they may knowingly 'play along', either critically or uncritically, with the illusion. Many of the themes of branded leisure emerge in the context of digital interactive media, considered in the next chapter.

on-screen interactivity   I'm flying through the solar system and
deciding which planet I want to have a closer look at. No, wait a minute, I'm re-mixing
Peter Gabriel's lates opus on a weeny four channel desk and, hey, it's sounding better
already. No, I'm swooping out of the stratosphere to look at the oil fields set alight by
the Iraqi army as they retreated from the Gulf War back in 1991. Then I'm having a gun-
battle with a would be assassin inside a film I'm trying to watch. And I'm doing it through
a television screen. Welcome to the world of interactive multimedia.

                                                                    (Horsham 1994: 25)

A flat, glowing screen and a disk spinning in the CD drive. And I'm waiting for a picture
to download while I 'stand' in the virtual basement of a virtual dinosaur museum. It looks
like how I remember natural science museums from my childhood: mysterious, echoey
hallways, rough edges and didactic exhibit captions. The difference is that these
dinosaurs are not silent, stuffed full-size reproductions, but animated, roaring beasts.
Meanwhile, I have a map to find my way through the maze of exhibition rooms, but I'm
not sure if I'd just prefer to get lost.

In the first of the above extracts, Michael Horsham reflects all the optimism and enthusiasm for immersive digital environments of the early 1990s.
They promised role-play and movement between distinctive, futuristic
scenographies, but also the interruption of the traditionally one-sided flow
of cultural production. The second is drawn from notes I wrote during an
encounter with the Dorling Kindersley *Dinosaur Hunter* CD-ROM at my
local library. Here the restrictions of screen and software and the possibility
that the experience is never fully immersive are acknowledged. Navigational
aids are necessary. In addition, the design language employed may seem at
odds with the medium – it exploits new technology to provide the virtual
environment, but it is an environment more redolent of a nineteenth-century
museum than a new interactive experience centre.

Views of Dinosaur
Hunter interactive
CD-ROM, designed
by Dorling
Kindersley in-house
team, launched
1996

Source: Guy Julier

167

This chapter deals with tensions between expectations of design for digital media and its realities. It focuses on the minutiae of navigating interactive software – clicking on hyperlinks, moving through virtual spaces, waiting for downloads – in order to address the limitations and challenges that both its designers and consumers face. The rapidity with which the various platforms for on-screen design have developed has left designers struggling to ascertain a critical discourse and language for it while at the same time their job has been to act as its technological and cultural intermediaries. This state of affairs is echoed in wider discussions where a libertarian enthusiasm for everything on screen is countered by those who strive to place its cultural and social import back in the real world.

By 'on-screen' I refer to the smaller rectangle of the video display unit (VDU) as opposed to the larger cinema screen and am concerned with the interactive applications on screen such as hypertext, CD-ROM, internet and convergent media. It is often difficult to separate out these different platforms, however, as technological and commercial development conspires to fuse more often than distinguish them. Two examples bear this out. In October 1999, Sega released its much anticipated Dreamcast, a computer game console – usually supported by ordinary televisions – that plugs into a telephone line and allows users to challenge other players worldwide via the internet. This was closely followed by Open, a new service offered by Sky, the satellite broadcasting company, that allows digital television viewers armed with their TV remote control to shop or check their bank accounts from home and send e-mails. These innovations anticipated fully-convergent media where the boundaries between areas of digital cultural production disappear. Likewise and relatedly, commercial developments tend towards their integration rather than compartmentalization. January 2000 saw the merger of AOL (America On Line), the internet service provider, and Time Warner, the entertainments conglomerate. Again, this points towards the continued integration of broadcast media and interactive systems.

From the early development of human computer interfaces for personal computers to the most recent trends in convergent media, designers have played a crucial role in shaping their content. The demands of the medium have provoked, to some degree, a reconfiguration of their role, requiring them to work in collaborative networks with a wide range of professionals and to regard the relationship with their end-user differently.

computers and graphic design   Within graphic design, the growth of desktop publishing since the mid-1980s has facilitated a reconfiguration of the relationship between designer and client. Prior to the advent of the Apple Macintosh, artwork and copy for a piece of design for print would be specified and marked up by a graphic designer, and then the typesetter, either by using metal type or photosetting, would prepare the finished graphic work for printing. However, the launch of the Macintosh personal computer in 1984 made a desktop computer accessible to many designers. Its key feature was its PostScript page layout system, developed by Adobe, which, unlike IBM compatible software, faithfully showed what was to be finally printed (such as the shape of distinct fonts) on the screen. By allowing the designer to input copy and arrange it on screen the need for specialist typesetters was dispensed with. In taking out a layer of production, designers and clients were one step closer to the finished article within the design process itself.

The growth of computer technology as a design tool provoked a flurry of debate among its commentators and educationalists which continued through the late 1980s and well into the 1990s (see, for example, Kinross 1997). Some of graphic design's traditions were directly translated from their metal-based origins into the digital format as Apple and its followers adopted much of the traditional terminology inherited from typography. For example, we still use the term 'leading' to describe how tightly or loosely individual characters of a word may be set together, a term inherited from typesetting wherein lead spacers would be introduced to separate characters. On the other hand, the new production system was much faster, implying that it might become a less contemplative act than hitherto. More shocking to traditionalists was the fact that the software came with a repertoire of basic shapes, layouts and fonts to choose from. The designer could therefore assemble elements on-screen according to pre-ordained patterns. It was feared that those traditional 'hand and eye' skills, such as drawing, which were thought to be the bedrock of design and thus invention, would be overrun by 'quick-fix' graphics which was tied by the parameters of the software available rather than the imagination and creativity of the designer. This alarm was further compounded by the fact that desktop publishing allowed non-professionals access to design tools. The graphic design profession was no longer protected by its own technology.

This debate was partially superseded by the fact that in addition to being a design tool, computers became a design medium. This was precipitated by the introduction of hypertext, via Apple's release of the HyperCard system in 1987, which allowed designers to write multimedia programs. Rather than functioning as a conduit towards print graphics, the computer screen itself became an immediate context for viewing by the end-user. Hypertext refers to software capabilities which allow readers supposedly non-linear forms of access to information via personal computers and terminals. It contains authored links which the user may follow and that create associations between different instances and forms of text. The term 'hypermedia' is conventionally used to describe hypertexts which incorporate other media, such as video, photographic images, sound, graphics, and so on. Crucially, then, it is computer-mediated and thus remains in an electronic format.

The arrival of hypertext instigated a more profound set of changes for the graphic designer. On the one hand it offered the restricted format of the video display screen itself, usually not much bigger than 28 cm × 21 cm. On the other, the designer now had to consider the structure and organization of elements to make up a document and the way the user would navigate through these. Obviously these are questions which also confront print graphics. By the arrangement of graphic elements on a page – the relationship of type to images, the emphasis given to different parts of the copy, and so on – the designer is structuring the reader's experience of it. There is a time element involved in moving from page to page or scanning a layout. But while a book or magazine normally involved a progressive linear narrative for the reader to follow, a hypermedia document provides a multi-linear format where the user may move through a variety of pathways. The physical make-up of print media gives the reader an idea of the position of an individual part of it in relation to the whole. As separate 'pages' of a hypermedia document appear on screen then previous pages are often obscured. In addition, by combining a range of media into the document – text, graphics, moving images, music, voiceover and so on – the designer has to consider their relationship to each other and how the narrative unfolds. In other words, the designer takes on a larger and more challenging role in the editorial arrangement of content. Production and distribution costs may be dramatically cut in digital media, but with the integration of moving image, music, narration and other forms, there is often more intense investment in the origination and editing of content. Finally, the designer's relationship to the client changes. Often the designer may only be providing an overall structure for the client to then fill in or update the detail. Ultimately, though, what either the designer creates on screen or what the client fills in is what the end-user gets. Production and distribution processes do not intervene to modify the look of the article. This has led some commentators (e.g. Myerson 1997) to equate computer interface and software design with craft. The digitized commodity may be serially reproduced, unlike in craft making, but the designer has the same direct relationship with the end-result as, say, potters have with their wares.

technological development and consumer growth   Opportunities for developing, distributing and accessing hypertext products of increasing sophistication subsequently facilitated an enormous growth in this sector of the design industry. The introduction of the CD-ROM provided a format on which a much greater volume of interactive material could be stored and accessed than could by storage on floppy or hard-disk drives. For ordinary home consumers, the CD-ROM delivered the most powerful format for integrating different media into the interactive experience through the 1990s. It was none the less limited. A CD-ROM disk can only store less than an hour of compressed video; as a result they use a lot of text, stills, and some sound, but only short, and often low resolution video-clips (Holtzman 1997: 161). By 1995 it was widely accepted that standalone CD-ROMS would largely be unprofitable (Herz 1998). The range and depth of skills required in their development mitigated against their widespread commercial exploitation. By contrast less elaborate interactive entertainment could as easily be put on the internet. Notably, then, it continued to be used only in specific markets. In the music industry promotional video and sound could be repackaged into a visual/audio format of CD-ROM. It also favoured large-scale documents such as encyclopaedias which involve multi-linear navigation. It was used for promotional means to be given away, where the data already existed – thus designers use it to show-off the outer limits of their work. Finally, it maintained its market among children's multimedia: its contained nature, as opposed to the open network of the internet, meant that parents would be reassured that their offspring did not stray onto 'unsuitable' material and that specific material deemed suitable by parents could be chosen. In practically all cases, children's CD-ROM titles were linked to other merchandise within its brand.

As internet technology developed, so it began to supersede or, at least, stand alongside the CD-ROM. In the later 1990s, the 'hybrid' CD-ROM emerged which combined its strength with the internet network. This meant that users could interact with other people or information online in combination with the offline format of the CD-ROM.

The establishment of the World Wide Web (WWW) in 1991 provided the first global hypertext environment. The internet was the result of a steady development dating back to the 1940s which is well documented (e.g. Kitchin 1998: Ch. 2) and was largely exploited for military and academic purposes. With the possibility of two-way communication across a network, it should be likened more to the telephone than the radio or television. The WWW allowed for the transmission of text, images and sound across its network. It also supported hypertext documents so that users had a direct link to other relevant sites. In the same year Gopher, a system for searching and retrieving information was circulated. This was soon followed by Mosaic, an internet interface which by 1993 became the standard on-screen format for the WWW. Netscape Navigator, which was to dominate web-browsing software, was released in 1995.

Internet use during the 1990s grew at a staggering rate. In 1981 there were just 213 hosts globally (hosts are computers that offer some sort of service to networked users). By 1994 there were 3,864,000; by 1997 there were 19,540,000 (http://nic.merit.edu/nsfnet/statistics/history.host: 1997). A commonly used method of estimating the total number of internet users is to multiply the number of host computers by ten. Internet pages themselves have to perform varied functions. They are used for publishing (such as online journals or product information sites), interaction (for instance Multiple User Domains such as online social groups), commerce (primarily mail order) and databases (often for sharing detailed specialist information across a wide network of organizations) (Lycett 1999).

Internet authoring software such as Dreamweaver allows ordinary PC owners to design their own web pages within a dictated format. More importantly for professional designers, internet growth has been fuelled by business use. Throughout the 1990s the number of business personal computers in Europe with internet access outstripped home PCs (Thackara 1997: 388).

professional practices   With the growing complexity and size of corporate and institutional websites and the increased consumer use of the internet, a digital media design industry had emerged by the late 1990s. In 1998 a reported 24 per cent of British design consultancies offered 'multimedia' design among their services (CITF 1998). In the majority of cases this was an add-on feature to the multidisciplinary offer of a consultancy, often in response to client demand. A typical scenario would be that a client would ask for a website or a multimedia station to be designed as an extension to a material-based project though often there wasn't a deep rationale for this except the feeling that they ought to have one. Theoretically speaking, the design consultancy could subsequently apply their understanding of the client's brand values to the patina of a website, thus extending them further into another domain. A more advanced instance would be where, say, a website or an intranet system would be integral to the strategic development of the client's internal communications being undertaken by the design consultancy.

While the majority of design consultancies may include individuals drawn from a range of design disciplines, the digital media teams are invariably more open in their constitution, sometimes incorporating software programmers, musicians, artists, video-makers, writers, architects, psychologists and traditional designers. The range of skills which are drawn from in this area means that it is more common for individuals to work in flexible networks according to the demand of particular projects. This typifies the post-Fordist system of design practice which emerged after the early 1990s recession. It also reflects the need to constantly reconfigure working practices in the face of voracious technological development of the medium and the attendant changes in demands made by clients. Even Britain's largest and best-known digital studio, Deepend, with 120 employees was organized into flexible and continuously changing subgroups according to both the particular medium – be it, say, website or convergent media – and/or the demands of specific projects (Waterfall 2000).

An understanding of the client's brand is important to the design process but few designers within digital media undertook systematic brand development – this was more frequently left to brand strategists. While on-screen design for a known brand certainly will no doubt modify its image, generally speaking designers in this domain provided a mixture of technological know-how and narrative creativity (good storytelling, in other words) rather than a more holistic market research and product management strategy.

Thus, to extend from Bourdieu's proposition, designers become both cultural and *technological* intermediaries. They serve to broker new developments in electronic media and indeed its own development requires them to be constantly at its cutting edge – or at least just behind it – as access grows. As Steve Grand, British designer of the Creatures program, which generates virtual pets which are maintained online, stated, 'I'm rushing to capitalise on [the innovation] . . . before increases in computer power make the problem so easy everyone will be doing it!' (Grand quoted in Schofield 2000).

critical reflection   It may hardly be surprising that given the rapidity of change in the technological platforms of design for digital media, it is marked by constant articulation and self-analysis by its practitioners although like their practice this was largely restricted to the discussion of what was happening on screen rather than the wider commercial or ideological ramifications of cyberculture. Many of its figurehead designers and consultancies regularly publish essays or journals – almost entirely on the internet – which explore their medium. This would include Andy Cameron, founder of the London-based collective Anti-Rom (see http://www.hrc.wmin.ac.uk/), the Amsterdam consultancy Mediamatics (see http://www.mediamatic.nl/magazine), or the American consultant Jakob Nielsen (see http://www.useit.com/alertbox).

This enthusiasm for critical reflection on practice can be read in several ways. First, it may merely be a reflection of the access that these specialists have to digital publishing which may at times be less subject to editorial controls of traditional print media. Secondly, it might be seen as a self-legitimating approach in a nascent profession whose participants are anxious to promote itself and its intellectual capital. Thirdly, and more benignly, it is born of a consciousness that normative discourses are still being established (Dew 1999). In the words of digital-media communictions consultant Kevin Lycett, 'We are producing this stuff, but we are also constantly thinking about what it is. It is an alien thing we are designing on and for, and so we need to get to grips with it, in our working practices, our technological know-how, but also in how we conceptualize it' (Lycett 1999). Or as interactive media designer, Nico Macdonald wrote, 'Developing a language to criticize and understand design in this media is the basis for moving it forward' (Macdonald 1997: 6). Similarly, Andy Cameron, of Anti-Rom, explained that, 'We have found that designing for a medium so new that it has not yet evolved into a cultural form, or a language of its own, is almost impossible' (Cameron 1998a: 7).

Overarching positions on digital media within the design profession, such as they are, range from the optimistic, if not utopian, through the pragmatists to the hopelessly pessimistic. Parallel positions may be found in a wider discussion of the social and cultural impact of information technology systems and are discussed towards the end of this chapter.

The optimists regard digital-media as a liberating format where technology can be exploited to limitless effects. For some, such as designer David Collier, this optimism underlines its potential both as a communicative and interactive tool, to the extent that it literally becomes embodied. He explains, 'Interactivity is the sixth sense that we're now developing and beginning to explore and use. We've had sound and vision and all those tactile things; interactivity is actually the first sense that really engages your mind' (Collier 1993). For others, the possibilities of this technology seem to be constantly just around the corner. In his book *Digital Mosaics: The Aesthetics of Cyberspace* (1997), Californian digital-media designer and writer Steven Holtzman also claims that new forms of cognition will arise with this technology. He looks to a future where he imagines himself to be, 'curled up in bed with laser images projected on my retinas, allowing me to view and travel through an imaginary three-dimensional virtual world' (1997: 186). As if the technology, however, is somehow separate from ideological or social influences, he demands that the reader, 'Keep in mind, these digital worlds are not bound by the laws of the real world. All bets are off. Anything can happen' (1997: 101). Thus utopianism, futurism and technological determinism are melded into a single, seemingly science-fiction driven belief system which is expressed in a semi-mystical way.

For many rank-and-file designers for the small screen, there is a clear realization that the day-to-day realities of developing interactive digital media do not offer such scope. Designers may have access to sophisticated authoring software but they know that their end-users will generally make different demands. In terms of websites, it is claimed that average users will spend less than one second on a homepage and will be reluctant to pursue the information they seek if it is more than four links away (Lycett 1999). Logging on to the internet is a private act, not requiring the niceties of ordinary social interaction; it is a brutal relationship. In this sense, the consumer is sovereign.

Moreover, ordinary home computer users rarely possess the software for rapid and trouble-free viewing of sophisticated graphics. For example, the dominant Web browsing system, Netscape, was released in successive upgrade versions in the late 1990s. But as the total number of internet users grows it is assumed that an increasing majority are in fact less likely to upgrade to versions which can handle sophisticated online data. Early internet users were more technologically sophisticated and demanding; later arrivals were, however, less concerned with and less interested in upgrades. According to web design consultant Jakob Nielsen (1999), Netscape 5, launched at the beginning of 1999, would never get more users than the Netscape 4 which pre-dates it by more than two years. In turn he advises that advances in Web design can only be incremental. Formal developments such as greater use of moving image and interactive sound have to be put on hold. Free downloadable software such as Flash or Shockwave which supports moving image is readily accessible, but is none the less slow and cumbersome for many domestic users who own low specification computers. In the meantime improvements in content, such as better writing, can increase a site's usability (Nielsen 1998).

For Nielsen the call to minimalism in website design is based on the pragmatism that 'the user is always right'. For others, such as New York-based digital-media designer Jessica Helfand, it may contain an implicitly Modernist stance which eschews ill-conceived decorative effects and promotes a more rationalistic, geometric approach. Indeed, she cites the Dutch interwar movement De Stijl as inspiration in the way they deal with, 'the relationships between structural form and transient content, between cyclical time and infinite space' (Helfand 1997: 9).

In whichever case, this tempered approach to on-screen design is not only at odds with the more aesthetic ambitions of some designers, but may also conflict with the corporate client's desire to weave something of the 'brand experience' into a website. While moving image clips and sound may provide a scene-setting mood for a site, this may in fact detract from the motivation of visitors who merely want to get at basic information or make purchases. Nielsen criticizes the American bookseller Barnes and Noble as a company making this marketing mistake on its website. He has suggested that:

> They weren't focusing on how to buy a book, they were focusing on building their brand, which is so arrogant. They were saying: 'Because we are a famous bookstore, you should buy from us and not [Amazon].' Everybody who tried the two sites decided it was enormously easier to buy the book from Amazon, so that's what they did.
>
> (Nielsen quoted in Schofield 1999)

Finally, the pessimists do not eschew digital-media. Rather these designers envisage a highly limited role for themselves in this medium. This was starkly apparent in the declarations and activities of the groups of well-known designers involved in the Fuse project as discussed in Chapter 4. It was driven by a philosophical position – influenced not least by Jean Baudrillard and Paul Virilio – which identified digital technology in its militaristic roots and claimed its impoverishment of everyday life as an instrument of surveillance, commercialization and banality (King 1995). (Virilio (1997) in particular presents a bleak picture of social destruction brought by the loss of geographical spaces, distance and intimacy as the result of information technology.) But the Fuse position was perhaps also driven by a realization that the days of the celebrity graphic designer were limited in the face of the widening of access to their tools, the growing consumer sovereignty over the design process and the range of specialisms required to deliver substantive digital-media design products.

authorship   The crisis expressed by the Fuse members was symptomatic of a wider problem facing typographic designers. Before digitization, typefaces had been held in material form, for instance, as metal type in its traditional format or from the 1970s in Letraset. This allowed typefoundries – the companies that manufactured and distributed these – to control their circulation. In turn, typeface designers could benefit from the return of royalty payments on sales from these foundries. However, with digitization a number of its characteristics confound copyright laws. These include: the falling cost of reproduction and increasing speed by which 'perfect' copies can be made; the interconnectedness of machines which means that works can be transferred with impunity and without the knowledge of their creators; the ability of computer software to mask original authorship. To put it otherwise, fonts can freely be downloaded from the internet or copied from CD-ROMs.

By focusing on the designer's role as an originator of typefaces or other primary forms the Fuse team seemed to be missing the point as to their potential role in a digitized age. Since these were instantly accessible on the computer desktop, the designer would now be more involved in the *selection* rather than the *creation* of forms (Manovich 1997: 293). An extreme example of this is in a website which consists entirely of links to other sites. The designer arranges an environment within and through which the user navigates. Authorship resides less in the object but rather in the presentation of a situation, in the provision of structures, sets of relationships and possibilities of narratives and flow which are experienced through them.

Design process expert Tom Mitchell (1988) locates historical precedents to this attitude in the composer John Cage and painter Robert Rauschenberg. Cage's composition *4'33"* involves four minutes and thirty-three seconds of silence while Rauschenberg's *White Paintings* consist of seven canvases each of which is uniformly covered with white house-paint. In each case the audience is left to experience the silence or space left in their own way. The musician or artist gives up their traditional role as the provider of the prime object of contemplation. Having set the situation up, they hand over the management of the aesthetic experience entirely to their viewers or listeners. In a similar spirit, from 1995 on artist/musician Brian Eno developed software with Tim Cole which produced ever-changing interactive music. This is part of a long interest in a systems approach to composition. He had written in the sleeve notes to his album *Discreet Music* in 1975, 'I have always preferred making plans to executing them. I have gravitated towards situations and systems that, once set into operation, could create music with little or no intervention on my part. This is to say I tend toward the role of planner and programmer, and then become an audience to the results' (Eno quoted in Mitchell 1988: 213). More specifically in relation to visual interactive media, Andy Cameron suggests that design work should be considered more in terms of a model than a proposition. In his estimation, the designer's voice is displaced (1998a: 7). Thus the designer may provide the language and its syntax, but users find their own voice within these frameworks.

readership   By providing a model for the user to navigate through and interact with, rather than a sequential narrative, the author/reader relationship is modified. Some commentators (e.g. Poster 1990; Landow 1992; Lanham 1993) explore the possibility that this indeed frees users to determine meaning to the extent, in some cases, that they actually become authors themselves. Among these, Landow is particularly vigorous in arguing this case. In the first instance, he aligns the emergence of hypertext and its implications with elements of poststructuralist theory. He notes how Jean Baudrillard, Jacques Derrida, Jean-François Lyotard and Marshall McLuhan all argue against the future importance of print-based information techno-logy. For Landow, Derrida (1976 [1967]) in particular points to how, 'new practical methods of information retrieval extends the possibilities of the "message" vastly' (Derrida quoted in Landow 1992: 29). This process con-tributes to the 'decentring' of the message so that not just one, but several messages may be configured by the reader. He also draws attention to Roland Barthes's notion of 'writerly' and 'readerly' texts, first articulated in *S/Z* (1975 [1970]). Barthes suggests that readers react to written texts by, in a sense, producing their own text through reading, deriving a multitude of readings from it – polysemy in other words.

For Landow, hypertext is an, 'embarrassingly literal embodiment' of Derrida's and Barthes's theories (1992: 34). From this position he pursues a vision of hypertext as a liberational medium by arguing that the various on-screen blocks of texts – or 'lexias' as he terms them – and the links between them allow for a radical repositioning of the reader's status. Lexias disperse and atomize any possible sequentialism so that users are free to assemble their own meanings. Hierarchy in terms of what are the important points of a document and what takes precedence is destroyed thereby making hyper-text a democratized medium.

Such optimistic and ambitious claims, however, are problematic. McHoul and Roe (1996) in particular take issue with Landow. They point out that in the first place, the parallels he draws between hypertext and post-structuralist theorists are premised on a misrepresentation of their argu-ment. Roland Barthes, in McHoul's and Roe's estimation, was concerned with exposing the fact that readers are slaves to a tyrannical text. Any amount of reading does not allow access to writing *per se*. In this vein they go on to note that hypertext authoring programs such as Authorware Professional, Macromedia Director and Toolbook do not come cheaply. Likewise, Derrida was discussing the general pre-conditions of writing rather than outlining a manifesto for reader's liberation. Finally, they point out that reading may be undertaken in several ways. They cite Wittengenstein (1968) in arguing that reading, even of the most uniformly arranged printed page is not a singular process with a particular 'essence' to it. Instead, reading may be performed in a variety of ways – from word-for-word to scanning – and may be experienced in different ways regardless of the medium which is read.

In the light of these objections to a 'libertarian' view of hypertext one might be guarded in claiming any particular qualities for interactive digital media. None the less, some tentative suggestions may be made which point to a middle-ground between either the author's or the reader's sovereignty.

consuming interactivity   A non-interactive form of cultural production usually only allows space for interpretation and reaction on the part of its audience. Interactivity, however, involves a dialogue of control and feedback between a user and a program. It means that the user is able to intervene in the representation itself. Thus in a mature form, 'interactivity allows narrative situations to be described *in potentia* and then set into motion – a process whereby model building supersedes storytelling, and the what-if engine replaces narrative sequence' (Cameron 1998b). Importantly the user is not presented with an entirely non-linear situation. The linearity of traditional storytelling is substituted by a multi-linear network through which the audience navigates.

A hypertext document presents a variety of pathways through it. One chooses the route at specific junctions within it by clicking on links. Rather than a strictly textual presentation, a spatio-temporal representation may be offered – often described as 'Virtual Reality' – in which the user moves through a series of virtual spaces. In this instance, a 'real-time' simulation of moving through them is provided: doors open, brickwork and floor-tiling trail past, sound grows on approach and recedes on departure. The user has, albeit momentarily, something of the sensation of actually being in this virtual space. This is what is commonly described as the immersive experience.

Clearly the user's relationship to the interface changes in the immersive situation. In the traditional narrative of cinema or theatre the user is outside the time of the narration, unable to control the speed of its flow or its direction. In the interactive environment, the user is inside the time of the events being described, able to dictate their movement through it by pausing to take decisions, moving backwards, sideways, diagonally as well as forwards. Indeed, while in modern literature, theatre and cinema the audience watches the plot being built around the interaction and tension between characters, in the immersive environment, the narrative is driven by the spatial movement of the user (Manovich 1997: 290–1).

This is particularly noticeable in computer games where often the player is encouraged to role-play into the hero or heroine's viewpoint. Their progress is measured in terms of their movement through different levels, each featuring tasks to perform in order to move on. In discussing video games Fleming argues that objective, environmental detail is invariably stripped back so that there is just enough to suggest movement through it (such as exploring caverns or leaping over crevasses) understandable (1996: 191). It is a cartoonesque world with the outlines and geometry of objects given, but little of their texture or hues. The player thus does not focus on the detail of this virtual world, rather he or she appreciates its geometry. It is a framework for movement. This environment of immersion is not unmediated, though. Rather simulation is encoded, planned and structured by its designer.

In these gameworlds, one's success depends on a degree of mastery over its geometry at two levels. Intensive and frequent engagement with its systems, rules and structure builds a set of intuitive responses (Weinbren 1995). If repeated without progression, it becomes either addictive or uninteresting. But often the player's interest is maintained by the unexpected appearing (Fleming 1996: 188). Working up an overall sense of how both the obvious features and the unexpected elements function is part of the game's challenge. It is perceived both from within, as the player discovers more about it through playing it, and outside it in the way the player conceptulizes its overall configurations. Computer games designer J.C. Herz describes this process in terms of 'hacking' the game:

> And what you're doing, what I'm doing, what a lot of kids are doing, when they play video games is there's a certain amount of model making that goes on. What you have in a video game is a system, it's a model of some reality, someone's reality. And what you have as a player, is a model that you're making in your head about how the game works. And when the model in your head matches the model in the computer, then you figured out the rules of the game, you figured out the system. And a lot of people actually don't finish playing computer games because to a large extent, the process of figuring out how it works, is the game . . . you've cracked it, once you've hacked it.
>
> (1998).

In a simpler way, a hypertext document encourages a similar approach. Skilled copywriters approach the hypertext medium with this in mind. Copy is shorter as there is less space to get the reader's attention. As copywriter Carol King states, 'what is written may only be a path to getting the reader to go somewhere else' (King quoted in Jones 1999: 30). By contrast, traditional narratives employ techniques to associate concepts together through, for instance, contrasting sections ('however'), consolidating ideas ('for example') or extending arguments ('moreover'). Hypertext links are rarely so explicit about their function. If overused they can merely assemble interconnected text-fragments in a meaningless trail of 'ands' (Mason and Dicks 1999). They carry meanings for example by the very act of associating one page with another. But the emphasis in building narrative is passed to the reader. First, readers find their way through and 'master' the data given. Secondly, they structure their own mental map of the various pages given and routes between them.

Manovich (1997: 297) observes that when web-surfing, a typical user may be reading a page while waiting for another to download. The user keeps checking the progress of this communication by looking at the toolbar which gives the percentage of download achieved. This act of communication – sending and reading the information which tells us about bytes being transmitted down wires – in turn becomes the message to supersede the web-page information. Likewise, Virtual Reality simulations constantly remind the user of the system in use. These three-dimensional environments are often designed so that the faster one moves through them, the less visual detail of objects is given. QuickTime VR, which by morphing a set of images of a space together allows one to navigate around a panoramic view, similarly, 'deconstructs its own illusion' (Manovich 1997: 298). The more one zooms in to view objects, the more one is left with oversized pixels. This reveals the artifice of constructing on-screen images. Rather than give over more quidity to the viewer, instead we are confronted with apparently abstract shapes which we know are assembled to represent reality. Overall, then, the illusion of another free space on the computer interface is constantly jammed by menus, icons, texts, pixels – information telling us about what is happening in terms of the program and which returns us from the three-dimensional virtual world to the flat, glowing screen. Human computer interfaces can never be totally immersive. Instead, cognition lies on two levels, between concentration and detachment, between the status of user and viewer.

cybernetic loss   In moving from the real to the virtual world, losses have to be acknowledged and compensations devised. Since the launch of the Apple Macintosh computer in 1984 and the Microsoft Windows operating system for IBM computers and their clones in 1985, these systems and their descendants have provided the user with an array of visual devices for navigating and reading the computer interface. On the Mac, for instance, we have a trash can icon which tells us where and how to throw away files; in Windows 97, more bizarrely, we have a 'recycle bin'. Buttons appear to be raised in relief, notepads have their spiral binding, communication is represented by a quaint old-fashioned telephone. This interface encourages the user to find their way round it by trying things out, clicking on what seems to be the appropriate icon and working through menus. Navigation, using a mouse, is essentially a two-dimensional act as one moves between applications. As Turkle observes, 'The user was presented with a scintillating surface on which to float, skim, and play. There was nowhere visible to dive. Yet strictly speaking, a Macintosh, like all computers, remained a collection of on/off switches, of bits and bytes, of traveling electrons . . .' (1997: 34).

By contrast, previous operating systems, such as CP/M and MS-DOS, required the user to type in instructions to the computer in order to access and open files or modify data. The experience was decidely un-visual and yet by being forced to learn and speak a specific computer language, the user was drawn into the idea that they were actually interacting with and commanding the software system. Turkle (1997: 36–47) likens this practice to a modernist conception of computer interfaces wherein the user has access to and a measure of the aesthetic/intellectual experience of the machine's functional workings. It was something that the user could control and modify. It follows, in her estimation, that the Macintosh interface is postmodern in that all the user gets is surface and simulation to be enjoyed. By extension, she compares the 'modernist' IBM corporation, whose personal computers ran on MS-DOS systems (and indeed, whose corporate identity was developed by arch-modernist Paul Rand) and the 'postmodernist' Apple corporation in the same way. Ultimately, the Macintosh model of the computer interface has prevailed. From 1995 the Windows interface provided the same basic features as the Macintosh, but was an overlay onto the MS-DOS system. This allowed the best of both worlds in giving access to the operating system, while those who sought greater ease of use, could remain on the surface.

In either the Macintosh or the Windows interfaces, the metaphors of trash can, file, briefcase and so on serve to fill in for what has been lost in a process of dematerialization. Tasks which had previously been undertaken in a more material form – such as writing a book, involving the textures of paper and ink, the scratch of pens or the clatter of typewriters – are transferred into a digital format. In essence this information consists of a binary code of noughts and ones, of the tiny electrical impulses of microchip technology. In shifting away from the material world of weight, texture, smell or incidental sound, much is lost. On screen this 'cybernetic loss' (Thackara 1988) is compensated for by giving a heightened allusion to materiality. This may be in the icons to be seen (as in the trash can), but also in the array of clunks, thuds and whirrs that the desktop sound system delivers. Make a mistake on a Macintosh and you get the sound of bedsprings or a toy trumpet; pull down on a menu in Windows and the dull thud of a chord played on a marimba accompanies you. We saw in Chapter 5 how the widespread use of plastics in product design meant that much of the communicative function of objects was thrown onto their surfaces and how in turn this gave way to an increasing sophistication in the use of semantic encoding. Associative imagery is likewise heavily inscribed into the computer interface as a way of explaining and enabling some experiential cognition of what cannot be seen, or at least, what has been lost in the transfer to digitally-based representation.

Similarly, the worlds inhabited by the heroes and heroines of most video games are densely material and textural. Sonic the Hedgehog in the Sega series, or SuperMario of the Nintendo games both work through a world redolent of H.G. Wells or Jules Verne, where the ordinary mechanical laws of leverage and elasticity, weight and gravity, momentum and force are still present. They inhabit a two-dimensional environment filled with springs, ratchets and pulleys that speaks in exaggerated tones of the industrial material culture of the near-past rather than William Gibson's science fictional cyberspace of lightness (Weinbren 1995: 403).

Screengrabs from

Dinosaur Hunter

Source: Guy Julier

The representation of material reality connects the interface to the more known world of everyday life. It takes a language which is already understood and then sets it up on screen. But it is also exaggerated, made hyperreal. Often this is not so much in the forms presented – we have already established that the digital domain will strip textures and detail down to leave one with geometry – but in their content. The Mac interface presents us with a trash can drawn in outline form with little textural detail, but it alludes to a heavy old-fashioned one, rather than a plastic wheely-bin.

The designers of the Dorling Kindersley *Dinosaur Hunter* CD-ROM went to extraordinary lengths in order to make the virtual museum environment believable. In particular, the detail of the spaces is pre-rendered as opposed to live-rendered (Harris 1999). Pre-rendered is when a detailed computer model is rendered at high quality a frame at a time and is stored as a series of picture files or a quicktime movie. Each frame takes many minutes or hours to render, allowing greater detail, but the finished rendered pictures can be called back quickly in succession to give the impression of a walkround, for example. Live rendering uses a more basic, less detailed, but 'on-the-fly' approach to render a computer model from any angle the user chooses. It allows for more interaction with an object, as opposed to pre-rendering, which has a fixed number of views to choose from. TV graphics, such as flying logos and title sequences, use pre-rendering. VRML (Virtual Reality Modelling Language, a system which allows users to navigate virtual spaces on the internet, conceived in spring 1994) and CD-ROM based-games like Quake and Tomb Raider use live-rendering. The *Dinosaur Hunter* CD-ROM is therefore sold partly on its technological capital. Its packaging boasts, '30 interative 3D consoles . . . 15 video segments, 340 fully rendered views, 650 screens and pop-ups' and appreciating the extent of its high-technology crafting is integral to the consumer experience.

The product has interesting coincidences with the visual hardware and thematic software of the international expositions stretching from the Crystal Palace Great Exhibition of 1851 to the New York World's Fair of 1939. Their common attributes included the fetishization of their own technology, their mixture of education and entertainment and their encyclopaedic content and format, providing scenarios where all knowledge is knowable and measurable (Greenhalgh 1988). Both the CD-ROM product and its historical forerunner of the international exposition indulge in presentation of Umberto Eco's notion of the hyperreal (Eco 1986). Exhibits in both contexts were/are presented to be more visceral, authentic and compliant to the viewers' expectations than their original (in the case of the dinosaur, this is perhaps inevitable, given its extinction). What is lost in moving from nature to its representation is compensated for by upping the aesthetic pleasure of looking. Pre-rendering the virtual environment helps this effect along.

A rendered look would have allowed the user greater freedom of movement through, and indeed scope to get lost in, the museum. Instead then, the user may be immersed in distinct environments – once they've downloaded – but also maintain their own mental map of its cybernetic architecture, backed up by on-screen navigational aids such as a museum plan. Likewise, expositions involved guidebooks, route-planning and signposting through a set of discreet situations.

Digital interactive environments frequently oscillate between delivering an immersive fantasy or imagined world, but also alluding to the raw qualities of the real world. A prime internet-based example of this is AlphaWorld which first appeared in 1995 (formerly at http://www.worlds.net/alphaworld, subsequently at http://www.activeworlds.com). This was a Multiple User Domain (MUD) where visitors could 'chat' with each other. It was configured in a Virtual Reality format so that participants could choose an avatar to represent themselves; they could then claim their own plot of land within a virtual neighbourhood and construct a homestead for themselves. In the process, they could get to know their neighbours and interact with them. The scenario was clearly similar to that of a frontiersland of the American Wild West made up of an unplanned space measuring 655 square kilometres – more or less, significantly, the same size as California. It was progressively colonized by people, their homesteads, ranging from ranch style tract homes to impenetrable stone fortresses to underground caverns and services such as bars. Users could create their virtual structures using objects from a library of more than 3,000 objects and textures. As of 30 June 1999, users had placed more than 30 million building blocks on AlphaWorld. The open space scenario contrasts with the fact that users actually construct their fantasy environment through the sweat of their brow and the click of the mouse.

liberation and regulation: the bigger picture   In its early days, AlphaWorld, could be read as a metaphor for the pioneering of cyberspace in general on the World Wide Web (Huxor 1995). There were the same myths of unregulated space into which individuals could stake their claim and the same infinite possibility of constructing a world afresh. Just as the user was free to navigate through AlphaWorld, talk to whoever they wish, build whatever they fancied, untrammelled by planning consent or aesthetic norms, so in some quarters, the internet and other hypermedia forms are seen to provide some form of liberation.

Such claims resonate with a wider ideological position which views electronic information technology as decentralized and open. This attitude was particularly prevalent during the early years of the internet (Sassen 1999). It was promoted by the California-based *Wired*, a magazine which glorifies the latest technological breakthroughs, the corporate spirit of leading-edge Information Technology industries and the hero worship of (nearly always male) software developers and business whizz-kids. Furthermore, much of its editorial content ascribes the technology and its content with a certain sense of autonomy. Its position is epitomized in the words of one of its columnists John Perry Barlow, who claimed that, 'Information is a life form . . . information wants to be free' (Barlow 1994: 89). Drawing from Richard Dawkins's notion of 'memes', he argues that information is self-reproducing and adaptable to the environments it inhabits. This implies that it can escape the normal structures of power and inequality and that, more ordinarily, technological platforms (such as the agility of web-browsers) or consumers' motivation (or lack of it) does not actually constrain its circulation. Such politically utopian views are matched by economic aspirations, held particularly strongly in the USA, that offer the prospect of the Web providing the basis for a new, democratic free market. Indeed, one time Vice-

Structures built by the 'inhabitants' of AlphaWorld

Source:http://www.jaring. nmhu.edu/future/pages/ alpha.htm

President of the USA, Al Gore famously declared at a world congress on information technology in 1994 that, 'families and friends will transcend the barriers of time and distance', and that also, 'it will make possible a global marketplace' (Gore quoted in Schiller 1995: 17–18).

The disembodying of information in the context of digital media and its treatment as apparently independent of any productive system smack precisely of Marx's notion of 'commodity fetishism'. Here we might call it 'info fetishism' (Henwood 1995). The difference, then, is that while in the first volume of *Capital* Marx wrote about how the relationship between commodities in the market appears to stand in for social relations, in the digital context, the information fetish appears as a relationship between bytes. Needless to say, the hypertext system on the internet, of endless links between pieces of information and whose relationship appears to be unstructured and unregulated, may well encourage such a conception. Any productive activity seems to reside in the consumer's domain: surfing between sites becomes the labour, waiting for downloads is time spent. The real producing agents who design and upload the website or even those who lay the fibre-optic cables to convey the information are strangely invisible.

In parallel with the view of information technology facilitating economic freedom is one which regards it as a space for personal liberation. In cyberspace, some claim (e.g. Plant 1993; Turkle 1997) individuals can experiment with identities, posting messages, joining chat groups, colonizing virtual worlds anonymously or under guises. It can also allow, as others argue (e.g. Rheingold 1994), for the creation of new networks of groups and individuals, through, for instance, the foundation of internet discussion groups.

Access to digital media is still governed by traditional spatial and social divisions. In the first instance, before any digital software can be viewed and interacted with, the user requires the hardware to run it on. While a market for second-hand low specification computer gear may put it within the financial reach of many people in the developed world, Kitchin reports that, even in the USA 50 per cent of all internet hosts are located in just five states (1998: 111). Even by the late 1990s, computer usage was dominated by white, middle-class males from Western nations who spoke English (see http://www.gvu.gatech.edu/user_surveys/). Thus cyberspace is, in fact, concentrated along geographical, demographic, gender, class and cultural lines.

It is not just access to computer hardware or the cultural biases of its software that exclude users. It is also dependent on the hardware of cabling to deliver significant bandwidth. Particular geographical nodes, such as major cities of New York or London are relatively well-served in this respect. Consequently, the nodes which are well connected become information rich. Meanwhile, locations that lie outside these nodes and the lines between them are left as information poor (Graham and Marvin 1996: 189–206). It seems, then, that just as life 'on screen' is in fact restricted by the available formats and technologies, so it is also constrained and regulated by a range of issues outside the box.

bytes and brands In reality, the topography of electronic space, 'weaves in and out of non-electronic space' (Sassen 1999: 62). This is the case as much for the social divisions relating to information technology as for the pragmatic organization of managing branded digital spaces. For example, from 1995 companies began using the Web for communicating with customers, partners and investors leading to the enormous growth of electronic commerce in 1999. In some cases, strings of information may be channelled through corporate alliances which connect up advertisers, products and media. Helen Nixon (1998) discusses how in 1996 Australian snack-food brand Twisties was promoted in conjunction with a 'Cyberheads surf the Net for free' ad campaign. Associative links were made through packaging and advertisements between 'Net surfing' and surfing and skateboarding, both of which are central themes of Australian youth culture. The campaign was run by Smith's Snackfood company in partnership with Compaq, the world's number one PC-systems retailer whose end-aim was the promotion of the Compaq Presario, a personal multimedia computer aimed at the home market. By tying the use of information technology up with a practice of everyday life, in this case the consumption of snack-food, then it is instituted into the cultural norms of youth. Rather than being free-flowing, information is directed along specific routes between corporations and niche markets.

In the case of the Dorling Kindersley *Dinosaur Hunter*, the product constantly reconfirms the generic brand identity of its publishers. It refers 'back' to other products, being sold with a 3D press-out stegosaurus skeleton and a free copy of the DK Pockets series *Dinosaurs* book. It extends outwards in that the disk is a hybrid CD-ROM, meaning that it can link to an online website which gives access to further dinosaur information and activities. Visually, the product coincides with the DK design ethic, using the same typography, palette and high production values as all its publications. The virtual museum is structured in the shape of the Eyewitness 'EYE' logo created for Dorling Kindersley interactive packages.

For its proponents, electronic commerce was expected to fulfil a strong role in bridging producers and consumers, and thus develop brand awareness. In the same way that we have seen how on-screen design facilitated a more immediate relationship between designer, client and end-user in the design process, so e-commerce effectively took out layers of mediation between the marketer and the customer. Rather than the traditional channels of distribution, media and sales forces, the marketer–customer gap could be replaced by an electronic 'market space', according to Nicholas Rudd, of marketing communications consultancy Wunderman Cato Johnson (Rudd 1999). This facilitates a more direct relationship so that consumers may have a more direct relationship with the brand and can, indeed, personalize their relationship with it. For example, in 1997, global management consultants Ernst and Young launched a service which gave unlimited consultancy advice online to small businesses for an annual fee of just $6,000. It used an internet system which was configured to route questions to specific, appropriate experts within the organization (Morris 1997: 28–9). This leads some commentators to place great emphasis on the design of interfaces as they are perceived to be the only point where the product, customer relationship and brand personality are defined (Hanna 1997: 35).

Other specialists in the design and marketing of internet products and services foresaw the medium as an effective tool for consolidating brand experience. Michael Moon, President of GISTICS Incorporated, a high-technology market research company based in California, argues that while traditional media such as television, direct mail and print can be used to create brand awareness, websites can create one-to-one relationships with customers (and indeed collect market information on them) (Moon 1999: 63). Websites can become what he calls, 'deep gravity wells', which offer, 'bright compelling cyberspace destinations around which stakeholders can take orbit' (1999: 61). He goes on to suggest that websites can also act as, 'theater', functioning as a stage and offering performances that keep audiences coming back. Other media, such as mailshots or e-mails containing hyperlinks can be used to, 'drive people into the deep gravity well' (1999: 64). The language Moon uses is revealing in the way it refers to customers or visitors as 'stakeholders', implying their greater participation in and, perhaps, ownership of the brand. The notion that these 'destinations' are 'compelling' implies that engagement is immersive and inevitable while at the same time, subtle strategies have to be adopted in order to induce consumers into visiting and revisiting branded websites.

conclusion   It appears, then, that specialists in the design of commercial websites demand that they be both informational and inspirational. On the one hand they exist as points for the interchange of data between corporations and their public. On the other, they must convey the emotional appeal of the brand. This double-edged exigency runs throughout interactive digital media. Like the exposition and guidebook, they promise both immersion and detachment, random sensual chaos and structured mediation and regulation.

The immediacy of the medium forces designers to adopt the role of the user – what they see on screen the user gets, and vice versa. This has the potential for reconfiguring the performer/audience divide. Users can partake in the forging of personal aesthetic pleasure and identity. Or they can access corporate information and entertainment relating to their favourite brand articulated in a highly visual format. And yet it also remains a flat, glowing, sensorially enervated image on a small screen. The loss of artefactual information – smell, tactility, presence – can only be made up for by a dense packing of artifice.

communications and management

It's a party. And yet the guests are in their office gear: suits, skirts, ties, shirts, lapel-badges. In other words, then, it is a corporate bash. This is no ordinary occasion, however: each event may combine such features as artists' installations, illusions, interactive technology pieces, psychologists, light and laser sculptures, reflexology practitioners and a stylish array of cocktails and canapés to produce a multi-layered creation. Guests wander through a series of spaces, each one rich with extraordinary displays and surprising encounters. Even the bartenders and cooks wear specially designed outfits and turn the serving of food and drinks into a performance in itself: a virtual waiter wall where individual canapés are dispensed from perspex windows; an eat me wall where boxed puddings are plucked from a velcro surface. It's almost as if a 1960s alternative *happening* has gatecrashed a corporate board meeting.

These are not gratuitous entertainments, however. Each party is orchestrated around corporate messages such as 'virtuality', 'liquidity', 'borderlessness' or 'transparency' which are then threaded through the scenography and performance of the event. To underline the more serious aims of the party and reinforce product by-lines, an introductory speech is made before the event gets underway. 'Enjoy yourselves and Xpand your Horizons', announces the host. He is Dr Francioni of Deutsche Börse Group, Europe's leading facilitator of equity capital.

From 1996, when the Deutsche Börse Group established an office in London, these events have been organized by Vamp, a consultancy specializing in the design and implementation of one-off productions. Vamp seeks out empty warehouses or office blocks – neutral spaces – turning them into multimedia environments that, 'embody the corporate culture' of the client (van den Munckhof and Dare 2000). In the case of the Deutsche Börse Group, Vamp deals with a multinational organization comprising three divisions. Collectively, these provide an information technology-based cash and derivatives market trading system and a range of information products and consultancy to players in financial markets. Its core business is therefore entirely built around online services and products which, by their very

Views of parties for Deutsche Börse Group organized in London by Vamp from 1996.

Source: Vamp

191

definition, seem intangible. It is also a complex organization with several layers and types of activity. The Vamp events provide an opportunity for the Deutsche Börse Group's international marketing and sales teams to meet with other group members and outside corporate partners. They usually coincide with important announcements such as new product launches or mergers. The parties offer an environment to encourage corporate bonding while immersing guests and employees in visual and material manifestations of company values. These aims and objectives are constituted in a more direct and simplified form than are usually experienced in their workaday lives. At the same time, it is hoped that the cultural capital of the organization is reinforced and that values of modernity and creativity are communicated both externally to guests who have come from outside the company, and internally among its professionals.

The Vamp/Deutsche Börse Group parties are perhaps an extreme example of a nascent arena of design intervention from the late 1990s where consultancies are directly involved in formulation of strategies to develop the corporate culture of a client. This focuses on the 'below the line' elements of a company, that is the parts that ordinary customers do not see. In design terms this may embrace the aesthetic environment of a company, but in turn it is expected that this has an attitudinal effect on the way employees see themselves, interact with each other and with their clients and customers.

internal brand building   Traditionally corporate identity has been regarded as a design tool by which both employees and their public relate to an organization. This is where the overall 'personality' of a company – its values and attitudes, its 'ways of doing things' – is communicated through a range of signifying data: logos, uniforms, letterheads, buildings and so on. Internal brand building draws a closer relationship between the employee and the products or services it purveys, and ultimately closer to its audience. It may therefore put the employee in the shoes of the consumer. Put otherwise, it aspires to inculcating an emotional investment in, as well as intellectual knowledge of what it is hoped that the consumer eventually experiences.

As such, internal brand building represents an attempt to achieve coherence between the products or services of an organization and their mediation at all levels. This is effectively done through the collapsing of a series of boundaries. In the design profession this is done in some instances through amalgamating advertising, communications and design consultancy. For the client company this strategy may be seen as part and parcel of the shifts in management theory and practice instigated in the 1990s. An important effect of this is that traditional distinctions between producer and consumer are increasingly blurred. In turn, for both the employee of a company and the end-user, the domains of 'public representation' and 'private life', as articulated in Johnson's 'circuit of culture' (see Chapter 3) appear to converge. The rest of the chapter explores the background to these changes and some further examples which illustrate them.

the end of advertising   Among many large corporate clients in the 1990s, responsibility for brand development and management ceased to rest solely in marketing departments, and by extension with their advertising agency. By 2000, a survey of 200 senior UK managers revealed that 73 per cent anticipated restructuring their companies, putting the brand at the heart of the organizations and building its working structure around it (Manuelli 2000). With a greater fluidity as to the internal ownership of brands, it may subsequently be anticipated that corporate consciousness of it and action on its behalf pervade the organization more fully.

Despite this development, statistical indications are that advertising expenditure by no means receded during the 1990s – economic expansion and emerging global markets ensured continued growth for Western advertising agencies (CITF 1998). However, much has emerged to challenge any assumption that advertising is the sole guardian and mediator of brand values. (Within this discussion we must be careful to separate the notion of pure sales from brand values. Sales are dependent on a range of issues stretching from product origination through advertising to promotions, positioning and pricing – all those elements of the 'marketing mix', in other words. Brand values refer more to the qualitative elements of recognition, emotional response, aesthetic appeal and, indeed, aesthetic illusion.) Schudson (1993 [1984]: 74–89) presents a convincing picture of an advertising industry which is fraught with divisions as to the efficacy of different techniques, in particular the question as to whether ads should be informational or emotional. Following his discussion, it appears that scientific approaches to the creation of ads, which would include market surveys or pre-testing of ads on focus groups as part of the planning, vie with questions of intuition and artistry; this is typified by the creatives-versus-researchers tension in ad agencies. In turn, a lack of clarity as to what actually works and what doesn't calls into question advertising's efficacy. This leads to the often quoted and widely attributed remark on the part of a client that, 'I know that at least half of my advertising money is being wasted. My problem is – I do not know which half' (quoted in Schudson 1993 [1984]: 85).

Schudson goes on to consider the consumer's information environment, that is, the methods by which the audiences receive data about products or services against which they set their advertising. His list of nine resources begins with the consumer's personal experiences of products or related products and ranges through government reports and consumer group information through to their interpretation of price (1993 [1984]: 90–1). This sets up powerful and constantly variable criteria by which consumers may challenge the claims of an advertisement. The growing sophistication of consumers in piecing together and interpreting different aspects of their respective information environments, means that ad agencies have an ever-increasingly difficult job in producing plausible ads. This may lead them to be increasingly explicit and reflexive by developing a language which comments on the mechanics of advertising while purveying an ad at the same time (see Williamson 1988 [1978]: 7). Another response has been to deliver advertising in unexpected or novel contexts – ambient advertising as it came to be known in the late 1990s – such as by projecting it onto the sides of buildings or printing it on the back of bus tickets. In either case, it seems that some ad agencies began to take some desperate and extreme measures to get their message seen and talked about by an increasingly critical audience.

In terms of the nuts and bolts of how advertising agencies and design consultancies make their money, there is a clear delineation between the two. Broadly speaking, the majority of design consultancies work on a fee basis whereby payment is made by the client which is agreed prior to or in the early stages of a project. On the part of the consultancy, this is calculated on the basis of such variables as time spent on the project, the expertises required, specialist subcontracting needed and other project expenses such as travel. (An exception to this occurs among some product and furniture designers who work on a royalty percentage of value of units sold.) By comparison, ad agencies derive their income from a percentage commission of the media space bought for a specific campaign. Even while from the mid-1980s the level of this commission became more frequently negotiable, the impetus for the ad agency is to achieve high acquisition of media space and go for high expenditure forms of diffusion in order to maximize profit (Leiss et al. 1990: 161).

In order to defend this financial basis of their existence, but also their own integrity and raison d'être, representatives of the advertising agencies campaign hard to sell the idea of publicity. This may not necessarily be in the face of any perceived threat from other practices in the creative industries, including design consultancy. More often this is directed at other elements of marketing used to secure brand loyalty, such as product promotions or customer loyalty schemes (see, for instance, Bond 1998 and Crosthwaite 1999). Equally, however, letters to the professional design and communications press reveal considerable discomfort with the shift of some design consultancies repackaging themselves as brand consultancies (see, for instance Massey 2000), many arguing that the need to integrate marketing, strategy and design requires more than mere repositioning but considerable internal restructuring instead.

brand and communications consultancy   From the 1990s representatives of sectors within the creative industries would provide evidence and counter-evidence to maintain their market share. On the other hand, fragmentation of working practices within the creative industries allowed groups to reconstitute their professional aims and the constellation of skills required to achieve these. This was matched by changes in internal brand ownership among clients and perceived developments in terms of the public reception of brand identity.

To focus on just one example as evidence of this shift on might cite communications and brand consultancy Circus, founded in 1998. With some 20 employees, Circus was not set up to carry out the specific making of design work themselves, rather they formed partnerships with a network of some 50 other design studios and consultancies in the creative industries. Their aim, then, was to bridge the gap between 'thinking' and 'doing' – and thus between strategic knowledge and design action – by carrying out design auditing, project development and, more straightforwardly, developing design briefs alongside clients. As such, the design outcomes of these collaborations would be characteristically diverse according to the desired end-results and require the consultancy to partner with a broad range of design and communication disciplines. Circus could therefore stray across professional demarcations between design and advertising.

In this way consultancies conspire to broaden the means by which brand values are held, managed and mediated. To return to the example of Circus, just as their working practices were mixed by collaborating with a wide range of other consultancies, so the design platforms onto which solutions were placed varied. In essence, they worked from a model which involved the exploration of the relationship between the brand and its 'community'. Between the two, it took into account notions of 'place' (meaning the forms by which the brand was communicated), 'voice' (being the various details which make up its content) and 'structure' (the systems, both internal and external to a company, that manage the communication of the brand). As such, a complex matrix of relationships linking both the hardware (for instance anything from a company's corporate logo to its buildings) and software of a client (such as the organizational structure of a company or even the way its products are viewed by its workers) are considered (Mottram 2000).

Shifts away from either advertising or design in their traditional senses towards communications and branding infer that an artefactual outcome – in the shape of an advertisement or a new retail scheme, for instance – does not always predominate. If, after all, the ultimate role of a consultancy in the commercial arena is to maximize profits then it is incumbent on it to seek the most effective device in order to achieve this. An example of this is in Wolff Olins's development of a brand identity for the mobile telephone group Orange in 1993. In positioning the company in a highly competitive market they identified Orange's proposition as being 'outstanding value' and 'future-proof', supported by five values which were meant to describe the way customers should experience the brand. These were: 'straightforward', 'refreshing', 'dynamic', 'honest' and 'friendly'. The consultancy originated a tightly managed visual identity to reflect this. However, a key feature of the brand positioning was in advising that Orange adopt 'per second billing'. At the time, Orange's competitors all used billing systems which rounded call-time up. The insistence on 'per second billing' not only gave the brand a 'unique selling proposition' but served to reinforce the brand values in the way the company did its business (Hamilton and Kirby 1999). Thus a 'weightless' solution was employed to consolidate the client's external brand image. In turn this innovation served to re-invigorate the reputation of Wolff Olins among its own competitors as an organization which delivered imaginative and holistic brand consultancy (Vinogradoff 1999).

In other instances, highly artefactual design interventions may be mobilized in order to create brand awareness internally to a company's representatives so that this may be directly communicated externally. Imagination employs up to 400 professionals to specialize in the creation and management of events, environments and experiences. Their activities include communications planning, retail and leisure design, project management, television productions, films, touring shows and theatrical events. They therefore move fluidly between the upstream elements such as the staging of corporate events and training, trade shows or conferences for companies to the downstream public face such as retail environments and experience centres. In doing so, Imagination strove to achieve a coherent fit between brand identity as understood by a client's representatives and brand image as perceived by end-customers.

One of Imagination's important long-term clients is the car manufacturer Ford. As with all automative producers, Ford experienced increasingly refined competition for market-share in the late 1990s. In part this can be attributed to production outstripping overall demand, particularly in Europe. But it was also because by this stage – after nearly a century's development – potential buyers took it for granted that a modern car was safe, well-equipped, economical and reliable. Small cars perform beyond what is actually required while extended warranties even made the few less reliable cars still attractive. Within product types, many makes have become almost indistinguishable in their overall look and performance. With a level playing field between manufacturers in terms of product performance, distribution networks and post-purchase backup, they are therefore forced towards using branding strategies more intensively than ever before. Part of the strategy for ensuring this was massively increased spending on publicity. In the mid-1990s industry analysis calculated that between £200 and £600 of the cost

'Project Aurora'
developed by
Imagination for Ford
Europe, staged in
Berlin, 1998
Source: Imagination

197

of a new car was attributable to the manufacturer's advertising budget (Copps 1996). However, given the limitations of advertising as the sole guardian of brand identity, other systems of diffusion had to be sought.

Into this context Ford launched the Cougar and the Focus cars in 1998. For this, Ford and Imagination developed the 'Project Aurora' in order to establish awareness of a set of new brand identities for the corporation. The cars were featured on Imagination-designed stands at the major European automobile trade fairs through that year. In addition, however, they set up a major event in Berlin during July of that year which was visited by 20,000 representatives of the Ford dealer network of franchises throughout Europe with the aim of instilling brand awareness upstream, among Ford's salespeople.

Staged in a disused factory, visitors entered the site via a 65 meter bridge. A bridge was also used in the trade shows to signify the continuity between the heritage of the Ford brand and its future as embodied in the new Ford Focus. In an area of 25,000 square metres, the Aurora Centre comprised a presentation arena, four areas which featured audio-visual shows, computer stations and sculptural arrangements carrying the brand message (brand 'DNA rooms' in Ford parlance), offices and meeting rooms, a restaurant and kitchens. It was also surrounded by a kilometre long drive familiarization circuit (Imagination 1998).

In common with all franchise systems, the core corporation's job is not just to market products to customers, but to provide its distributors with the necessary knowledge and experience of it in order to make all aspects of its provision appear seamless. While part of the Project Aurora was also to provide basic product information for its sellers, it was also to train them up in the appropriate brandspeak. To this end the primary Ford brands (being 'design and package', 'driving dynamics', 'ingenuity' and 'accessibility') which make up its 'DNA' were translated into the artefactual data of the Aurora Centre. Direct experience and knowledge of the cars was layered with visual and textual metaphors which would communicate the emotional appeal of the brand to its human mediators – the dealers themselves. In addition, through careful copywriting of speeches and textual information they would be given a language of description which could subsequently be used on prospective customers in the selling process (Pickering 1999).

employees as consumers   In the case of the Deutsche Börse Group events created by Vamp we saw how the informal context of the company's party was used to facilitate business networking and reinforce corporate messages. In doing so, the boundaries between the public representation and the private life, both of a company and its individual employees, are relaxed. Guests from other firms are invited to the parties; they are fed something of the inside atmosphere of the group and see its members at play; but this is also within the parameters of the corporate event. Equally, the highly textured, sometimes intimate patina of the events with their heady mixture of interactive features encourage subjectivity and, to some degree, self-actualization; but again, this is mustered as an integral aspect of the corporate culture. Paul du Gay (1997: 316–18) lays emphasis on how a consequence of globalization of finance has meant that, in fact, elements of communications, display and presentation have become more important. Transactional relationships of trust and affability between corporate players are highly valued. Financial networks are therefore, in essence, socio-cultural networks.

This example is also indicative of a shift towards a more complex and, indeed, aestheticized worker–employer relationship. This is where management interest has extended from creating and controlling the basic activities of work – what people do in their jobs – into managing its *meaning* with increasing vitality. Management has always entailed an element of ensuring its 'morality', as Salaman argues, but now, 'they [also] seek to define the workers' emotions and relationships' (1997: 239–40). This therefore entails the development and management of 'meanings', 'feelings' and 'beliefs' which are important to the quality of service they deliver (du Gay 1996: 130). This evidences a shift from an authoritarian JFDI (Just Fucking Do It!) culture to one which is calculated to motivate employees into personal engagement with and self-actualization within the attitudinal framework of the company. Furthermore, since the early 1980s this practice has been supported by the theories of corporate culture consultants such as Peters and Waterman (1982) and Deal and Kennedy (1982). They have advocated a 'hearts and minds' approach to corporate management in which the attitude and voice of employees are sought, won over and made loyal. Corporate culture therefore entails the self-conscious production of particular relationships between workers and the company, its products and services, and between each other.

Similarly, the Project Aurora to promote the Ford brand among its dealers was concerned with building enthusiasms and belief structures around a brand. A key feature, however, was that these ideas were being sold to them – albeit in a more spectacular fashion – as the dealers sell the product to their customers. This system of internal branding might have been done through direct mail or presentations to convey the key messages, but as the project's originators declared, 'it would have fallen short of delivering the essential degree of motivation' (Imagination 1998). So momentarily, members of the producing system become consumers. Again, the scenario of the event focuses on building emotional ties between corporation, product and employees. Within this process, subjectivity, normally associated with consumption, is found within the productive sphere. As du Gay states,

> The relationship to self that the employee is expected to develop builds upon and extends the identity he or she is deemed to have as a consumer: both are represented as autonomous, calculating individuals in search of meaning and fulfilment, looking to 'add value' to themselves in every sphere of existence, whether at work or at play.
>
> (1996: 79)

By taking part in the construction and implementation of systems, environments, ideas and values within organizations which communicate to and on behalf of individuals, design consultants are indulging in what Buchanan (1998a: 14) calls 'fourth order design'. In his estimation this evidences a mature state of design practice. In first and second order design, practitioners are engaged in problem-solving towards the creation and implementation of signs, symbols and images ('first order design') and physical objects ('second order design'). In 'third order design' they are involved in a more strategic decision-making mode which originates activities, services and processes for their client. Within fourth order design they ensure systems for the incorporation and functioning of those decisions. Both the Vamp and Imagination practices aspire to this fourth level: they are instrumental in ascertaining particular management messages but also devise ways of making them work.

The distinction between third and fourth order is fine. The former may provide a set of goals but does not necessarily guarantee their achievement. Fourth order design however proposes enabling a transition with the organization towards those goals. This transition, 'depends on discovering the core idea, values, and thought which organize a culture or system and propel it forward in a new search for expression in appropriate activities and products' (Buchanan 1998a: 16). Ultimately, this form of design practice does not exclude the other three; rather it is hoped that it integrates all four orders in a complex, interdisciplinary approach which extends through pre-existing systems of provision and circuits of culture and in doing so, alters their configuration. It follows, then, that if either Vamp or Imagination were to extend their service further backwards towards originating and shaping core products for their clients, then they would be covering all four of Buchanan's bases.

concluding remarks   While researching this book I often asked the designers I interviewed how far they saw the integration of the different domains of design, branding, marketing, management and distribution. Do they aspire to orchestrating a complete product in all its aspects, from the orgination of form to organization of its production, through to its mediation and after-sales strategy so that they might retain a seamless coherence throughout its lifecycle? The majority of respondents in fact considered this unviable and most did not either see it as desirable. Some admitted that this was too great a task for one consultancy to undertake alone and that in any case, their value was in contributing highly focused skills. Others merely regarded such a situation as lacking interest. To see this as an ultimate destination of the design profession for the near future would disregard the culture of its working practices and the various contexts in which it works. As consultants, many see their role as 'trainers' rather than 'players', providing support and advice for clients. They are not there to play the whole game for them by, for example, taking on the long-term management of their internal communications systems (Allen 2000).

'Designer-heroes' such as Peter Behrens, who brought together product form and corporate identity for the German company AEG in 1905, or Raymond Loewy, who, as we have seen, integrated product development, marketing and advertising into his consultancy, represent historical points of reference in this discourse. But whatever their realities were – and I question the claims made of the consistency they acheived – they seem to have passed into myth. Behrens is invoked as a forerunner to the Central European development of the modern movement (Heskett 1986) with all the claims to decompartmentalization between design disciplines and between spheres of everyday life that this implies. Loewy apparently shaped the aesthetic and commercial modernity of major twentieth-century corporate powers (Leiss et al. 1990: 84–6). While at times both may be cited as precursors to a mature state of design culture, where management theory and disciplines in the creative industries are integrated, I question whether, deep down, anyone actually wants to entirely reproduce their models.

A contemporary design industry dedicated to differentiation, disembedding itself from its own professional structures and, to a large extent, 'thinking through doing', is unlikely, in practice, to mimic the Loewy-myth. I asked a senior consultant at a major branding consultancy what he thought of the role of planners in the design process. He took a dim view of their contribution, replying that, 'They are there to iron out the surprises'. Similarly, clients aspire to greater consistency, but are aware of its pitfalls. As ownership of brands is diffused more throughout the internal structure of a company or institution, so there is more scope for misinterpretation, modification or contestation of its values. Managers and designers alike know that in a dynamic economy a balance between corporativism and individualism must be struck. Overlaps, misapprehensions, compromises, misfits and deliberate interruptions of meaning are probably more likely in an era of disorganized capitalism.

It is worth remembering that designers and producers are also consumers. While their experience as consumers may be restricted to the parameters of their socio-economic background, they none the less hold in regard and use their status as consumers. They may be equally, if not more questioning of the power that brand strategists, advertisers and indeed designers hold of their public. They might invariably suspend a critical viewpoint of their role in pursuit of profit. But they are sometimes also aware that the influence they hold over consumer habits is limited.

Much of this book has traced the threads, narratives, strategies or coincidences by which design values are implanted in its audience and its proponents. By extension, it has reviewed systems whereby designers, producers and consumers are brought closer together. As part of this culture of design, various activities conspire to break down the temporal, spatial and cultural separation between these domains. Therefore I have concentrated on their interaction and, more generally, on relationships of nodes in the 'circuit of culture'. Conversely, when a wide separation between designer, producer and consumer does happen, it results in poor products or services, business failure and/or ignorance of user-needs. In turn this may lead us towards considering discourses of 'good design' and 'bad design' to be centred less on the form of the artefact but on the relationships it instigates. As seen towards the end of Chapter 2, tendencies towards this attitude are manifest both in design management thinking for profit maximization and in enthusiasms for social and environmental agency.

The flows of these exchanges are not always equal or coherent. An enquiry which quantifies whether consumers are duped or empowered is therefore not useful. In the same way that designers, corporations and institutions are often contradictory and ambivalent, so consuming is multifaceted. Yes, we/I use a lot of our/my hard-won cash to visit leisure experiences, buy flashy products or upgrade our software. No, we don't like paying over the odds for a brand name. But yes, we try and enjoy it. At times we are immersed in the design values. At others we self-consciously play along with them. And sometimes we ignore them.

On a more localized scale, the majority of the objects, images and spaces discussed in this book invite multi-layering in their cognition. We have seen high design which deliberately destabilizes its own ideals. We have considered domestic products which are heavily elaborated with sign-value through their own form and the narrative systems around them, but which are also objects of intimate use. Likewise elements of urban design may communicate to users on a direct visceral level – they may be touched, leant on, felt through your shoes – but they may communicate the identity of a place on a global scale. Branded leisure spaces may offer spatially and temporally bounded experiences in which visitors immerse themselves while knowing that this is a temporary state of affairs. Users of computer gaming programs or informational documents engage at intuitive levels with them while keeping an eye on navigation bars and thinking about their overall configuration. We are knowing consumers and as such, mobilize different forms of engagement and interpretation in different scenarios.

The conditions of disorganized capitalism lead to a more aestheticized, sign economy, we are told (Lash and Urry 1987; 1994). Certainly many of the individual features of design conspire towards this conclusion. Designer products achieve most widespread recognition through the pages of lifestyle publications. The use of plastics throws product values onto their outer surface. Places are arranged for visual consumption. Interaction in digital media takes place on a flat surface. As such products and services are liable to constant layering of their mediation as sign is applied on top of sign. The range of moments and locations at which they are produced and consumed has been ignored by historians and commentators who pursue an essentialist view of design which focuses on them as individualized, singular objects.

This is not to say, though, that design has become entirely a question of visual representation. While it is necessary to illustrate it through photographs in a book, it must be remembered that design has many forms. Its interdisciplinary practice means that it may amalgamate a range of sensory features – of sound, smell, touch, feel, weight, movement and sight. These are always referential, by assimilating and arranging data of the known world into new configurations, or more straightforwardly by simulating pasts and places. So while design may reproduce and refine pre-existing situations, it may also aspire to the invention of new ones. It is the stuff both of illusion and allusion.

references

Abbott, Howard and Tyler, Mark (1997) *Safer by Design: A Guide to the Management and Law of Designing for Product Safety*, 2nd edn. London: Design Council.

Abrahams, Charlotte (1998) 'Not Just a Pretty Place', *The Guardian* Weekend, 19 December.

Adorno, Theodor and Horkheimer, Max (1979 [1947]) *Dialectic of Enlightenment*. London: Verso.

Aldersey-Williams, Hugh (1987) 'Starck and Stardom', *Industrial Design*, 34: 46–51.

Aldersey-Williams, Hugh (1993) 'Reponse to Myth', in Susan Yelavich (ed.) *The Edge of the Millennium: An International Critique of Architecture, Urban Planning and Communication Design*. New York: Whitney Library of Design, pp. 139–44.

Alessi (1983) *Tea and Coffee Piazza: 11 Tea and Coffee Sets*. Milan: Alessi.

Alessi (1996) *L'Oggetto Dell'equilibrio*. Milan: Electra/Alessi.

Alexander, C., Ishiwaka, S. and Silverstein, M. (1977) *A Pattern Language: Towns, Buildings, Construction*. New York: Oxford University Press.

Allen, Tony (2000) Managing Director, Interbrand/Newell & Sorrell. Interview with the author 11/01/00.

Appadurai, Arjun (1990) 'Disjuncture and Difference in the Global Cultural Economy', *Theory, Culture & Society*, 7: 295–310.

Argent, Patrick (1998) 'Graphic Design is Engulfed in Self-disillusionment', *Design Week*, 13: 42.

Artus, Mark (1999) 'That's Entertainment', *Fitch Flypaper: The 'E' Issue*. Columbus: Fitch.

Ashworth, Gregory (1990) 'The Historic Cities of Groningen: Which Is Sold To Whom?', in Gregory Ashworth and Brian Goodall (eds) *Marketing Tourism Places*. London: Routledge, pp. 138–55.

Attfield, Judy (1989) 'FORM/female FOLLOWS FUNCTION/male: Feminist Critiques of Design', in John A. Walker (ed.) *Design History and the History of Design*. London: Pluto, pp. 199–225.

Baker, Nicholson (1988) *The Mezzanine*. London: Granta.

Baker, Steve (1989) 'Re-Reading *The Corporate Personality*', *Journal of Design History*, 2(4): 275–91.

Balcioglu, Tevfik (1994) 'On Transformations of the Term Design with Reference to Mass Produced Objects', in Gulay Hasdogan (ed.) *Design Industry and Turkey: Proceedings of International Product Design Symposium, Middle East Technical University, Department of Industrial Design, 1994*. METU: Ankara, pp. 253–63.

Banham, Reyner (1960) *Theory and Design in the First Machine Age*. London: Architectural Press.

Banham, Reyner (1981 [1965]) 'The Great Gizmo', in Penny Sparke (ed.) *Design by Choice*. London: Academy Editions, pp. 108–14.

Banham, Reyner (1996 [1973]) 'Power Plank', in *A Critic Writes: Essays by Reyner Banham*. Berkeley: University of California Press, 184–7.

Barbacetto, Gianni (1987) *Design Interface: How Man and Machine Communicate. Olivetti Design Research by King and Miranda*. Milan: Arcadia Edizioni.

Barberis, Peter and May, Timothy (1993) *Government, Industry and Political Economy*. Buckingham: Open University Press.

Barlow, J.P. (1994) 'The Economy of Ideas', *Wired*, 2.03: 84–90, 126–9.

Barnard, Matt (2000) 'Make Your Mark', *Design Week*, 24 January.

Barrick, A. and Thorp, D. (1989) 'Leeds: Awakening to the Possibilities', *Building Design*, 18 June: 24–5.

Barthes, Roland (1975 [1970]) *S/Z*. London: Jonathon Cape.

Barthes, Roland (1983 [1957]) *Mythologies*. London: Jonathon Cape.

Baudrillard, Jean (1988) *Jean Baudrillard: Selected Writings*, ed. Mark Poster. Cambridge: Polity Press.

Bayley, Stephen (1979) *In Good Shape: Style in Industrial Products 1900–1960*. London: Design Council.

Beck, Ulrich (1992 [1986]) *Risk Society: Towards a New Modernity*, trans. Mark Ritter. London: Sage.

Benjamin, Walter (1970 [1936]) *Illuminations*. London: Fontana.

Benson, Richard (1999) 'Flexible Friends', *The Guardian* G2, 4 February.

Berger, John (1972) *Ways of Seeing*. London: Penguin.

Berger, Suzanne and Piore, Michael J. (1980) *Dualism and Discontinuity in Industrial Society*. Cambridge: Cambridge University Press.

Berman, Marshall (1983) *All That Is Solid Melts Into Air: The Experience of Modernity*. London: Verso.

Best, Michael H. (1990) *The New Competition: Institutions and Industrial Restructuring*. Oxford: Polity Press.

Betsky, Aaron (1999) 'Ontario Mills, California: Castle of Consumption in the Empire of Signs', in Rowan Moore (ed.) *Vertigo: The Strange New World of the Contemporary City*. London: Laurence King, pp. 192–203.

Betsky, Aaron (2000 forthcoming) 'All The World's A Store: The Spaces of Shopping', in Jane Pavitt (ed.) *Brand New*. London: V&A Publications.

Bianchini, Franco (1995) 'Night Cultures, Night Economies', *Planning, Practice and Research*, 10(2): 121–6.

Bianchini, Franco and Parkinson, Michael (eds) (1993) *Cultural Policy and Urban Regeneration: The West European Experience*. Manchester: Manchester University Press.

Billig, Michael (1995) *Banal Nationalism*. London: Sage.

Blackwell, Lewis (1995) *The End of Print: Graphic Works of Dave Carson*. London: Laurence King.

Blackwell, Lewis (1997) *David Carson: 2nd Sight: Grafik Design After the End of Print*. London: Laurence King.

Blauvelt, Andrew (1994) 'An Opening: Graphic Design's Discursive Spaces', *Visible Language*, 28(3): 207–17.

Bloch, Peter (1995) 'Seeking the Ideal Form: Product Design and Consumer Response', *Journal of Marketing*, 59: 16–29.

Block, Fred (1990) *Postindustrial Possibilities: A Critique of Economic Discourse*. Berkeley: University of California Press.

Bond, Julian (1998) 'Multibuy Now, Pay Later', *Atticus: The Journal of Original Thinking in Communications Services*, 4: 16–17.

Booth, Peter and Boyle, Robin (1993) 'See Glasgow, See Culture', in Franco Bianchini and Michael Parkinson (eds) *Cultural Policy and Urban Regeneration: The West European Experience*. Manchester: Manchester University Press, pp. 21–47.

Bourdieu, Pierre (1984) *Distinction: A Social Critique of the Judgement of Taste*, trans. Richard Nice. Cambridge, MA: Harvard University Press.

Boym, Constantin (1992) *New Russian Design*. New York: Rizzoli.

Branzi, Andrea (1984) *The Hot House: Italian New Wave Design*. London: Thames & Hudson.

Branzi, Andrea (1988) *Learning from Milan: Design and the Second Modernity*. Cambridge, MA: MIT Press.

Branzi, Andrea (1989) 'We Are the Primitives', in V. Margolin (ed.) *Design Discourse: History, Theory, Criticism*. Chicago, IL: University of Chicago Press, pp. 37–42.

Branzi, Andrea (1993) 'Design and the Second Modernity: Theorems for an Ecology of the Artificial World', in Susan Yelavich (ed.) *The Edge of the Millennium: An International Critique of Architecture, Urban Planning and Communication Design*. New York: Whitney Library of Design, pp. 125–7.

British Tourist Authority (1997) *Branding Britain*. London: British Tourist Authority.

Brown, Julian (1999) Studio Brown. Interview with the author, 5/8/99.

Buchanan, Peter (1986) 'Spain: Poetics of Modernism', *Architectural Review*, CLXXIX: 1071, May: special edition.

Buchanan, Richard (1998a) 'Branzi's Dilemma: Design in Contemporary Culture', *Design Issues*, 14(1): 3–20.

Buchanan, Richard (1998b) review of J. Woodham (1997) 'Twentieth Century Design' in *Journal of Design History*, 11(3): 259–63.

Buckley, Cheryl (1998) 'On the Margins: Theorizing the History and Significance of Making and Designing Clothes at Home', *Journal of Design History*, 11(2): 157–71.

Business Ratio Plus (1998) *Design Consultancies*. London: ICC Business Publications.

Cameron, Andy (1998a) 'The Medium is Messy', *Eye*, 30: 6–7.

Cameron, Andy (1998b) 'Dissimulations', http://ma.hrc.wmin.ac.uk/kids/ma.theory.3.2.db

Campbell, Colin (1998) 'Consumption and the Rhetorics of Need and Want', *Journal of Design History*, 11(3): 235–46.

Capella, Juli (1997) 'Rinuncio al design e mi metto a disposizione della società', *Domus*, 794: 52–6.

Carr, Raymond and Fusi, Juan Pablo (1981) *Spain: Dictatorship to Democracy*. London: Allen and Unwin.

Carrington, Noel (1976) *Industrial Design in Britain*. London: Allen and Unwin.

Castells, Manuel (1996) *The Rise of the Network Society*. Oxford: Blackwells.

de Certeau, Michel (1984) *The Practice of Everyday Life*. Berkeley: University of California Press.

Chaney, David (1996) *Lifestyles*. London: Routledge.

Clegg, Sue and Mayfield, Wendy (1999) 'Gendered by Design: How Women's Place in Design is Still Defined by Gender', *Design Issues*, 15(3): 3–16.

Coates, Nigel (1988) 'Street Signs', in John Thackara (ed.) *Design after Modernism: Beyond the Object*. London: Thames & Hudson, pp. 95–114.

Cohen, G.A. (1978) *Karl Marx's Theory of History: A Defence*. Oxford: Clarendon.

Collier, David (1993) 'Visual Metaphors for Interactive Products'. Paper given at *Doors of Perception 1* conference, Netherlands Design Institute. Conference proceedings published at http://www.doorsofperception.com

Consultancy Survey (1996) in *Design Week*, 26 March.

Copps, Alan (1996) 'This is a sequence from an action-packed movie . . . it is selling a new car as drama', *The Times* Car, 3 February.

Corrigan, Peter (1997) *The Sociology of Consumption: An Introduction*. London: Sage.

Cousins, Mark (1994) 'Danger and safety', *Art History*, 17(3): 418–23.

Crace, John (1999) 'Whose Bright Idea is it Anyway?', *The Guardian* Education, 5 October.

Creative Industries Task Force (CITF) (1998) *Creative Industries Mapping Document*. London: British Government, Department of Culture, Media and Sport.

Crilley, Darrel (1993) 'Architecture as Advertising: Constructing the Image of Redevelopment', in Gerry Kearns and Chris Philo (eds) *Selling Places: The City as Cultural Capital, Past and Present*. Oxford: Pergamon Press, pp. 231–52.

Crosthwaite, Andrew (1999) *How Advertising Affects Customer Loyalty* (pamphlet). London: Institute of Practitioners in Advertising.

Crowley, David et al. (1992) *Design and Culture in Poland and Hungary, 1890–1990*. Brighton: Brighton University.

Csikszentmihalyi, Mihaly (1975) *Beyond Boredom and Anxiety: The Experience of Play in Work and Games*. San Francisco, CA: Jossey-Bass.

Csikszentmihalyi, Mihaly (1991) 'Design and Order in Everyday Life', *Design Issues*, 8(1): 26–34.

Davenport, Russ (1999) Project Leader, Leeds Landmark, FaulknerBrowns. Interview with the author, 22/11/99.

Davidson, Martin (1992) *The Consumerist Manifesto: Advertising in Postmodern Times*. London: Routledge.

Deal, T.E. and Kennedy, A.A. (1982) *Corporate Cultures: The Rites and Rituals of Corporate Life*. Reading, MA: Addison-Wesley.

Derrida, Jacques (1976 [1967]) *Of Grammatology*, trans. G.C. Spivak. Baltimore, MD: John Hopkins University Press.

Design Continuum (1999) http://www.dcontinuum.com/do/capabilities.html#pl

Design Council (1998) *Design in Britain 1998–9: Facts, Figures and Quotable Quotes*. London: Design Council.

Design Exchange (1995) *Design for a Strong Ontario: A Strategy for Ontario's Design Sector*. Toronto: Design Exchange.

Design Week (1998) 'Consultancy Survey', 26 March.

Dew, Tom (1999) 'Developing a Critique of New Media', unpublished essay, Leeds Metropolitan University.

Dilnot, Clive (1984) 'The State of Design History, Part II: Problems and Possibilities', *Design Issues*, 3(2): 3–20.

Dormer, Peter (1990) *The Meanings of Modern Design: Towards the Twenty-First Century*. London: Thames & Hudson.

Drakulic, Slavenka (1988) *How We Survived Communism and Even Laughed*. London: Vintage.

Dyer, Gillian (1982) *Adveertising as Communication*. London: Methuen.

Dyson, James (1998) *Against the Odds: An Autobiography*. London: Orion Business Books.

Eco, Umberto (1986) *Faith in Fakes*. London: Bracken Books.

Edwards, Barry (1999) Project Manager Dynamic Earth, Event Communications. Interview with the author, 8/10/99.

Ellwood, Iain (1998) 'The Future of Retail Sites, a Paradigmatic Shift from the Retailing of Commodities to the Commodification and Consumption of Brand Experiences'. Paper given at 'Design Innovation: Conception to Consumption' 21st International Annual Conference of the Design History Society, University of Huddersfield.

Espada, Arcadi (1997) *Contra Catalunya: Una Crónica*. Barcelona: Flor del Viento.

Featherstone, Mike (1991) *Consumer Culture and Postmodernism*. London: Sage.

Feifer, Maxine (1985) *Going Places: The ways of the Tourist from Imperial Rome to the Present Day*. London: Macmillan.

Fernández, Josep-Anton (1995) 'Becoming Normal: Cultural Production and Cultural Policy in Catalonia', in Helen Graham and Jo Labanyi (eds) *Spanish Cultural Studies: An Introduction: The Struggle for Modernity*. Oxford: Oxford University Press, pp. 342–5.

Fine, Ben (1995) 'From Political Economy to Consumption', in Daniel Miller (ed.) *Acknowledging Consumption: A Review of New Studies*. London: Routledge, pp. 127–57.

Fine, Ben and Leopold, Ellen (1993) *The World of Consumption*. London: Routledge.

Fischer Fine Art (1991) *Pioneers of Modern Furniture*. London: Lund Humphries.

Fiske, John (1989a) *Understanding Popular Culture*. London: Routledge.

Fiske, John (1989b) *Reading the Popular*. London: Routledge.

Fitch (1999) 'Reality Bites', *Fly Paper: The 'E' Issue*. Columbus: Fitch.

Fleming, Dan (1996) *Powerplay: Toys as Popular Culture*. Manchester: Manchester University Press.

Flusty, Steven (1997) 'Icons in the Stream: On Local Revisions of Global Stuff', in Aaron Betsky (ed.) *Icons: Magnets of Meaning*. San Francisco, CA: Museum of Modern Art and Chronicle Books, pp. 52–65.

Forty, Adrian (1986) *Objects of Desire: Design and Society since 1750*. London: Thames & Hudson.

Foucault, Michel (1977) *Discipline and Punish*, trans. Alan Sheridan. London: Allen Lane.

Frayling, Christopher (1999) 'Flight of the Phoenix', *RSA Journal*, 3/4: 48–57.

Friedel, Robert (1996) *Zipper: An Exploration in Novelty*. New York: Norton.

Frith, Simon and Horne, Howard (1987) *Art into Pop*. London: Routledge.

Gabra-Liddell, Meret (ed.) (1994) *Alessi: The Design Factory*. London: Academy Editions.

Galbraith, J.K. (1958) *The Affluent Society*. London: Hamish Hamilton.

Galbraith, J.K. (1967) *The New Industrial State*. London: Hamish Hamilton.

Galbraith, J.K. (1969) *The Affluent Society*, 2nd edn, revised. London: Hamish Hamilton.

Gardner, Carl and Sheppard, Julie (1989) *Consuming Passion: The Rise of Retail Culture*. London: Unwin Hyman.

du Gay, Paul (1996) *Consumption and Identity at Work*. London: Sage.

du Gay, Paul (1997) 'Organizing Identity: Making Up People at Work', in Paul du Gay (ed.) *Production of Culture/Cultures of Production*. London: Sage/The Open University, pp. 285–344.

du Gay, P., Hall, S., Janes, L., Mackay, H. and Negus, K. (1997) *Doing Cultural Studies: The Story of the Sony Walkman*. London: Sage/The Open University.

Gibson, William (1994) *Virtual Light*. London: Viking.

Giddens, Anthony (1991) *Modernity and Self-Identity: Self and Society in the Late Modern Age*. London: Polity Press.

Gideon, Sigfried (1948) *Mechanization Takes Command: A Contribution to Anonymous History*. New York: Oxford University Press.

Goldman, Robert and Papson, Stephen (1998) *Nike Culture: The Sign of the Swoosh*. London: Sage.

Gottdiener, Mark (1997) *The Theming of America: Dreams, Visions and Commercial Spaces*. New York: HarperCollins.

Graham, Stephen and Marvin, Simon (1996) *Telecommunications and the City: Electronic Spaces, Urban Places*. London: Routledge.

Greenhalgh, Paul (1988) *Ephemeral Vistas: The Expositions Universelles, Great Exhibitions and World's Fairs, 1851–1939*. Manchester: Manchester University Press.

Guterson, David (1995) *Snow Falling on Cedars*. London: Bloomsbury.

Hajer, Maarten A. (1993) 'Rotterdam: Re-designing the Pubic Domain', in Franco Bianchini and Michael Parkinson (eds) *Cultural Policy and Urban Regeneration: The West European Experience*. Manchester: Manchester University Press, pp. 48–72.

Hall, Peter (1996) 'Strange Fruit', *ID Magazine*, 43: 78–81.

Hamilton, Doug and Kirby, Keith (1999) 'A New Brand for a New Category: Paint it Orange', *Design Management Journal*, 10(1): 41–5.

Hanna, Jeannette (1997) 'The Rise of Interactive Branding', *Design Management Journal*, 8(1): 34–9.

Harris, Nick (1999) Executive Producer, Acquisitions & Licensing, DK Interactive Learning. Correspondence with the author, 20/12/99.

Harrison, Bennett (1994) *Lean and Mean: The Changing Landscape of Corporate Power in the Age of Flexibility*. New York: Basic Books.

Harvey, David (1989) *The Condition of Postmodernity: An Enquiry into the Origins of Cultural Change*. Oxford: Basil Blackwell.

Harvey, David (1989) *The Urban Experience*. Oxford: Basil Blackwell.

Haug, W.F. (1986) *Critique of Commodity Aesthetics: Appearance, Sexuality and Advertising in Capitalist Society*. London: Polity Press.

Hayward, Stephen (1998) ' "Good design is largely a matter of common sense": Questioning the Meaning and Ownership of a Twentieth-Century Orthodoxy', *Journal of Design History* 11(3): 217–33.

Hebdige, Dick (1979) *Subculture: The Meaning of Style*. London: Comedia.

Hebdige, Dick (1988) *Hiding in the Light: On Images and Things*. London: Comedia.

Helfand, Jessica (1997) 'Geometry is Never Wrong', *Eye*, 24: 6–7.

Henwood, Doug (1995) 'Info fetishism', in J. Brook and I. Boal (eds) *Resisting the Virtual Life: The Culture and Politics of Information*. San Fransisco: City Lights, pp. 161–71.

Heron, Steve (1999) Senior Designer, IDEO. Interview with the author, 2/11/99.

Herrmann, M., Millard, A. and Royffe, C. (2000 forthcoming) 'Sustainable Landscape Design in Practice', in John Benson and Maggie Roe (eds) *Landscape and Sustainability*. London: E & FN Spon.

Herz, J.C. (1998) 'Toggle your Joysticks with Pride'. Paper given at 'Doors of Perception 5: Play', Netherlands Design Institute. Conference proceedings, published on CD-ROM, Amsterdam: Netherlands Design Institute.

Heskett, John (1986) *German Design: 1870–1918*. New York: Taplinger.

Heskett, John (1989) *Philips: A Study of the Corporate Management of Design*. London: Trefoil.

Hess, Allen (1993) *Viva Las Vegas: After-hours Architecture*. San Francisco, CA: Chronicle Books.

Heward, Tony (1994) 'Retailing the Police: Corporate Identity and the Met.', in R. Keat, N. Whiteley and N. Abercrombie (eds) *The Authority of the Consumer*. London: Routledge, pp. 240–52.

Hewison, Robert (1987) *The Heritage Industry: Britain in a Climate of Decline*. London: Methuen.

Hewison, Robert (1997) 'Fool Britannia', *Blueprint*, 144: 30–1.

Hollington, Geoff (1998) 'The Usual Suspects', *Design*, Summer: 62–3.

Hollington, Geoff (1999a) Interview with the author, 25/6/99.

Hollington, Geoff (1999b) Correspondence with the author, 5/11/99.

Holtzman, Steven R. (1997) *Digital Mosaics: The Aesthetics of Cyberspace*. New York: Simon & Schuster.

Horsham, Michael (1994) 'The Great i AM', *Blueprint*, May: 25–6.

Howard, Elizabeth and Davies, Ross (1988) *Change in the Retail Environment*. Harlow: Longman.

Hsiao, S. and Chen, C. (1997) 'A Semantic and Shape Grammar Based Approach for Product Design', *Design Studies*, 18(3): 275–96.

Huxor, Avon (1995) 'Virtual Worlds: Design as a New frontier'. Paper given at 'Futures: Visions and Revisions', Design History Society 18th Annual Conference, Middlesex University.

Huygen, Frederique (1989) *British Design: Image and Identity*. London: Thames & Hudson.

Imagination (1998) *Building Bridges: A Year in the Life of the Aurora Project* (unpaginated in-house publication). London: Imagination.

Jackson, Peter and Thrift, Nigel (1995) 'Geographies of Consumption', in Daniel Miller (ed.) *Acknowledging Consumption: A Review of New Studies*. London: Routledge, pp. 204–37.

Jacobs, Jane (1961) *The Death and Life of Great American Cities: The Failure of Town Planning*. New York: Random House and Vintage.

Janson-Smith, Deirdre (1999) Event Communications. Interview with the author, 8/10/99.

Jessop, Bob et al. (eds) (1991) *The Politics of Flexibility: Restructuring State and Industry in Britain, Germany and Scandinavia*. Aldershot: Elgar.

Johnson, Richard (1986) 'The Story so Far: And Further Transformations', in David Punter (ed.) *Introduction to Contemporary Cultural Studies*. London: Longman, pp. 277–313.

Jones, Helen (1999) 'The Write Stuff', *Design Week*, 17 September.

Jones, Mike (1991) 'Going Public, Going Bust', *Design*, January: 13–19.

Julier, Guy (1991) *New Spanish Design*. London: Thames & Hudson.

Julier, Guy (1993) *Thames & Hudson Encyclopedia of 20c. Design and Designers*. London: Thames & Hudson.

Julier, Guy (1995) 'Design Institutions and the Transition to Democracy: A Comparative Case Study of Spain and Hungary'. Paper given at 'Design,

Government Initiatives and Industry' International Conference, Brighton University.

Julier, Guy (1996) 'Barcelona Design, Catalonia's Political Economy and the New Spain', *Journal of Design History*, 9(2): 117–28.

Julier, Guy (1998) *The Teapot: An Appreciation*. London: Aurum.

Kearns, Gerry and Philo, Chris (eds) (1993) *Selling Places: The City as Cultural Capital, Past and Present*. Oxford: Pergamon Press.

Keat, Russell and Abercrombie, Nicholas (1991) 'Introduction', in *Enterprise Culture*, London: Routledge, pp. 1–20.

Keat, R., Whitely, N. and Abercrombie, N. (eds) (1994) *The Authority of the Consumer*. London: Routledge.

Key Note Report (1990) *Advertising Agencies: An Industry Sector Overview*. Hampton: Key Note Publications.

Key Note Report (1996) *Market Report: Design Consultancies*. Hampton: Key Note Publications.

King, Emily (1995) 'The End of Print?'. Paper given at 'Futures: Visions and Revisions', Design History Society 18th Annual Conference, Middlesex University.

Kinross, Robin (1992) *Modern Typography: An Essay in Critical History*. London: Hypen Press.

Kinross, Robin (1997) 'Where the Dear God Lives', in Steven Heller and Marie Finamore (eds) *Design Culture: An Anthology of Writing from the AIGA Journal of Graphic Design*. New York: Allworth, pp. 199–202.

Kitchen, Sarah (1990) 'Leeds: The Smotherer of Invention', *Building*, 23 February: 24–5.

Kitchin, Rob (1998) *Cyberspace: The World in the Wires*. Chichester: Wiley.

Kochan, Nicholas (1996) *The World's Greatest Brands*. London: Macmillan Business.

Kopytoff, Igor (1986) 'The Cultural Biography of Things: Commoditization as Process', in Arjun Appadurai (ed.) *The Social Life of Things: Commodites in Cultural Perspective*. Cambridge: Cambridge University Press, pp. 64–94.

Krippendorf, Klaus and Butter, Reinhart (1984) 'Product Semantics: Exploring the Symbolic Qualities of Form', *Innovation*, Spring, 4–9.

Landow, George P. (1992) *Hypertext: The Convergence of Contemporary Critical Theory and Technology*. Baltimore, MD: John Hopkins University Press.

Landscape Design Associates/Bioscan (UK) Ltd (1992) *Center Parcs: An International Approach to Environmental Issues*, unpublished internal report.

Lanham, Richard (1993) *The Electronic Word: Democracy, Technology and the Arts*. Chicago, IL: University of Chicago Press.

Lash, Scott and Urry, John (1987) *The End of Organized Capitalism*. London: Polity.

Lash, Scott and Urry, John (1994) *Economies of Signs and Spaces*. London: Sage.

Laurier, Eric (1993) ' "Tackintosh": Glasgow's Supplementary Gloss', in Gerry Kearns and Chris Philo (eds) *Selling Places: The City as Cultural Capital, Past and Present*. Oxford: Pergamon Press, pp. 267–90.

Leeds City Council (LCC) (1998) *Leeds Economic Handbook*. Leeds: Leeds City Council.

Lees, Grace (1997) 'Balancing the Object: The Reinvention of Alessi', *Things*, 6: 74–91.

Lefebvre, Henri (1994 [1974]) *The Production of Space*, trans. Donald Nicholson-Smith. Oxford: Blackwell.

this figure had risen to 11 million (Urry 1990: 48). Tourism, and leisure more generally, has subsequently become a more fragmented but also more tightly managed commodity.

Rojek (1985: 18–23) identifies four key features of contemporary leisure. First, it is a privatized affair which has become increasingly focused on the home rather than the public sphere. No doubt this has been encouraged by the development of radio, television, then teletext, video, internet and computer games. It is the job of leisure entrepreneurs to get people out of their homes, but also to give leisure spaces the same security, exclusivity and 'buzz' available at home. Secondly, leisure is more individuated: it is more subject to personalization. Leisure spaces must deliver a menu of choice without destabilizing the core values of the brand. Thirdly, Rojek believes that leisure has become much more commercialized, becoming a major industry in itself. Fourthly, leisure is more pacified: it entails more complex and encultured expression through activities which require learning, practice and mastery. Whether it's appreciating high cuisine or trying out a new sport, leisure activities are, in fact, more restrained and regulated than ever.

As work patterns in the late twentieth century have become more fragmented and varied, so has leisure. Paradoxically, while there has been an overall decline in the length of the working week, for those in employment the total amount of leisure time – that is, time spent in unproductive activities – has diminished. Leisure entrepreneurs increasingly take seriously the notion of 'time squeeze': in a Henley Centre survey published in 1998, 59 per cent of respondents agreed that 'I have never had enough time to get things done'. This is particularly so among working women. They report only 13.5 hours per week free as against the 60 hours average (Rees 1998). This time-squeeze has given rise to the development of one-stop leisure complexes, or so-called E-zones (as in Entertainment), which incorporate a variety of leisure activities into one branded site. This allows consumers the most efficient use of their precious leisure time as they move from cinema to pizza restaurant to bowling alley or from swimming pool, to tennis court to health spa. In such circumstances, some design consultancy work is dedicated to achieving the right constellation of retail and leisure brands within a single branded space. These would provide sufficient variety of resources while maintaining the overall character of the leisure complex. Here the designer is not just originating new shapes, colours and names but is working rather like an image consultant by advising on the appropriate off-the-peg brands to combine into the leisure offer (within the design industry this is frequently referred to as 'brand marrying').

In a later discussion, Rojek asks whether all leisure provides is endless but temporary distraction. He argues that dedicated leisure activity is quite rare (1993: 216). Compulsive hill-walkers or serious amateur musicians

Leiss, W., Kline, S. and Jhally, S. (1990) *Social Communication in Advertising: Persons, Products and Images of Well-Being*, 2nd edn. London: Routledge.

Leonard, Mark (1997) *Britain™: Renewing Our Identity*. London: Demos.

Lévi-Strauss, Claude (1969) *The Raw and the Cooked*, trans. by John and Doreen Weightman. London: Cape.

Lloyd Jones, Peter (1992) 'Time and the Perception of Everyday Things', in Susana Vihma (ed.) *Objects and Images: Studies in Design and Advertising*. Helsinki: University of Industrial Arts, pp. 58–75.

Lloyd Morgan, Conway (1999) *Starck*. New York: Universe.

Loewy, Raymond (1951) *Never Leave Well Enough Alone*. New York: Simon & Schuster.

Lorenz, Christopher (1986) *The Design Dimension: Product Strategy and the Challenge of Global Marketing*. Oxford: Blackwell.

Lury, Celia (1996) *Consumer Culture*. Cambridge: Polity Press.

Lycett, Kevin (1999) Communication Design Solutions. Interview with the author, 2/12/99.

McAlhone, Beryl (1987) *British Design Consultancy*. London: Design Council.

McCoy, Michael (1993) 'Design and the New Mythology', in Yelavich, Susan (ed.) *The Edge of the Millennium: An International Critique of Architecture, Urban Planning and Communication Design*. New York: Whitney Library of Design, pp. 132–8.

McCracken, Grant (1990) *Culture and Consumption: New Approaches to the Symbolic Character of Consumer Goods and Activities*. Bloomington and Indianapolis: Indiana University Press.

Macdonald, Nico (1997) 'Not As Other Media', *Eye*, 26: 6–7.

McDonough, Michael (1993) 'Gods Too Ancient and Contradictory: in Response to Andrea Branzi', in Susan Yelavich (ed.) *The Edge of the Millennium: An International Critique of Architecture, Urban Planning and Communication Design*. New York: Whitney Library of Design, pp. 128–31.

McGrane, Sally (1999) 'For a Seller of Innovation, a Bag of Technotricks', *New York Times*, Circuit, 11 February.

McHoul, Alec and Roe, Phil (1996) 'Hypertext and Reading Cognition', in B.L. Gorayska and J.L. Mey (eds) *Cognitive Technology: In Search of a Human Interface* (Advances in Psychology 113). Amsterdam: Elsevier Science, pp. 347–59.

Mañà, Jordi (1983) *Diseño y la Exportación*. Barcelona: Centro de Estudios Internacional.

Manovich, Lev (1997) 'The Aesthetics of Virtual Worlds: Report from Los Angeles', in Arthur Kroker and Marilouise Kroker (eds) *Digital Delirium*. Montréal: New World Perspectives, pp. 288–300.

Manuelli, Sara (2000) 'Searching for an Identity', *Design Week*, 14 January.

Manzini, Ezio (1986) *The Material of Invention*. Milan: Arcadia.

Manzini, Ezio (1992) *Artefactos: Hacia una Nueva Ecología del Ambiente Artificial*, trans. Cristina Ordóñez and Pierluigi Cattermole. Madrid: Ediciones Experimenta.

Manzini, Ezio (1998) 'Products in a Period of Transition: Products, Services and Interactions for a Sustainable Society', in Tevfik Balcioglu (ed.) *The Role of Product Design in Post-Industrial Society*. Ankara: Middle East Technical University, pp. 43–58.

Margolin, Victor (1995) 'A Reply to Adrian Forty', *Design Issues*, 11(1): 19–21.

Marling, Karal Ann (1997) *Designing Disney's Theme Parks: The Architecture of Reassurance*. Paris: Flammarion.

Martín, Jesus (1992) 'De potencia industrial a economía de servicios', *Economics*, 55: 30–40.

Marx, Karl (1957 [1867]) *Capital: Volume One*. London: Everyman.

Mason, Bruce and Dicks, Bella (1999) 'The Digital Ethnographer', *CyberSociology*, 6, August, http://www.socio.demon.co.uk/magazine/6/issue6.html

Massey, Simon (2000) 'There's More to a Good Brand Than Design', *Design Week*, 21 January.

Meikle, Jeffrey (1998) 'Material Virtues: On the Ideal and the Real in Design History', *Journal of Design History*, 11(3): 191–9.

Meggs, Philip B. (1983) *A History of Graphic Design*. London: Allen Lane.

Metz, Christian (1974) *Language and Cinema*, trans. Donna Jean Umiker-Sebeok. The Hague: Mouton.

Miller, Daniel (1987) *Material Culture and Mass Consumption*. Oxford: Basil Blackwell.

Miller, Daniel (1988) 'Appropriating the State on the Council Estate', *Man*, 23: 353–72.

Mitchell, C. Thomas (1988) 'The Product as Illusion', in John Thackara (ed.) *Design After Modernism: Beyond the Object*. London: Thames & Hudson, pp. 208–15.

Mitchell, C. Thomas (1993) *Redefining Designing: From Form to Experience*. New York: Van Nostrand Reinhold.

Molotch, Harvey (1996) 'L.A. as Design Product: How Art Works in a Regional Economy', in Allen J. Scott and Edward W. Soja (eds) *The City: Los Angeles and Urban Theory at the End of the Twentieth Century*. Berkeley: University of California Press, pp. 225–75.

Moon, Michael (1999) 'Branding in the Networked Economy', *Design Management Journal*, 10(2): 61–70.

Morris, Kenneth (1997) 'Shake Hands with the Brand: Crafting the Message for the Medium', *Design Management Journal*, 8(3): 27–32.

Morris, L., Rabinowitz, J., Myerson, J. (1998) 'No More Heroes: From Controllers to Collaborators', *Design Management Journal*, 9(2): 22–5.

Mottram, Simon (2000) Consultant, Circus. Interview with the author, 11/01/00.

Moulaert, F. and Swyngedouw, E.A. (1989) 'A Regulation Approach to the Geography of Flexible Production Systems', *Environment and Planning D: Society and Space*, 7: 327–45.

Muller, W. and Pasman, G. (1996) 'Typology and the Organization of Design Knowledge', *Design Studies*, 17(2): 111–30.

van den Munckhof, Crissij and Dare, Lucy (2000) Vamp. Interview with the author, 11/01/00.

Murray, Richard (1998) 'Jumping on the Brand Wagon', *Design Week*, 27 March.

Myerson, Jeremy (1990) 'All's Fair in Love and War', *Design Week*, 27 April.

Myerson, Jeremy (1997) 'Tornadoes, T-squares and Technology: Can Computing be a Craft?', in Peter Dormer (ed.) *The Culture of Craft*. Manchester: Manchester University Press, pp. 176–85.

Myerson, Jeremy (1999) 'Class of the Century', *Design Week*, 17 December.

Napier, Christopher (1994) 'Brand Accounting in the United Kingdom', in Geoff Jones and Nicholas Morgan (eds) *Adding Value: Brands and Marketing in Food and Drink*. London: Routledge, pp. 76–102.

Narotzky, Viviana (1998) 'Going Public: Design, Consumption and Urban Identity in Barcelona'. Conference paper given at 'Design Innovation: Conception to Consumption' 21st International Annual Conference of the Design History Society, University of Huddersfield.

Nederveen Pieterse, Jan (1991) 'Fictions of Europe', *Race and Class*, 32(3): 3–10.

Nederveen Pieterse, Jan (1995) 'Globalization as Hybridization', in Mike Featherstone, Scott Lash and Roland Robertson (eds) *Global Modernities*. London: Sage, pp. 45–68.

Netherlands Design Institute (1994) *Design Across Europe: Patterns of Supply and Demand in the European Design Market*. Amsterdam: Vormgevingsinstitut.

Nevett, T.R. (1987) *Advertising in Britain: A History*. London: Heinemann.

Nevins, James and Whitney, Daniel (eds) (1989) *Concurrent Design of Products and Processes*. New York: McGraw-Hill.

Nielsen, Jakob (1998) 'The Increasing Conservatism of Web users', Alertbox for 22 March, http://www.useit.com/alertbox

Nielsen, Jakob (1999) 'Stuck With Old Browsers Until 2003', Alertbox for April, http://www.useit.com/alertbox

Nixon, Helen (1998) 'Fun and Games Are Serious Business', in Julian Sefton-Green (ed.) *Digital Diversions: Youth Culture in the Age of Multimedia*. London: UCL Press, pp. 21–42.

Nutley, Michael (1998) 'Health and Fitness', *Design Week: The Big Picture: Leisure*: 49.

Nuttgens, Patrick (1979) *Leeds: The Back to Front Inside Out Upside Down City*. Otley: Stile Publications.

Offe, Claus (1985) *Disorganized Capitalism*. Oxford: Polity.

Olins, Wally (1978) *The Corporate Personality: An Inquiry into the Nature of Corporate Identity*. London: Design Council.

Olins, Wally (1982) 'How Wolff Olins Learnt about Corporate Identity', *Penrose Annual*, 74: 221–9.

Olins, Wally (1988) *A Force for Change*. London: Metropolitan Police Force.

Olins, Wally (1989) *Corporate Identity: Making Business Strategy Visible through Design*. London: Thames & Hudson.

Olins, Wally (1999) *Trading Identities: Why Countries and Companies are Taking on Each Others' Roles*. London: The Foreign Policy Centre.

Øresund Committee (1999) *Hello* (pamphlet). Copenhagen: Øresund Committee.

Packard, Vance (1957) *The Hidden Persuaders: On Psychology and Advertising*. London: Longmans, Green & Co.

Papanek, Victor (1972) *Design for the Real World*. London: Thames & Hudson.

Papanek, Victor and Hennessey, James (1974) *Nomadic Furniture: How to Build and Where to Buy Lightweight Furniture*. London: Studio Vista.

Pawley, Martin (1998) *Terminal Architecture*. London: Reaktion Books.

Peters, Tom and Waterman, Robert (1982) *In Search of Excellence*. New York: Harper and Row.

Petroski, Henry (1996) *The Pencil: A History of Design and Circumstance*. New York: Alfred A. Knopf.

Pevsner, Nikolaus (1936) *Pioneers of the Modern Movement: From William Morris to Walter Gropius*. London: Harmondsworth.

Phelan, Cel (1999) Marketing Director, Event Communications. Interview with the author, 8/10/99.

Pibernat, Oriol (ed.) (1999) *Dissenyadors a Ciutat Vella*. Barcelona: Ajuntament de Barcelona.

Pickering, John (1999) Copywriter, Imagination. Interview with the author, 7/10/99.

Pilditch, James (1970) *Communication by Design: A Study in Corporate Identity*. New York: McGraw-Hill.

Pilditch, James and Scott, Douglas (1965) *The Business of Product Design*. London: Business Publications.

Plant, Sadie (1993) 'On the Matrix: Cyberfeminist Simulations', in Rob Shields (ed.) *Cultures of Internet: Virtual Spaces, Real Histories, Living Bodies*. London: Sage, pp. 170–83.

Policy Research Institute (PRI) (1996) *The Cultural Industries in Leeds*. Report, Leeds Metropolitan University/Leeds City Council.

Poster, Mark (1990) *The Mode of Information: Poststructuralism and Social Context*. Cambridge: Polity Press.

Powell, Kenneth (1989) 'The Offense of the Inoffensive', *Architects' Journal*, 8.189: 24–9.

Powell, Kenneth (1992) 'What Have we Done to our Cities', *Daily Telegraph*, 11 April.

Poyner, Rick (1991) 'The Designer as Author', *Blueprint*, May: 30–1.

Poyner, Rick (1999) 'Publishing by Numbers', *Eye*, 8(31): 6–7.

Project on Disney (1995) *Inside the Mouse: Work and Play at Disney World*. Durham, NC: Duke University Press.

Raban, Jonathon (1974) *Soft City*. London: Hamish Hamilton.

Reavley, Gordon (1998) 'Inconspicuous Consumption'. Paper given at 'Design Innovation: Conception to Consumption' 21st International Annual Conference of the Design History Society, University of Huddersfield.

Rees, Emma (1998) 'Leisure Futures', *Design Week: The Big Picture: Leisure*, October: 24–5.

Relph-Knight, Linda (1998) 'Team Leaders', *DesignWeek*, 27 March.

Rheingold, Howard (1994) *The Virtual Community*. London: Secker and Warburg.

Richardson, Darren (1999) Director, Gardiner-Richardson, interview with the author, 13.1.99.

Robertson, Keith (1994) 'On White Space/When Less is More', in M. Bierut, W. Drenttel, S. Heller and D.K. Holland (eds) *Looking Closer: Critical Writings on Graphic Desin*. New York: Allworth, pp. 61–6.

Robins, Kevin (1997) 'What in the World's Going On?', in Paul du Gay (ed.) *Production of Culture/Cultures of Production*. London: Sage/The Open University, pp. 11–47.

Rojek, Chris (1985) *Capitalism and Leisure Theory*. London: Tavistock.

Rojek, Chris (1993) *Ways of Escape: Modern Tranformations in Leisure and Travel*. London: Macmillan.

Rudd, Nicholas (1999) 'Going Direct: Design and Digital Commerce', *Design Management Journal*, 10(1): 17–22.

Russell, Beverly (1996) 'Starck Raving Genius of Design', *Graphis*, 52: 30–41.

Sabel, Charles (1982) *Work and Politics: The Division of Labour in Industry*. Cambridge: Cambridge University Press.

Salaman, Graeme (1997) 'Culturing Production', in Paul du Gay (ed.) *Production of Culture/Cultures of Production*. London: Sage/The Open University, pp. 235–84.

Salvador, Tony, Bell, Genevieve and Anderson, Ken (1999) 'Design Ethnography', *Design Management Journal*, 10(4): 35–41.

Sassen, Saskia (1999) 'Digital Networks and Power', in Mike Featherstone and Scott Lash (eds) *Spaces of Culture: City, Nation, World*. London: Sage, pp. 49–63.

Satué, Enric (1997) 'Lo "Stile Barcellona": un gioco da bambini', *Domus*, 794: 88–97.

Schiller, H.I. (1995) 'The Global Information Highway: Project for an Ungovernable World', in J. Brook and I. Boal (eds) *Resisting the Virtual Life: The Culture and Politics of Information*. San Francisco, CA: City Lights Books, pp. 17–34.

Schmitt, Bernd and Simonson (1997) *Marketing Aesthetics: The Stategic Management of Brands, Identity, and Image*. New York: Free Press.

Schofield, Jack (1999) 'It's so Smart to be Simple', *The Guardian* Online, 2 December.

Schofield, Jack (2000) 'Life with the Creature Feature', *The Guardian* Online, 13 January.

Schön, Donald A. (1991) *The Reflective Practitioner: How Professionals Think In Action*. London: Basic Books.

Schudson, Michael (1993 [1984]) *Advertising, the Uneasy Persuasion: Its Dubious Impact on American Society*. London: Routledge.

Scott, Allen (1998) *The Regions and the World Economy: The Coming Shape of Global Production, Competition, and Political Order*. Oxford: Oxford University Press.

Shields, Rob (1991) *Places on the Margin: Alternative Geographies of Modernity*. London: Routledge.

Slater, Don (1997) *Consumer Culture and Modernity*. London: Polity.

Smales, Lindsay (1994) 'Desperate Pragmatism or Shrewd Optimism? The Image and Selling of West Yorkshire', in Graham Haughton and David Whitney (eds) *Reinventing a Region: Restructuring in West Yorkshire*. Aldershot: Avebury, pp. 35–60.

Smales, Lindsay and Whitney, David (1996) 'Inventing a Better Place: Urban Design in Leeds in the Post-War Era', in Graham Haughton and Colin C. Williams (eds) *Corporate City: Partnership, Participation and Partition in Urban Development in Leeds*. Aldershot: Avebury, pp. 199–218.

Sontag, Susan (1978) *On Photography*. London: Allen Lane, Penguin Books.

Southgate, Paul (1994) *Total Branding by Design: How To Make Your Brand's Packaging More Effective*. London: Kogan Page.

Sparke, Penny (1988) *Italian Design: 1870 to the Present*. London: Thames & Hudson.

Sparke, Penny (1990) ' "A Home for Everybody?": Design, Ideology, and the Culture of the Home in Italy, 1945–72', in Paul Greenhalgh (ed.) *Modernism in Design*. London: Reaktion Books, pp. 185–202.

Sparke, Penny (1995) *As Long as it's Pink: The Sexual Politics of Taste*. London: HarperCollins.

Sparks, Leigh (1994) 'Delivering Quality: The Role of Logistics in the Postwar Transformation of British Retailing', in Geoff Jones and Nicholas Morgan (eds) *Adding Value: Brands and Marketing in Food and Drink*. London: Routledge, pp. 310–35.

Spencer, Herbert (1969) *Pioneers of Modern Typography*. London: Lund Humphries.

Spivak, G.C. (1988) 'Can the Subaltern Speak?', in Carey Nelson and Lawrence Grossberg (eds) *Marxism and the Interpretation of Culture*. London: Macmillan, pp. 271–313.

Sudjic, Deyan (1985) *Cult Objects: The Complete Guide to Having it All*. London: Paladin.

Sushi (1999) 'X Factor', *Sushi*, 3: (unpaginated).

Suskind, Patrick (1987) *Perfume*. London: Penguin Books.

Sweet, Fay (1998) *Alessi: Art and Poetry*. London: Thames & Hudson.

Sweet, Fay (1999) *Philippe Starck: Subverchic Design*. London: Thames & Hudson.

Thackara, John (ed.) (1988) *Design after Modernism: Beyond the Object*. London: Thames & Hudson.

Thackara, John (1997) *Winners! How Today's Successful Companies Innovate by Design*. Aldershot: Gower.

Thackray, Rachelle (1999) 'Me and My Partner: Michael Wolff and Piers Schmidt', *The Independent*, Business Review, 7 April.

Toffler, Alvin (1980) *The Third Wave*. London: Collins.

Tomes, A., Oates, C. and Armstrong, P. (1998) 'Talking Design: Negotiating the Verbal–visual Translation', *Design Studies*, 19(2): 127–42.

Toporowski, Jan (1989) 'The Financial System and Capital Accumulation in the 1980s', in Francis Green (ed.) *The Restructuring of the UK Economy*. Hemel Hempstead: Harvester Wheatsheaf, pp. 242–62.

Touraine, Alain (1995) *Critique of Modernity*, trans. David Macey. Oxford: Blackwell.

Trias, Josep Maria (1988) 'El logotipo olímpico', *On*, 91: 15–20.

Tso, Judy (1999) 'Do You Dig Up Dinosaur Bones? Anthropology, Business, and Design', *Design Management Journal*, 10(4): 69–74.

Turkle, Sherry (1997) *Life on the Screen: Identity in the Age of the Internet*. London: Phoenix.

Turner, Louis and Ash, John (1975) *The Golden Hordes: International Tourism and the Pleasure Periphery*. London: Constable.

Urry, John (1990) *The Tourist Gaze: Leisure and Travel in Contemporary Societies*. London: Sage.

Urry, John (1995) *Consuming Places*. London: Routledge.

Valentine, Matthew (1998) 'Creative mind games', *Design Week*, 6 November.

Van Doren, Harold (1940) *Industrial Design: A Practical Guide*. New York: McGraw-Hill.

Van Hinte, E. (1990) 'The Limits of Flexibility', *Industrieel Ontwerpen*, 3: 45–6.

Veblen, Thorstein (1970 [1899]) *The Theory of the Leisure Class*. London: Unwin.

Venturi, R., Scott-Brown, D. and Izenour, S. (1972) *Learning from Las Vegas: The Forgotten Symbolism of Architectural Form*. Cambridge, MA: MIT Press.

Vergo, Peter (ed.) (1989) *The New Museology*. London: Reaktion.

Vinogradoff, Paul (1999) Consultant, Wolff Olins. Interview with the author, 2/11/99.

Virilio, Paul (1997) *Open Sky*, trans. Julia Rose. London: Verso.

Walker, John A. (1983) *Art in the Age of Mass Media*. London: Pluto Press.

Walker, John A. (1989) *Design History and the History of Design*. London: Pluto Press.

Ward, Stephen (1998) *Selling Places: The Marketing and Promotion of Towns and Cities, 1850–2000*. London: E & FN Spon.

Waterfall, Simon (2000) Creative Director, Deepend. Interview with the author, 11/01/00.

Weibull, Jörgen et al. (1993) *Øresund: Past, Present and Future*. Svedab: Corona/Norden.

Weinbren, Grahame (1995) 'Mastery: Computer Games, Intuitive Interfaces and Interactive Multimedia', *Leonardo*, 28(5): 403–8.

Wells, John (1989) 'Uneven development and de-industrialisation in the UK since 1979', in Francis Green (ed.) *The Restructuring of the UK Economy*. Hemel Hempstead: Harvester Wheatsheaf, pp. 25–64.

Wernick, Andrew (1991) *Promotional Culture: Advertising, Ideology and Symbolic Expression*. London: Sage.

Whitely, Nigel (1991) 'Design in Enterprise Culture: Design for Whose Profit?', in Russell Keat and Nicholas Abercrombie (eds) *Enterprise Culture*. London: Routledge, pp. 106–205.

Whitely, Nigel (1993) *Design for Society*. London: Reaktion Books.

Whitely, Nigel (1994) 'High Art and the High Street: The "Commerce-and-Culture" Debate', in R. Keat, N. Whitely and N. Abercrombie (eds) *The Authority of the Consumer*. London: Routledge, pp. 119–37.

Whittaker, Mary (1990) 'Leeds. Has the Renaissance Started?', *Architecture Today*, 5: 15–16.

van der Will, Wilfried (1990) 'The Body and the Body Politic as Symptom and Metaphor in the Transition of German Culture to National Socialism', in Brandon Taylor and Wilfried van der Will (eds) *The Nazification of Art: Art, Design, Music, Architecture and Film in the Third Reich*. Winchester: Winchester Press, pp. 14–52.

Williams, Raymond (1974) *Television, Technology and Cultural Form*. London: Fontana.

Williamson, Judith (1988 [1978]) *Decoding Advertisements: Ideology and Meaning in Advertising*. London: Marion Boyars.

Wittgenstein, Ludwig (1968) *Philosophical Investigations*, trans. G.E.M. Anscombe. Oxford: Blackwell.

Wolff Olins (1999a) *Britain. Bye bye Bulldog* (pamphlet). London: Wolff Olins.

Wolff Olins (1999b) *Deutschland als globale marke/A global brand for Germany* (pamphlet). London: Wolff Olins.

Wollen, Chad (1998) 'The Hurricane of Innovation', *Atticus: The Journal of Original Thinking in Communications Services*, 4: 8–9.

Wood, S.L and Ullman, D.G. (1996) 'The Functions of Plastic Injection Moulding Features', *Design Studies*, 17(2): 201–13.

Woodham, Jonathon (1997) *Twentieth-Century Design*. Oxford: Oxford University Press.

Woudhuysen, James (1998) 'Beyond the Dogma of Globalisation', in Tevfik Balcioglu (ed.) *The Role of Product Design in Post-Industrial Society*. Ankara: Middle East Technical University, pp. 93–112.

Wozencroft, Jon (1987) *The Graphic Language of Neville Brody*. London: Thames & Hudson.

Wozencroft, Jon (1994) *The Graphic Language of Neville Brody 2*. London: Thames & Hudson.

Wren, Phil (1999) Director, Fitch. Interview with the author, 7/10/99.

York, Peter (1984) *Modern Times*. London: Heinemann.

York, Peter (1988) 'Culture as Commodity: Style Wars, Punk and Pageant', in John Thackara (ed.) *Design After Modernism: Beyond the Object*. London: Thames & Hudson, pp. 160–8.

Zukin, Sharon (1991) *Landscapes of Power: From Detroit to Disney World*. Berkeley: University of California Press.

Zukin, Sharon (1995) *The Cultures of Cities*. Cambridge, MA: Blackwell.

Index

Note: Illustrations are indicated by page references in *italics*.